HERE AM I!

HERE AM I!

A Christian Reflection on God

Adrio König

Translated from Afrikaans

WM. B. EERDMANS PUBL. CO., GRAND RAPIDS

MARSHALL MORGAN & SCOTT, LONDON

Copyright © Adrio König 1982
First published by Marshall Morgan & Scott 1982
All rights reserved

This edition printed in the
United States of America for
Wm. B. Eerdmans Publishing Company
255 Jefferson Ave. S.E., Grand Rapids, MI 49503
and Marshall Morgan & Scott, 1 Bath Street, London EC1V 9LB

ISBN: 0 551 00856 3

Phototypesetting in England by
Nuprint Services Limited, Harpenden, Hertfordshire

Library of Congress Cataloging in Publication Data

König, Adrio.
Here am I!

Translation of: Hier is ek!
Bibliography: p. 225
Includes indexes.
1. God. I. Title.
BT102.K5613   1982   231   82-11377
ISBN 0-8028-3551-1 (pbk.)

Contents

Foreword

I wish most cordially to recommend this book to a wide reading public. In order to appreciate its significance, it is in fact necessary to grasp something of the theological situation in South Africa, and particularly its historical development.

Theology, as it has been pursued in the three Afrikaans-speaking Calvinist churches in South Africa, has hardly been known outside its own realm. This is partly due to its language, and partly to its almost exclusive orientation towards the conservative reformed traditions of the Netherlands, particularly as these were embodied in the 'Neo-Calvinism' of Abraham Kuyper (1837-1920) which was taught in his foundation, the Free University of Amsterdam. A dominant feature of this theology was its doctrine of 'the ordinances of creation', which refers to institutions such as the family, education, the state, society, science, and so on. All these are corrupted by sin, but can, and must be purified by the influence of Christ and the Bible. In this process real Christians, the regenerated ones, are instrumental. This theology, supported by a Calvinistic philosophy, a Christian school system, a Christian political programme and other similar aids had, as one of its aims, the restoration and maintenance of God's ordinances in the midst of a Europe which, as Kuyper saw it around him, was shaken to its foundations. This theology was characterized by its static nature and concepts, and a looking back to what was supposed to have been in the beginning. Many of the more gifted students of the three Afrikaans churches were sent to the Free University, or to the more conservative state faculty of Utrecht. Later, as pastors and professors, they developed this theology.

There are various phases which we ought to distinguish in this period of Dutch Calvinist influence of Afrikaans theology. In the years before the Second World War the influence of Kuyper and his disciples, with their rather scholastic presentation of calvinist doctrine, was direct. In the post-war epoch the chair of dogmatics at the Free University was occupied by G. C. Berkouwer, who was born in 1903, and retired in 1973. Berkouwer was orientated towards another great Neo-Calvinist theologian, Herman Bavinck (1854-1921) rather than towards Kuyper. Bavinck had offered a more dynamic and existential reinterpretation of classic reformed doctrines in his four volumes of *Reformed Dogmatics* (in Dutch). As Berkouwer explored further along this path he drew, particularly during the second half of his professorship, very near to Barth. Many brilliant Afrikaner students sat at his feet, and prepared dissertations under his guidance.

This period during which Afrikaans theology was fertilized rather exclusively by the Dutch has now almost passed. The successors of Berkouwer, especially H. M. Kuitert, have gone beyond his position and attached the Calvinist heritage of their university as unable to cope with the increasing tempo of secularization in the Netherlands.

As a consequence of these recent developments two things are happening in the Afrikaans Churches. On the one hand their official leadership tends to turn its back on theological developments in the Netherlands, and for that matter, on all major developments overseas, except the remaining fundamentalist trends. They are disinclined to expose their students to these influences and are satisfied simply to repeat more or less unaltered, the theology of a bygone Dutch generation (Kuyper, Bavinck). This has been so particularly since the sixties, when the Free University abandoned its traditional fundamentalist approach to the Bible, and simultaneously developed a theology which could hardly be harmonized with the underlying principles of the South African establishment.

On the other hand the influence of Berkouwer and other leading Netherlands theologians has broadened the outlook of the younger generation of Afrikaans theologians who occupy several of the chairs of theology in South Africa. They are no longer satisfied simply to repeat what a previous generation of Netherlands theologians have said. They display a stronger self-assurance than before and increasingly attempt to think through the gospel in terms of the situation in South Africa. In this they make use of a far wider theological spectrum than merely the Netherlands, and exhibit strong signs of an independent reworking of the leading European theologians of all traditions. Afrikaans theology is indeed now in a process of coming of age and the time has come for theologians in other areas to study what is happening in this Afrikaans-speaking tradition.

Among those who are seeking new ways, intent upon reaching the very frontiers of contemporary theological thinking, Prof. dr. Adrio König, Professor of Systematic Theology at the University of South Africa, plays a conspicuous role. At an early stage his dissertation on *Jesus Christ, the Eschatos – the foundation and structure of eschatology as teleological Cristology* (Pretoria, 1970, in Afrikaans) aroused my interest. This dissertation has since been revised and is to be published shortly as *Jesus the Last, A Christian Reflection on the End.* Alongside faithfulness to the Bavinck tradition it showed reasonings and perspectives of remarkable originality. Since then, every new book from this passionate and hard-working thinker has testified to new discoveries. While eager to learn from many others, especially protestant thinkers in Germany and the Netherlands, he increasingly shows his independence and courage in going new ways.

Foreword

I feel that this book you have in your hands is a real climax to this process. It is the first of a series of monographs, and deals with the doctrine of God. This he does in a manner which is both biblical and exciting, and which is intelligible not only to advanced students of theology but also to the educated layman. In König's book God is no longer the Unmoved First Mover spoken of in scholastic and classical protestant theology. Again and again he performs new deeds and creates fresh relationships. He is a living and acting God, whose fields of work are the ever-changing scenes and challenges of history. Therefore König has the courage to relate God not only to concepts such as being, immutability, transcendence and so forth, but also to change, history and even passion. It is clear that he has learned much from Berkouwer and his consistent de-scholasticizing of Calvinistic theology. Nevertheless, he goes much further on many points, often inspired by Moltmann, Pannenberg and many others. This book is imbued with a sense of what the Germans call *Geschichtlichkeit* ('historicity'). I admire him for his gift of assimilating so many trends, but even more for avoiding elevating any of them into blinding ideologies. König maintains his independence. He defines, criticizes and limits all concepts by what he understands of the character of the living God in the Bible – particularly the Old (!) Testament.

Although this book has no political aspirations, it is clear from several passages that many of these concepts, and particularly the underlying idea of *Geschichtlichkeit*, also have clear and highly relevant consequences for obedience to God in the present social and political life of South Africa.

I consider this book one of the most inspiring studies of the doctrine of God to have been published in recent years. It deserves to be read in far wider circles than can be reached by the Afrikaans language, and I therefore warmly welcome the fact that this English translation opens the door to a greater part of the theological world. A thorough study of this book will not only be illuminating for many students of theology, but will also help preachers and teachers in the church to open new perspectives for faith and action.

HENDRIKUS BERKHOF
Professor of Biblical and Dogmatical Theology
Leyden University

Preface

The main title *Here Am I!* is the introduction of God to his discouraged people in exile (e.g. Isa. 52:6). This title has been chosen because it so vividly expresses God's involvement with his people in their misery. This is one of the main thrusts of the book.

What one would further normally write in an introduction I have decided to put at the end of chapter 4. I have done that because this book is also meant for non-theologians; for people who may not be interested in the more technical aspect of theology. This arrangement makes it possible for them to delve at once into the main content of the book.

For the benefit of readers who may not read European languages with ease I have as far as possible confined myself to English when quoting from texts which were originally written in another language.

This book is the first of a series dealing with the more important aspects of the Biblical message. The next in line is *Jesus the Last, A Christian Reflection on the End.* i.e. eschatology. This means that in the first two books the beginning and the end points of the Biblical message will be considered. In subsequent books I will deal with the other major themes of our faith, beginning with creation, man and election.

This book appeared for the first time a few years ago in Afrikaans. Thereafter an English translation was published by the University of South Africa. I am grateful to Marshall Morgan and Scott who have taken the initiative to make this series available internationally. I also wish to thank Prof. dr H. Berkhof of the Netherlands for writing the foreword.

Department of Systematic Theology　　　　　　　　　ADRIO KÖNIG
University of South Africa
Pretoria
February 1980

1

God and the gods

The incomparableness of God

INTRODUCTION

We live in times in which the world has become small. Quite under-
standably, then, it is a time of contact, dialogue, co-operation. But this
fact also presents us with new questions about God, especially the
question concerning the relationship between God and the gods of the
philosophers and of the religions of the world. It is sometimes said that to
be unknown is to be unloved. The opposite can also be true: to be known
is to be loved. This would suggest, then, that it was easier in earlier days
to maintain the uniqueness of God as against the gods. It was an easy
thing for a theologian to indicate and extol the incomparableness of God
against the background of his own ideas of the nature of the other gods.
But nowadays the smallness of the world has made available a great deal
more knowledge about other gods, and many similarities to the God of
Israel have been pointed out. Supported by a general sense of the
common lot of mankind, it is now – in contrast to former times – easier to
suggest a similarity between God and the gods, and from this to derive a
variety of conclusions regarding the message of the church: for example
that Christianity is no longer an 'export religion'![1]

Without implying that Holy Scripture contains answers to all questions,
the new ones included, it is still necessary to ask what the prophets and
apostles had to say about the relationship between God and the gods,
especially as this emerged in the history of Israel and in the first Christian
congregations.

There is a second reason why this investigation is important for our
times. When the early Christians carried the gospel into the world, they
did so in an environment that was characterised by definite streams of
Greek (particularly Platonic) philosophy. For understandable reasons
those who proclaimed and (later) defended the gospel, had to make their
message about God intelligible to this 'Greek' society. They linked up
closely with so-called neo-Platonism and appropriated a number of the
concepts that were used in this philosophical doctrine of God. Concepts
such as being, 'of-the-same-being', person, and (two) natures, which are
used in the doctrine of the Trinity and the doctrine of Christ, and
concepts such as the unchangeableness and self-sufficiency of God
(*immutabilitas, aseitas*) all derive from this source.

In recent decades there has been a renewed interest in this 'Greek'
heritage in the church in general, but more especially in relation to the

doctrine of God. The easy, almost facile association in early days between
the God of Israel and Platonic theology is still used today by certain
theologians to justify claiming strong similarities between God and the
gods, but other theologians query these similarities on the basis of the
Bible, and there are repeated pleas that the gospel should be set free from
its Greek mould.

This aspect especially is very important. In the following pages the
relationship between God and the gods will be traced in the Bible, and it
will be shown that apart from occasional and passing similarities, there is
a sharp antithesis between God and the gods. A strong question mark will
be placed against any facile association with Platonic philosophy. To
speak of Israel's God in Platonic terms is just as difficult (impossible?) as
it was for the prophets to speak of their LORD in terms derived from Baal
or Bel. In this light it will be shown that God's incomparableness and
uniqueness flow from his very being,[2] and that to surrender this would be
(even today) to surrender the God of Israel.

It will further be shown that the greatness of God, his incomparableness
and exaltedness (transcendence), come under consideration primarily in
his relationship with the gods – and not in the first place in his relationship
to man. This will allow us freedom when discussing the anthropomorphisms in a subsequent chapter, to make them an integral part of the
doctrine of God and to endeavour to overcome our doubts about them.

MOCKING THE GODS IN THE OLD TESTAMENT

The first monograph on this subject has only recently appeared, from the
pen of H. D. Preuss, and in the following pages considerable appreciative
use will be made of his work.[3]

Mocking the gods and their images occur frequently in the Old
Testament. Because this mockery occurs in various forms a reader will
sometimes pass over them unawares. Thus, the simple absence of the
names 'sun' and 'moon' in Genesis 1:14–18 is apparently a sharp challenge
to Babylonian astral religion,[4] in which the sun and the moon were
revered as gods giving light to the world. Against this, in Genesis 1 the
light does not come from the sun and the moon, but precedes them, and
is therefore independent of them. The LORD created the light and he
used the light to govern the separation between day and night (v. 4).
Later he made two 'lights' (a somewhat disrespectful word for the
Babylonian gods!) to take over the functions that he had exercised: to
provide light and to separate night from day (v. 14–15). In this way the
LORD would indicate to his humbled and dispirited people in exile that he
was the true God and that these Babylonian 'gods' were nothing more
than 'officials' in his service, doing what he himself had done earlier, and
for which he therefore did not even need them.[5]

When one investigates more closely the abundant evidence of the
mockery of the gods in the Old Testament, it is even more striking that

the peoples surrounding Israel never practised this and did not even know it. In order to understand this, one must see clearly the difference between the *nature* of their gods and the nature of the LORD.

The nations surrounding Israel deified various natural phenomena (e.g. the sun or the Nile).[6] Such gods had very limited functions and so from their very nature there arose the need for many of them. Peoples and nations had need of rain gods, fertility deities, gods of journeys (to protect them on their travels), war gods. Such gods did not exclude one another, but were complementary. Deity 'takeovers' and mergers were fully in order in the ancient east. Evidence of this is found in the composite names given to various deities, such as Amon-Re or Re-atum (Egypt). Marduk was known by fifty different names (some by combinations with other gods), of which Bel, in Isaiah 46:1, is one.

Radical mockery, such as is found in the Old Testament, could not occur in such circumstances. The mocking of the gods as this occurs in the Old Testament presupposes a denial and mocking of the *deity* of the gods. The implication of the mockery is that Israel's God alone is truly *God*. All other gods are non-gods, 'nothings'.[7]

Such mockery would be impossible among Israel's neighbours, for to them a *plurality* of gods was self-evident. A particular god could indeed be mocked at times, such as for example when the people who served him were defeated in battle. But in such mockery his deity was not denied. On the contrary he could in turn be assimilated by the (war)god of the conqueror.

Exclusivistic utterances would not be enountered in such situations either. The familiar exclamation to the LORD, 'Who is like you?' or 'Who can be compared with you?' is found among other people, but only as doxological hyperbole (an exaggerated form of glorification). That is, it would be used with reference to a particular situation in order to express how wonderful the help of the god concerned had been (e.g. after a great victory). The same people, however, would direct the same words of honour to another god in a different situation.

Another important element in the preaching of the prophets, that is absent from the peoples of the ancient east, concerns unfaithfulness to a god. People could quite calmly change their gods. When, for example, the raingod of a neighbouring people appeared to be more successful than their own, they could either exchange theirs for the other, or allow the two to merge. In addition they could accept and worship as many extra deities as their needs called for. The acceptance of yet another god did not imply any falling away from the old gods since they were all jointly honoured.

By radically opposing God to the gods, however, the prophets stressed the uniqueness and incomparableness of the LORD. When Israel conquered another people, or were delivered from the control of another people, it was not merely because the LORD was stronger than the other god, but because the other was not in fact God. And, when Israel turned to serve any other god, they could no longer serve the true God as well. He is the only true God. This he can be because he is essentially different from the other gods. He is not a mere personification of some natural force that is considered responsible for a particular aspect of the life of his people. He is the personal, living Creator God who holds the entire life of his people in his hands, who indeed creates their history. There can be room for no other god alongside him. This is the meaning of the first commandment: 'You shall have no other gods before me.' But this command is also gospel, good news, for it means: 'You do not *need* to have any other gods before me, since I accept responsibility for the *entire* life of my people.'

The uniqueness and incomparableness of the LORD has in recent times rightly been emphasised as a central element in the preaching of the Old Testament. The fact that it was only in the sixties that the first monograph on this subject appeared,[8] suggests that there was a major vacuum in this respect in the older theologies. The incomparableness of God, and the mockery of the other gods that accompanies it, is of basic significance for the treatment of the being (or the reality) of God. *A prophet would naturally mock the other gods about precisely those things which were strongest in his God.* Thus, for example, no nation is mocked in the Bible for having only one god (since the LORD is but one); but it is mocked because their gods cannot see, or hear, or help or open up the future. For just these reasons it is worthwhile to consider more closely what is involved in the mocking of the gods.

Mocking the gods in Deutero-Isaiah

It is no arbitrary choice to select the second part of Isaiah for this purpose (i.e. Deutero-Isaiah, comprising chapters 40–55). This prophet contains the greatest concentration of the mocking of the gods that is to be found in the Old Testament. In fact this element is as important in the message of Deutero-Isaiah as are the famous *ebed Yahweh* songs (the songs concerning the Servant of the LORD). And it is repeatedly evident that the prophet makes use of mocking motifs that are distributed elsewhere in earlier parts of the Old Testament.

The situation in which this unknown prophet prophesied is, as always, vital to a sound understanding of his message. He comes on the scene in Babylonia shortly before the end of the captivity (possibly about 545 BC). The people did not know, however, that the captivity was soon to end. They lived in humiliation, and by this time had for decades been helplessly handed over to Babylon and their faith was fading. If the LORD was still powerful, he had certainly forgotten them, and was in any event no longer concerned about them (40:27; 49:14; 54:7–8). *If* the LORD were still powerful – this had become the great cancer in their faith, for they could no longer suppress the doubt that the gods of Babylon were perhaps mightier than the LORD. Did not their history, now almost half a century under 'Bel and Nebo' (Isa. 46:1), indicate that God was like the other gods and could indeed be defeated? Against such consuming questions the prophet poses his decisive counter questions, in such passages as Isaiah 40:18, 25; 46:5.

It is in this situation that the prophet makes use of the mockery of the gods. This mockery is thus not to be understood as an independent literary form or matter – this is found nowhere in the Old Testament – but always exists in wider contexts and with a pastoral goal: to convince the dispirited, doubting people of the incomparableness of the LORD, so that they would overcome the temptation to idolatry and trust only in the LORD.

The most important pericopes in which the mocking of the gods occurs are: Isaiah 40:18–26; 41:4–7; 41:21–29; 42:8–17; 43:9–13; 44:6–23; 45:14–25; 46:1–13; 48:3–5, and actually as far as verse 22. The Living Bible can be used effectively for a rapid survey of these passages.

In all of them the LORD and the gods are continually contrasted with one another. The first absolute contrast is that the gods are *fashioned*, and are thus man's creations, while the LORD is *Creator* (40:19 f; 40:26; 41:6 f; 44:10 f; 44:21, 24; 45:18 f; 46:6; 48:13). When the prophet emphasises that the LORD also created the sun, moon and stars (40:26 'these' are the heavenly bodies), it is as in Genesis 1:14–18 a sharp taunt against the Babylonian astral religion, in which the heavenly bodies were gods. The images (identified by Deutero-Isaiah with the gods), however, do not even belong to the category of the things created by God, but have been made by goldsmiths (40:19), who in turn have been made by the LORD (54:16). Consequently the gods are not even only one remove, but in fact two removes from God. In Isaiah 44 the origins of the images are pushed to the ridiculous. From a single tree a man takes firewood to warm himself, to bake his bread and grill his meat (44:15–16), and from the rest he makes himself a god (44:17). Verses 18–20 elaborate on this absurdity. How inconceivable it is that the man cannot reflect on what he is doing! The sharp contrast follows immediately: 'Remember these things, O Jacob and Israel, for you are my servant; *I formed you*, you are my servant.' So far from Israel needing to make gods for themselves, they have been created by the LORD and have been brought into existence by him.[9]

A second contrast follows from the first. *Manufactured* gods are motionless, lifeless (40:20; 41:7; 46:7). Frequently they cannot even stand on their own and have to be nailed to the ground (41:7). In Psalm 115:4–8 this futility and lifelessness is developed more fully still. It is absolutely ludicrous to believe in a god that has no power to save its worshipper (46:7), and it is precisely this point that Israel must think over (46:8), because this above all is what the LORD has done, and promises to do again (soon!). 'The former things of old' (46:9) would seem to be the exodus from Egypt (cf. 43:18), but the new things that God will now do will be infinitely greater and more glorious – so much so that those former things could even be forgotton (43:18–21). What these new things are to be will become clear later. However, the 'former things' already done, have given a crystal-clear picture of his superior worth (41:8–10).

It is in contrast to the inertia of the gods that God's acts of salvation are arrayed. But these are more than isolated interventions in the lives of individuals or the history of the nation. God's acts control, indeed create, history. Against the gods who cannot even move (40:20) the LORD is presented as the one who destroys the work of the rulers of the world by simply blowing on them (40:23–24)!

For the prophet, what is of outstanding importance in this control of history by the LORD is the *new* thing that he is about to do. Not that this was the first time that the LORD had sent his messengers with an announcement of something that would happen in future. 'Behold, the former things have come to pass' (42:9) indicates former things that had also been announced in advance. From Isaiah 44:7–8; 46:9–10 and 48:3–5 (see the Living Bible) it appears that it was always a characteristic of the LORD that he announced beforehand what was going to happen.

In contrast to this are the gods, who are repeatedly challenged: 'Tell us what is to come hereafter, that we may know that you are gods' (41:23; cf. also 41:22; 43:9; 44:7; 45:21; 48:14). But they remain dumb, to such an extent that they cannot even relate past events – things known even to *men* (41:22).

In this light the prophet proceeds to proclaim that a decisive proof that the LORD is the only true God is the fact that events already taking place, that is the triumphant campaign of Cyrus, had been made known *in advance* by the LORD (41:25–28; 44:24–28; 45:21; 46:10–11; 48:14–15). Utterances such as 44:28 were in fact spoken years before Cyrus began his march.

This new act of the LORD was of decisive significance to the oppressed and downhearted people. It would be through Cyrus the Persian that the LORD would humble proud Babylon, break its power and grant Israel a triumphant 'second exodus' back to Jerusalem (43:14–21; 45:9–16; 47:1–15; 49:8–13). When one considers the decisive importance of the exodus from Egypt for the preaching of the early prophets,[10] and how this intervention on God's part in the history of Israel's origins continually reminded her of his love and faithfulness, it is breathtaking to hear Deutero-Isaiah declare that the exodus would be as nothing in comparison with the 'new exodus', the return journey, in which the LORD would lead his people back in festive joy (as against the tribulations of the wilderness journey of the first exodus).

The fact that *God* fashions the history of the world at definite and decisive moments becomes particularly clear from a comparison between Jeremiah 27 (especially v. 6–9) and Isaiah 45 (especially v. 1–4). (Cf. also Isa. 44:28.) Before the exile the LORD appointed the king of Babylon, Nebuchadnezzar, as his 'servant' and no nation could stand against him. But now, half a century later, he appoints Cyrus to his service, and even Babylon itself will not be able to withstand him.

This raises the old problem of the 'proofs of God' in a new (actually the original!) sense. The LORD calls repeatedly for a lawsuit between himself and his people on the one hand, and the gods and their worshippers on the other. The clearest example is recorded in Isaiah 41:21–9, but it appears elsewhere too, in 45:21 and less directly in 40:19 f and 41:6 f. In such a lawsuit judgment would be given and the guilty condemned. To this end witness and evidence are produced. In 41:21–9 the primary interest is in the 'proofs' (41:21), and these proofs are to show whether the gods or the LORD is truly God. Such a proof would be given if either party could demonstrate control of history, including the ability to announce the course of the future. The concern here is not with mere isolated 'predictions',[11] which might later evoke a debate as to whether the foreteller had manipulated things in such a way that the event took place, or whether it was by chance a good guess in the midst of many abortive predictions. Such isolated predictions abounded in Babylon (44:25; 47:13). Rather, the proof that is called for relates to the god who controls history: past, present and future. This is precisely what the LORD does.

Let us first look at his *future* dealings. In this court hearing, the issue is that the LORD had announced beforehand the triumphant campaign of Cyrus, who would subjugate all the nations in his path, *but would liberate Israel and let them return to Palestine*. This shows clearly that the LORD is not a mere opportunist who, with or without the aid of a little extra common sense, could guess correctly, but that he caused Cyrus to arise; indeed, that he used Cyrus to subdue the nations (in particular Babylon, who had oppressed Israel so savagely – Isa. 47) and equally to liberate his people and lead them back (41:25–27). As for the *past*, Israel always remembered the triumphant exodus from Egypt which itself had been a contest between God and the Egyptian gods, and in which none of them could withstand the LORD.[12] And finally as for the *present*, they are still in the exile into which the LORD had caused them to be taken by Nebuchadnezzar.

Taken in the context sketched above it is clear that we are dealing here with the broader movements of history, past, present and future. And in these historic dealings God is free at one time to punish his people by means of a heathen king (Nebuchadnezzar) and at another time to liberate them through another heathen king (Cyrus), and that out of the hands of their former oppressor. In a single event he uses the same king (Cyrus) to subdue and punish the nations, and to free Israel and bring her back to Jerusalem. Two things here serve to prove that God is the true God: the factual control of history, and the fact that he announced beforehand what he was going to do.

In sharp contrast to this is the powerlessness of the gods. When it becomes evident that they cannot open up the future and therefore are unable to determine history, Yahweh calls out in seeming despair: 'Do good or do harm, that we may be dismayed and terrified' (41:23). 'Do

good or do harm' is an idiomatic expression implying: 'Please do something, *anything*, just so long as you react' (cf. Jer. 10:5 and Zeph. 1:12).
In this lawsuit the judge is eager, almost too eager to accept virtually any
evidence. Even if it were but an indication that the gods can move,
Yahweh and his people would stand amazed. The verdict that the LORD
pronounces over them (41:24, 29) makes it clear, however, that they have
reacted in no way whatsoever – which makes the laughableness of their
'deity' all the greater.

This contrast presents the LORD as the *incomparable God*, especially in
the sense that *he intervenes in history as the saving and judging God*.[13] And
this presents a proof of God that is conclusive. It is a proof of God that
serves a different purpose from the proofs in the history of the church
(think of the famous five 'ways' of Thomas by means of which man by his
effort and reasoning endeavours to reach God). Here we have a proof of
God in which *God himself proves himself*, and consequently has no need of
our proofs. He does, however, give his people the privilege of being his
witnesses, testifying to his decisive acts in their history. In Isaiah 43:9–13
especially, God and the gods are once more contrasted with each other,
but this time by their witnesses. And it becomes evident that the gods can
call up no witnesses (v. 9) because they have never intervened decisively
in history. The people of Israel, on the other hand, are the LORD's
witnesses (v. 10 f), having testified for centuries to the way in which he
made history at the exodus (v. 16–17), and whose prophets witnessed to
his more recent intervention which had resulted in the exile. And, as
though these inteventions were of only minor importance Israel would
now be witness to his greatest and most decisive act (v. 18–21): the
triumphant return journey resulting from Cyrus's impending victories.

Here is no question of a *sacrificium intellectus* – a betrayal of the intellect
in order to believe in God. On the contrary. Far from it being a leap in the
dark to have faith in God, it would be a leap in the dark to trust in the
gods. But God had proved himself through that which he had done and
which was visible to the entire world, and he would prove himself in a
similar way once more, and was announcing his intention in advance.
Those who would not believe on the evidence of this self-attestation,
would only demonstrate how unfounded and therefore guilty was their
unbelief. A strong case can be made for the point of view that faith is the
normal and reasonable human reaction to God's revelation, and that
unbelief is an inconceivable and inexplicable, but for this reason also,
guilty reaction.[14]

It is now also clear that the various verbs that are used of God in
contradistinction to the gods, such as *save, hear, bear, liberate*, must not
be understood only in a general sense, but concretely in relation to
Israel's return to Jerusalem.

In Isaiah 44:17 and 22 the following are juxtaposed: On the one hand
there is the idol with its worshipper on his knees urgently crying:
'Deliver me, for thou art my god!' But it is a fruitless cry. On the other

hand there is the true God who has not even been called upon by his people but nevertheless proclaims to them the forgiveness of their sins. These sins are not mere sins in general. They are those sins which estranged them from their God and brought upon them the judgment of the exile (cf. Isa. 40:1–2). 'For I have redeemed you' is therefore a prophetic perfect tense (*perfectum propheticum*) which views a future act of the LORD (the return to Jerusalem) with as much certainty as though it had already taken place.

The other expressions of contrast also have this concrete meaning. And where is this mocking contrast more sharply portrayed than in Isaiah 46? The collapse of Bel and Nebo (apparently the most important of Babylon's deities) points to the attack by Cyrus on Babylon. (Whether this still lies in the future so that we have another prophetic perfect here, or whether the event has already taken place – the latter is less probable – is not important for the moment.) The gods were unable to *save* the situation (v. 2) (i.e. to protect their dependants), but had to be *carried* about by them (v. 1), as defeated gods, in the triumphal procession of the enemy. Against them stood the LORD who had *borne* his people from their mothers' womb (v. 3), and would continue to *carry* them to their old age; indeed 'I will *carry* and will *save*' (v. 4). The contrast speaks for itself. But we must not lose the concreteness of these concepts. The people who had been 'carried from the womb' had had a 'prenatal' life in Egypt and came to birth (became a people) through the exodus. So this *carrying* is also concrete: out of Egypt. Confident that God will continue to carry and save them, they can look forward to the spectacular return under a king who challenges and overcomes all the other nations.

In fact it is not only for *Israel* that the LORD intends to actually perform these deeds, but, by means of the return, he aims to summon the surrounding nations and move them also to seek their salvation in him. The most arresting example of this is Isaiah 45:20–25 (see the Living Bible for a survey). Those of the nations that had survived the hand of Cyrus (v. 20) – actually, that would survive – are called to a lawsuit. They must now come to a decision. If they can – even now! – show that their gods can do something, well and good. But is it not so that only the LORD had 'declared it of old' (namely Cyrus's victories, v. 21)? And does this not prove that he is the only true God? Furthermore: is he not the only '*righteous* God and *Saviour*'? In this he is incomparable. *Righteous* and *saving* are not opposed to each other but are closely linked. Israel had been more severely oppressed in Babylonia than was called for (47:6 f), and for this reason the LORD's salvation was 'righteous': that is, it gave justice to those who had suffered unjustly.

But because the LORD is righteous not only towards Israel, the heathen may also come to a decision: 'Turn to me and be saved all the ends of the earth! For I am God and there is no other' (45:22). Because God delivers his people with the repentance of the nations in mind (v. 23), he now expects of the nations a positive reaction (v. 24). Indeed, in raising up

Cyrus he had proved himself God in such an incontrovertible way (v. 21)
that a conversion to him on a massive scale might well be expected. The
nations would come to the realization that their gods had deceived them
and would turn their backs on them and stream to the LORD. In this way
they would become the witnesses of the LORD! (v. 24). See also Isaiah
45:14; 49:6–7, 22–3.

It is not necessary to take sides here with von Rad against the idea of
mission in Deutero-Isaiah.[15] Mission is not exclusively a going out to
other peoples. If in this situation Israel is such a witness to the LORD that
the nations see in her the wonders the LORD had performed and as a
result turn to him themselves, then the goal of all forms of mission is
achieved. One would rather agree with Blauw's distinction between
centripetal and centrifugal mission; that is, in the Old Testament, mission
was intended to be performed mainly in such a way that the unbelievers
stream to the people of the LORD in Jerusalem (centripetal) in order to
find their salvation there in the LORD, whereas after the outpouring of the
Holy Spirit the church went out to the heathen and there proclaimed the
salvation of the LORD (centrifugal).[16]

On the other hand, it is important to point with von Rad to the
radicalness of the LORD's turning to Israel, according to Deutero-Isaiah.[17]
Just as the mocking of the gods had to convince the doubting people of
the powerlessness of the idols and the power of the LORD, so the proclamation of the radical love of God would have to throw light on the bitter
half-century that they had had to endure in humiliation and oppression.
One of the most striking characteristics of the preaching of Deutero-
Isaiah is that he (unlike the prophets of the exile) no longer emphasises
the sins and the non-repentance of the people, but speaks of these sins
only as *forgiven* sins (43:25; 44:22), and even goes so far as to say that
Israel has suffered excessively for her sins (40:2). The gloom and God-
forsakenness through which the people had gone was but a moment in
God's wrath in comparison with the eternal love with which he would
have compassion on them (54:7–8). And now he unfolds to his people
what pain and suffering he went through in restraining himself so long
and hiding himself while his people were being oppressed (42:14), but
because he loves them (43:4) they need no longer fear (which is impressed
on them repeatedly, apparently because their fears had reached such a
pitch – 41:10, 13, 14; 43:4; 49:14–16).

Von Rad shows that no prophet had ever spoken like this before.
Never before had the LORD bowed himself so low through a prophet, and
endeavoured so hard to drive out all fear. Never before had God so
surrendered his heart and declared so pressingly his unconquerable love.
Although we are touching here on the content of chapter 2 (on the
anthropomorphisms), all this is appropriate to a discussion of the mocking
of the gods because it is these aspects which give the richest content to
God's incomparableness. Because God loves his people with a love which
cannot even be discussed in relation to the gods, he does immense,

unheard of things in order to restore them.

Mocking the gods according to Psalm 82

There are Old Testament scholars who argue that while the incomparableness and exclusiveness of the LORD over against the gods may well be the rule, the relationship between the LORD and El (a Hebrew word which in the Old Testament is translated either 'God' or 'god') constitutes an exception. On the grounds of this restful, peaceful relationship between the LORD and El they argue that a more positive relationship should be accepted today between God and the gods of the great world religions. One has the impression that Pannenberg bases his idea that the entire history of religion is the revelation of God – and that the archives of the world religions are therefore the subject of theology – on this supposed positive relationship between the LORD and El.[18]

However, because El does not play an important part in Deutero-Isaiah it is necessary to make a closer analysis of one of the most significant pericopes where both the LORD and El come under discussion. Psalm 82 has been chosen for this purpose.

Although the word LORD (Yahweh) does not occur in the psalm, it should be kept in mind that this is one of the so-called Elohistic psalms, that is, those psalms in which the name the LORD is replaced with the word God (*Elohim*). So in verse 1, as well as in verse 8, we can read 'the LORD' for 'God'.

According to verse 1 the LORD ('God') stands in the council of the gods (*Elohim*), and holds judgment over these assembled deities. Such assemblies of the gods were well-known in the world of Canaanite religion. The principal god, or president of the assembly, was a god named El. (There were actually many other gods bearing the name El, some important and some less important.[19] This fact is all too frequently overlooked when it is argued as though the contest was between the LORD and only one particular El).

Verse 1 indicates that what has now happened is that the LORD has assumed the place and function of this El. He now functions as chairman of the council of the gods. The assembly takes the form of a court action in which the LORD hears a charge against the gods.

Earlier Old Testament scholars attempted to make a strong case for the suggestion that these gods were actually judges.[20] Today however, it is fairly generally accepted that we have here a play on the familiar heathen idea of an assembly of the gods – an idea which occurs elsewhere in the Old Testament as well, under a variety of terms.[21] It will later become evident, however, that it makes little difference whether one accepts the first or the second interpretation.

There are two indications that the LORD actually takes the place of El and imparts his own content to the chairmanship of the gathering of the gods: first and foremost is the fact that he sacks the gods after he has found them guilty of mismanagement, and then secondly, there is the nature of the offence for which he finds them guilty. The latter is of great importance to our understanding of who God himself is.

The accusation against the gods is that they judge unjustly and show partiality to the godless (v. 2). As usual in a court action, the gods are given the opportunity to prove their innocence by doing what is appropriate to gods (cf. *Inter alia* Isa. 41:21 ff; 43:9 ff). This is demanded in verses 3–4:

> Give justice to the weak and the fatherless;
> Maintain the right of the afflicted and the destitute.
> Rescue the weak and the needy;
> Deliver them from the hand of the wicked.

By doing this, the gods would demonstrate their deity, would fulfil their task, and would be acquitted by the LORD. *This* is what is divine; *this* is God's appropriate action: justice and righteousness. But the gods are unable to do this (v. 5), and they are accordingly found to be no gods at all and are sacked from the assembly – the assembly over which the LORD had assumed the presidency – which implies that it was he who imposed the demand on the gods for justice and righteousness. In fact, it is exactly that which he requires of the gods ('give justice' v. 3) that he himself will do ('judge' v.8), 'for the judgment is God's (Deut. 1:17). On the basis of the structure of the psalm, which uses the same verb in verses 3 and 8, verse 8 should probably read:

> Arise, O God, *establish justice* on the earth;
> for to thee belong all the nations. [22]

The call to the LORD begins deliberately with the same verb as that demanded of the gods (*špṭ*), and the request to the LORD ('judge – establish justice for – the earth') is actually a summary of the *entire* demand addressed to the gods in verses 3–4. So the LORD will now do everything that the gods do not do, and will in this way prove that he is (the only true) God.

In the light of these considerations it is probable that the Psalm should be dated shortly before Josiah's reforms, and is specifically directed against polytheism and a tendency towards syncretism (the merging of gods and religions). But for this reason the exclusive strain of the psalm is of great significance. That is, the LORD took over the presidency of the council of gods, and did it in such a way that El was eliminated and no longer appeared in the picture. Other Old Testament traditions, in which the LORD takes over the name El, should be interpreted in this light. It is not the merging of the LORD with one or other god named El, but an elimination of El, with the LORD taking over his place and functions.

The history of Abram and Melchizedek provides an excellent example (Gen. 14). Melchizedek is introduced as a priest of 'God Most High' (v. 18–20): in Hebrew, *El Elyon*. This *El Elyon* was believed to be the creator of heaven and earth (v. 19). But when Abram answers Melchizedek, he refers to 'the LORD , God Most High, maker of heaven and earth' (v. 22). So if there is any reference to a most high God who is the Creator God, it must be the LORD, and the LORD immediately assumes the name and the function ascribed to this god.[23] Genesis 33:20 can be understood in the same way. Here it is literally stated: 'El (is) the God of Israel', and this comes down to the fact that the El to whom reference is made can only be the God of Israel. Deuteronomy 32:8–9 occurs in a song which begins with praise to the LORD (v. 3 f) and ends with a challenge to the other gods to do what befits a true God (v. 37–38) followed by a declaration concerning the exclusiveness of the LORD (v. 39). In this song in its present form (which is the revelatory witness to which the church gives attention), the Most High of v. 8 is identified with the LORD of v. 9. Consequently, even if it is true that it was only during the course of their religious development that Israel came to the awareness that their God was the only true god and that all the marvels ascribed to other gods were in reality works of the LORD, the church lives by this later testimony of Israel, and not by the earlier development phases which were deliberately discarded in the final witness.

MOCKING THE GODS IN THE NEW TESTAMENT

At first glance it seems that the mocking of the gods has moved into the background in the New Testament in favour of a more 'theoretical' doctrine of God. But this impression is shown to be wrong and disappears as soon as one begins to consider the relationship between Jesus and the evil powers. This relationship has a crucial role throughout the New Testament. Since I intend to go into this in some detail elsewhere,[24] only the results of that study will be taken up here and interpreted in terms of the doctrine of God.

Structurally there is a remarkable similarity between the mocking of the gods in the Old Testament and the triumph of Christ over the powers of evil in the New Testament. While a significant part of the synoptic gospels is devoted to the conflict between Jesus and the powers, it never develops into an actual bloody clash. Whenever Jesus appears on the scene, the powerlessness of the powers becomes apparent. Even as Jesus approaches they cry out in terror, acknowledge his sovereignty, entreat him not to destroy or hurt them, surrender their victims and make off. Read Mark 1:21–8; 1:34 v., 39; 3:10–12; 3:20–7; 5:1–20. In the letters it is emphasized that Jesus Christ is the Head of all 'principalities and powers' (indicating the powers of evil), and that he has disarmed them, making them a 'public spectacle' (TEV), and so has triumphed over them (Col. 2:9, 15). For this reason, believers really can 'stand firm' against all attacks of the evil powers, provided they take their stand 'in Christ' (Eph. 6:11 f). ('In Christ' is the comprehensive phrase for the full armour described in Ephesians 6.) And while the powers of evil are already radically subdued, they will in the future be totally destroyed, so that it will not be possible even to question the sovereignty of Christ (1 Cor. 15:24–6; Phil. 2:9–11). The ease with which the final destruction will take place is further testimony to the complete superiority of God in Christ (2 Thess. 2:8; Rev. 19:19–21; 20:7–8; indeed, consider all the 'wars' in Revelation).

The element of mockery is not so consciously and deliberately apparent, but is more hidden and implicit. And yet the total powerlessness of the demons, the concepts which Paul uses for example in Colossians 2:15, and especially the 'wars' described in the Revelation, all reflect the same structure as the mocking of the gods in the Old Testament: there is no talk of real opposition to Jesus Christ or of vicious conflicts. The evil powers make themselves laughable in their attacks on him. Their only effective recourse is to flee, and this they can do very well.

But the question that arises is whether it is correct to see the relationship between Jesus and the powers as an extension of the relationship between God and the gods in the Old Testament. On the one hand the question is whether in Jesus Christ we are confronted with God himself; and on the other, whether it is the gods that we encounter in the powers.

I presuppose here what I intend to put forward concerning the presence of God in Jesus.[25] It comes down to the fact that we do not merely have God's revelation of something (e.g. simply his 'revealed will') in Jesus Christ, but that in him is fully revealed that which makes God God: that is, his free love. Anyone who contemplates the life of Christ as a sacrifice of love for the salvation of the world knows who God is. God acts in the concreteness of the love of Jesus for sinners. While, alongside Jesus Christ, we read in the New Testament about the Father and the Holy Spirit, and there is thus 'more' in God than only Jesus, there is qualitatively nothing else in God than that which is revealed in Jesus. In Jesus God has poured out his heart, and now, through the Holy Spirit, he opens our hearts and helps us to speak from our hearts to him.

On the one hand it is true that various interpretations are possible when we consider the little word 'is' in the statement 'Jesus *is* God'. Just as there were complex discussions concerning the communion formula and the words of Jesus: 'This is my body', so too there will be further debates in reformed circles about the (ontological?) relationship between God and Christ, as, for example in Berkhof's Christology and Schoonenberg's defence of it.[26] Theoretically it would in fact be possible for someone to hold that in saying 'Christ is truly God' the church (merely) means that God acted through Christ, and that Christ, e.g. by his love for the lost, was revealing God's heart to the world. On the other hand, for the purposes of our present discussion, even this basic minimum would be sufficient to support an aspect of a particular comparison: in the actions of Christ in the New Testament, including his attitude towards the powers of evil, we learn to know God.

There is less clarity concerning the possible connection between the gods of the Old Testament and the demons and powers of the New.

First of all, it is mistaken to assert that the Old Testament knows nothing of evil powers and demons, or that the New Testament knows nothing of gods and idols.

While the gods do dominate the scene in the Old Testament, there are many references to demonic powers.[27] In Isaiah 13:21 f and 34:14 we read of satyrs and the night hag – both demonic powers. But there is a strong possibility that the other animals mentioned also represent demons or demon-possessed creatures (wild beasts, howling creatures, ostriches, jackals). Then too, Leviticus 16:8 mentions Azazel, which was possibly a Semitic god of the flocks which later took on demonic characteristics. Psalm 91:5–6 speaks of the 'terror by night', the arrow, the pestilence, the destruction, and should be interpreted demonically, and so too the 'leech' of Proverbs 30:15. Besides these, Satan appears three times: Job 1:6 f; 2:1 f; 1 Chronicles 21:1 and Zechariah 3:1 f.

There are a few further expressions of great importance. In Deuteronomy 32:17 and Psalm 106:37 it is said that Israel offered sacrifices to demons (*šdym*). In both cases the reference is made in contexts where the gods are being discussed, and from references such as Leviticus 18:21; Deuteronomy 12:31; 2 Kings 23:10 and Jeremiah 19:5 it is sufficiently clear that the child sacrifices were made to the gods (idols). Leviticus 17:7 also refers to sacrifices to satyrs (Isa. 13:21 and 34:14) and a similar reference can be found in 2 Chronicles 11:15. (Cf. also 2 Kgs. 23:8 and Hos. 12:12.) There is some uncertainty as to what it means when in these texts the gods are called demons or devils,[28] but the least that can be concluded is that there is a definite link between gods and demons, and that the later belief that there is indeed a much closer relationship between them was made possible by these utterances.

What makes these utterances so important is the fact that they are taken up in the New Testament in the same context. When Paul warns against idolatry in 1 Corinthians 10:14–22, he describes the sacrifices as being made to *devils* (demons). To emphasise the point he uses the idea of demons four times in this pericope when referring to idols: first he speaks of sacrifices to demons (v. 20), and from this he concludes that a sacrifice to demons implies fellowship with them. After this he goes into further details and speaks (in connection with communion) of the 'cup of demons' (as against the 'cup of the LORD'), and of the 'table of demons' (as against the 'table of the LORD' v. 21). It is generally accepted that Paul is referring here to Deuteronomy 32:17, and this is further evident, for example, in the fact that the LXX also uses 'demons' to translate *šd* in Deuteronomy 32:17. Revelation 9:20 also suggests a particular connection between gods and demons.

When, against this background, one considers the role that the exorcism of demons had in the earthly ministry of Jesus, it seems acceptable to consider the mocking of the evil powers in the New Testament as in essential continuity with the mocking of the gods in the Old Testament.

This does not mean that all the categories of evil powers in the New Testament can be equated with and regarded as a continuation of the gods of the Old Testament, but rather that there is in the New Testament a definite cleavage between two kingdoms, one under Jesus Christ and the other under Satan, and that little attention is given to the supernatural subjects of these two kingdoms.[29] The division and the boundaries, and especially the commanders, are central. The question then is not precisely what the relationship might be, for example, between the powers and principalities on the one hand, or the demons and the gods on the other, but that the gods of the Old Testament are classified quite clearly with Satan and his followers (inter alia through their being named as demons) and so become part of that total host of supernatural beings which under Satan are in opposition to Jesus Christ – and which through him are dethroned and made into a laughing stock.

On the other hand it should also be noted that the New Testament expands these hordes of evil spirits under Satan to include other powers too. Against the sovereignty of God are ranged: 'the belly' (Phil. 3:19); mammon (Matt. 6:24); government (Acts 4:19; 5:29); and the so-called 'elemental spirits' (Gal. 4:9).[30]

COMPARABLENESS AS WELL

The title of this chapter could be misleading. There is not only *in*comparableness between God and the gods – just as there is not only comparableness between God and man (chapter 2). While the emphasis certainly does fall on the incomparableness of God in relation to the gods, yet there is also a definite comparableness. And this is not confined to the 'positive' relationship between the LORD and El. Throughout the Old Testament points of comparison are drawn between the LORD and the various gods. And indeed, this is inevitable. The word El itself, used by both Jewish and other Semitic peoples indicates a specific agreement. Were *no* comparison possible, Israel would have found it impossible to explain the meaning of the word in speaking to the heathen about the LORD. Naturally, they had to stress his radical difference, but this they could only do on the basis of the common fact that when the heathen heard the word El (God) they thought of a 'divine being'.

This agreement is not merely formal, but has a clear content. Just as the LORD is known as the Creator of heaven and earth, the various Semitic peoples also believed in a god that was the creator. And, while the LORD was known as the one who directed nature (with rain and fruitful years), and the life of the people (with prosperity and freedom), so too did the heathen have gods that were responsible for these things.

What makes these substantial agreements even more important is that when the people of Israel came into Canaan and established themselves there, the LORD appropriated some of the functions of the Canaanite gods and in this way revealed his own being and qualities more clearly to

Israel. That these appropriations had a basis in principle and not only in merely co-incidental similarity is clear from the fact that the LORD took over names and attributes not only of El (in relation to whom there is little mention of antithesis or polemics), but also of Baal and other gods, against whom there were strong antithetical (hostile) attitudes.

It is helpful to consider some of these appropriations, and especially the way in which they occurred. The LORD takes over various names of El: e.g. *El, El Elyon* (Gen. 14:18–24), *El Shaddai* (e.g. Gen. 17:1; 28:3; 35:11). He also takes over certain functions, such as the presidency of the pantheon of the gods – a typical Canaanitic phenomenon (Psalm 82). But he also takes over a good deal from *Baal*, perhaps even more than from El. He (and not Baal) provides bread and water, wool and flax, oil and drink (Hos. 2:5, 8). The LORD, and not Baal, gives the dew of heaven, corn, wine, fruitfulness of land and flocks. He gives the rain and fruitfulness of mankind. In fact, it is probable that Psalm 29 was taken from an original Canaanitic-Syrian environment and adapted to the LORD.[31]

In this connection, two matters are of the greatest importance. These appropriations must not be thought of as features that were willy-nilly imposed on the LORD from without, merely because he was God, and these were things that other gods possessed or performed.[32] Far rather, the LORD takes over, or the people ascribe to him, that which he already is or has. A good example of this is the fact that the LORD is confessed as Creator. It is frequently assumed that the LORD was not held to be Creator from the earliest times and that this was the case only after the encounter with El (Gen. 14:18 f), who was described as the creator of heaven and earth. But Labuschagne has shown that this is an *argumentum e silentio* (argument from silence) and proves nothing beyond suggesting that through this contact with El, Israel became aware of a facet of their faith that was latently present all along.[33]

In fact, these appropriations took place in a unique manner. This is evident, for example, from the name *El Qanna* (a jealous God), as ascribed to the LORD. This name could not have been used previously for El since it presupposes the incomparableness of the LORD,[34] an incomparableness and uniqueness that was not encountered in Israel's environment, as has already been indicated. In other words, after El had been taken over as one of the names of the LORD, it acquired the addition 'jealous', since the LORD is jealous. The appropriations are determined then by the unique nature of the LORD.

The second aspect concerns the way in which these appropriations occurred. When, for example, the LORD assumes the place of the chief god El, and accordingly takes over the presidency of the council, he *replaces* El, and does not merely merge with him. In the mergers of the heathen gods the 'new' god assumes the names of both deities, with the result that in various religions gods have double names (e.g. Amon-Re or Re-Atum). In contrast, after such a takeover, the Old Testament confesses: 'The God of Israel is El' (Gen. 33:20).

Furthermore, the LORD does what was previously ascribed to El, in his own way. Under the LORD, the gods in the council lose their divine status.[35] Under El they were, it is true, minor deities who had to honour and make obeisance to their head, but they nevertheless remained gods. In Babylon it was Marduk that received the tribute of the pantheon of the gods. The Old Testament often speaks of these 'sons of the gods', as for example in Psalm 29:1, where they are called 'heavenly beings'. But under the LORD's authority they are no longer gods. They are either servant spirits of the heavenly world, that are obedient to the LORD (1 Kgs. 22:29; Job 1:6 f; 2:1 f; 38:7; Ps. 89:7; Isa. 6:2 f); or they are dethroned and humiliated because they do not do what the LORD expects of them (Ps. 82). While there would consequently be a fair amount of confusion during the course of such a takeover, it would in this case eventually become clear to the people that the LORD was different, and that he does not have a council of gods in which he is merely the *primus inter pares* (first among equals).

In the case of Baal the appropriations take place more polemically and antithetically, although not too much should be made of the 'peaceful' (non-polemical) takeovers from El. The explanation for the difference that is often given is that El did not actually threaten the position of the LORD in Israel and was no real danger. However, it should be kept in mind that the real confrontation between the LORD and El took place long before the Old Testament was committed to writing in the form that we have it today. One can therefore say no more than that *at the time when the Old Testament was committed to writing* El was no longer a serious threat, whereas Baal and the other gods were, and that as a result the attitude towards El was far less negative.

So far as the takeovers from Baal are concerned, the same matters become clear that have already been referred to. In 1 Chronicles 12:5 we find the name Bealiah, and this means 'The Lord is Baal'. Here too, the LORD remains subject, and takes Baal over. But he does it in such a way that he takes over and performs the good things that the heathen believed of Baal, while rejecting and condemning Baal's features that are inappropriate to himself. Since it was particularly believed of Baal that, as the god of nature, he could deliver those in natural dangers, the prophets proclaimed that in reality it was the LORD that did these things and not Baal (Hos. 2:5, 8); and indeed, in a most arresting way, the matter was demonstrated before the eyes of the people and the prophets of Baal (1 Kgs. 18). But when children were sacrificed to Baal (Jer. 19:5) or Moloch, this was rejected by the LORD as inappropriate to him.

Preuss offers several perceptive summarising comments on this whole matter.[36] Under the LORD's guidance, especially after the conquest of the land, Israel did not only reject the Canaanite world of gods and beliefs, but also took over some features which were appropriate to the LORD and could be absorbed into Israel's faith without affecting or destroying the essential structure of their belief in the LORD. That many dangers lurked in this is indisputable. And yet, even in the matter of images and metaphors, Israel knew very well what was suitable to the LORD, and what was not. This can be illustrated by the fact that many more comparisons and pictures for him are drawn from history than from nature. Because the LORD is the God of history, he had revealed himself more fully in the course of history; among other things by taking over from the gods new realms appropriate to his being. Thus far, Preuss.

One cannot simply accept all Preuss' formulations without qualification – e.g. the idea that the LORD became greater and stronger through these acquisitions. Theologically it seems preferable to treat these takeovers and their consequences epistemologically rather than ontologically, and thus not in relation to the being of God, but rather in relation to his revelation. Thus, it would seem that at an earlier stage Israel did not perceive clearly that the LORD also controlled nature, fruitfulness and harvest, until they were confronted by a people that believed these things of their god (Baal). This confrontation brought Israel to the awareness that their God, who had undertaken responsibility for their entire life, did in reality also control nature. And as soon as Israel perceived this (during the course of revelation), they also realised that the other gods did not in fact do so. Sometimes this realisation came to them through dramatic events (1 Kgs. 18). So then, God did not gradually become greater and stronger, but *revealed himself more fully* by way of particular things that other people believed of their gods.

Something of the same kind occurs several times in the New Testament, as in the letter to the Colossians. Whatever one must make of the powers in this letter, it is clear that the community cherished a real fear of them, and was under the impression that they should be honoured (2:18–23). The apostle makes use of this situation to proclaim and explain the sovereignty of Jesus Christ over these powers as well. Christ had triumphed completely over them – had in fact made a mockery of them (2:15), and he is accordingly head over all rulers and authority (2:10). Even as created beings, all these things are dependent on him (1:16–17). From this vantage point the community was given an entirely new insight into reality and into the significance of Christ and here, just as in the Old Testament, use is made of a situation in which powers with (supposed) authority were thought to have legitimate claims on obedience.

In the famous address on the Areopagus, too, use is made of a certain connection and similarity of ideas and comparison. Paul does not enter a zoo or botanic gardens as a preamble to speaking about God. He walks through the temples and among the idols (Acts 17:16), and makes his point of contact the altar with the inscription: 'To an unknown god' (v. 23) – not to mention the use he makes of their poets.

In the light of this (limited but substantial) comparableness between God and the gods, there can be no objection in principle to the use of terms taken from Greek philosophy. Even the Greek idea that God is the origin or explanation of reality, had to be taken into the church's message (and indeed, the monotheistic ideas of Greek philosophy were also used with great profit). As will appear later, the only objection is that the apologists (defenders of the Christian faith in the second century) did not do this critically enough. Instead of giving these Greek philosophical ideas a subsidiary role, they drew them into the very centre, so that for ages in some circles the doctrine of God was related more to an impersonal something (cause, ground, meaning) than to the living God.

In passing, there is something that is sometimes forgotten when this Greek idea (that God is the explanation, or origin of reality) is undiscriminatingly equated with the biblical message that God is the Creator of heaven and earth. This is the problem of faith that a Christian experiences when he perceives what it means to describe God as the explanation of all that is. Anyone who refuses to idealise or romanticise reality, but looks it straight in the eye, sees around him more signs of the demonic than of the true God. Indeed, there is more pain and misery, injustice and violence in this world than love, prosperity, justice and joy. So whoever names God the 'origin' of all that exists, has to reinterpret this Greek term radically in the light of the biblical message concerning creation, fall and redemption.[37]

But in spite of these and other similar dangers and warnings, it remains basically true that the church, like Israel, can learn something of the true God through contact with other religions – even though it will sometimes be negative and polemical. But such influences from the heathen gods must never be permitted to lead to syncretism; they must not be the *absorption* of these gods into God, but must remain *appropriations*. An appropriation of this kind can positively lead to a clearer understanding of the true God, but the heathen god is in the process excluded or replaced, not absorbed. El is eliminated, not taken in. 'The God of Israel is El'! (Gen. 33:20).

This will be considered more fully in the next paragraph where the incomparableness between God and the gods will be discussed.

BUT ABOVE ALL, INCOMPARABLENESS

During the course of the discussion of the limited comparableness between God and the gods, we came inevitably to the conclusion that the LORD is different. For example, he is not merely the first among equals in the pantheon.

That was a hint of the other, actual matter that becomes clear in a comparison of God with the gods: the incomparableness of the LORD. This is altogether the most important thing that emerges from the relationship between God and the gods, and the resulting mockery of the gods. It is in this context pre-eminently that we hear the question: 'To whom then will you liken God?' (Isa. 40:18, 25; 44:7; 46:5; Exod. 15:11; Deut. 3:24; Ps. 89:9).

The incomparableness of the LORD is not confined to a comparison with the gods. He is also incomparable in relation to the wise men of the world (Jer. 10:7; 1 Cor. 1:17–25). But that is not the usual way in which the relationship between God and man, and especially God and his people, is discussed. There the issue is rather of comparableness, as will emerge in chapter 2.[38]

A general impression of the complete incomparableness between God and the gods can be gained from the following brief summary of what Preuss says about the mocking of the gods in Deutero-Isaiah: The LORD elects a people; people choose gods. The LORD is Creator; people make gods. The LORD is the God that accompanies his people, escorting and bearing them; gods are immobile, can do nothing, and have to be carried. The LORD cannot be portrayed in images; the gods acquire their form in images. The LORD proves by his words and deeds that he is the only true God; the gods say and do nothing, and in fact cannot, and are in a mocking way identified with their images. What we have here then are not rational arguments, but powerful deeds which could be experienced. It is striking that Israel is never urged to draw these conclusions from what the LORD had done and what they had experienced. What God does speaks for itself. It should therefore be a self-evident conclusion that he is the only true God. He will prove himself, and that will be convincing.[39]

That the LORD is incomparable means that he is different from the gods and heavenly beings, cannot be compared with them, and must be described in terms different from those used for them. The question before us now is whether this incomparableness has had full justice done to it in the history of the church and theology. From the first centuries of dogmatic formulation, when the doctrine of God took shape, down to particular circles of theology in our own day, there have been strong and deliberate associations with certain streams of Greek philosophy.

In dealing with the 'incommunicable' attributes of God, H. Bavinck declares that 'philosophy often called and described God as the only, eternal, immutable, undisturbed Ruler, who ever remains like unto himself. According to Aristotle the perpetuity of motion in the universe presupposes a "first mover", an "eternal, immovable being", who was *one* and everlasting, necessary, immutable, free from all composition, devoid of "matter, capacity or potentiality"; pure "energy or activity", pure "idea or form", unadulterated essence, absolute form, "the very nature of a thing, the primary substance", Philo called God "unchangeable, consistent with himself, invariable, steadfast, firm, fixed, unalterable". And Christian theology was in thorough agreement with this view. According to Augustine, God's immutability ensues from the fact that he is the highest, perfect essence. It is "naturally and truly ingrafted in every creature that there is an altogether unchangeable and incorruptible God". This conception of an eternal and immutable being is not produced by the senses, for every creature, also man, is changeable; but within his soul man sees and finds that which is immutable, better and greater than all those things which are subject to change. If God were not immutable, he would not be God. His name is *being*, and this name is "an unchangeable name".[40] 'Every change is foreign to God. He transcends every change in time, for he is eternal; in space, for he is omnipresent; in essence, for he is pure being, whence Christian theology often called God "pure actuality". Aristotle so conceived of God's being. . . .'[41]

The direct link between Christian theology and Greek philosophy is immediately apparent here. What Greek philosophy had concluded about other gods was considered suitable for use with reference to the true God. There is surely no one today who would still believe that Plato could only speak so 'biblically' about God because he had read the Old Testament![42] And to bring general revelation into the picture at this point would be to forget that we are concerned here with central affirmations about God, affirmations which express his very being. General revelation can surely never be exalted to such an extent that it becomes the school to which Christian theology goes to learn from heathen philosophy that which makes God *God*.

For this reason it will be helpful to look more closely at the use Paul makes of Greek thought in his address on Mars hill (Acts 17:15–34). Even a short survey of this sermon and related passages elsewhere in Paul, makes it clear that this link-up ought not to be exaggerated. The point of contact for Paul in the concrete Athenian situation is their extreme religiousness (v. 22; a better translation would be their 'excessive deference to gods'), and more especially the alter dedicated 'To an unknown god' (v. 23). Linking up with this, Paul declares that it is this God, whom they *did not know*, whom he proclaims – 'What you worship but do not know'. What we have then is a formal point of contact, but nothing in respect of content.

In verse 24 the sermon makes conscious use of material from the Old Testament (just as in the parallel statement in Acts 14:15). The content is from Isaiah 42:5, and the first part is used in verse 24a and the second half is expanded in verse 25b. This message from the Old Testament provides an immediate opportunity to place the true God in contrast to the Greek gods (he 'does not live in shrines made by man'). Verse 26 in turn links up with Psalm 74:17, and means little more than that through Adam God made all mankind to inhabit all the earth (the first part of the verse) and that by means of seasons he made the earth habitable. ('Allotted periods' – cf. Ps. 74:17.) Against the threatening sea and sea monsters he provided limits to protect the habitable land ('their habitation'), so that the sea monsters would not wipe out mankind.[43]

Verse 27 also begins with a thought from the Old Testament, and even the second part of verse 27 could equally well be interpreted from the Old Testament (God who lives among his people), in spite of this being a well-known Hellenistic idea.

This brings us to the direct (and also more indirect) links between Paul and certain streams of Greek religion and philosophy. In verse 25a he makes use of an idea which cannot be traced back to the Old Testament, but in the second part of the verse he interprets it clearly in the light of the Old Testament (Isa. 42:5). In verse 28 he makes the clearest contact with Greek philosophy, but uses the thought (which can be readily interpreted in terms of the creation message of the Old Testament) to express criticism of Greek religion (v. 29). There are wide differences of opinion about what to make of this contact with Greek thought, but it is clear that the actual message of Paul ought not to be sought in it, since in verse 30 he returns to the idea raised in verse 23; viz. the times of *ignorance*. From here he proceeds to proclaim Christ and to call his hearers to repentance – features known to be his real concern from his other sermons and letters. Indeed, this is what his sermon in Athens is also concerned with, according to verse 18: 'he preached Jesus and the resurrection'.

And the most important aspect of the matter is the reaction to his sermon. When the audience began to mock (some openly and others less so), and it became clear that they were not willing to believe Paul's message, we read: 'So Paul went out from among them'. Those who will not come to repentance, who refuse to turn from their gods to God, stand outside of his salvation.

On the one hand there is here a certain comparableness in some sense. The apostle is able to link up with specific heathen ideas, but only in order to use them to show the absurdity of their own religion (v. 29). For the rest we find definite appropriations, which are immediately interpreted from the perspective of the Old Testament and applied to the living God; they are appropriations that are true of *him* (v. 25a, v. 27b, v. 28) and not of the gods. On the other hand it is clear that these points of contact are incidental and overwhelmingly formal in nature (v. 22, 23), and that what is actually at stake is a call to turn from the Greek gods *to* the true God, and that those who refuse to accept God through the life, death and resurrection of Jesus Christ, remain outside. The chief matter here too, which Paul was working towards throughout his sermon, was the incomparableness of God. The heathen do not know the true God. A knowledge of their gods is not a knowledge of the true God. This is almost a refrain in Paul's letters. In 1 Thessalonians 4:5 we hear of the 'heathen who do not know God' (also 2 Thess. 1:8); in Galatians 4:8 he explains that before their conversion the Christians 'did not know God', and in Ephesians 2:12 that they were then 'without God', and 'alienated from the life of God because of the ignorance' that was in them (Eph. 4:18). That the heathen do not know God is an idea derived from the Old Testament (Ps. 79:6; Job 18:21; Jer. 10:25) and recurs frequently in the New Testament (1 Cor. 1:21; 1 Pet. 1:14). In Romans 1:18–21 the apostle does indeed write about the heathen who 'knew God', but it is clear that we have here another perspective, a knowledge that, far from diverting the wrath of God, calls it down.[44]

Against this biblical background it remains inconceivable that theology should so easily and positively have linked up with the Greek philosophical doctrine of God. Naturally, there is a certain comparableness between

God and the gods, and by taking over certain aspects of El and Baal God gave a richer and more comprehensive revelation of himself to Israel. Similarly, in Colossians Paul could give a more radical interpretation of the headship of Jesus over *all* things by proclaiming it in terms of the confrontation between Jesus and the powers. It is possible therefore in principle to learn something more of the true God from the heathen gods, and also from the Greek philosophers. But these appropriations must be intentionally measured against the biblical witness to God, just as in the Old Testament Israel only took over what matched up with the being of God, and either changed the rest (the pantheon) or rejected it (polytheism).

So the question is: Has the Christian church adequately and satis-factorily measured its use of Greek religious thought against the biblical witness to God, or has the usage taken place more or less uncritically, so that its picture of God is actually in tension with the true God?

In endeavouring to answer this, it should first of all be noted that in the Old Testament God was incomparable with that which the prophets of Israel preached about the gods, but that the same prophets (at least in certain respects) took over certain things that the heathen confessed about their gods (but which the prophets denied concerning these gods). That is, there was a sharp difference between the heathen belief in their gods and the judgment of the prophets on these gods. The heathen believed that Baal did indeed bring the rain, and the spring and prosperity. This awakened Israel to the fact that it was the LORD who did these things. But at the same time this led to the prophetic denial that the gods had the power to do these things (1 Kgs. 18 and Hos. 2:4–8). One may therefore conclude that, while the LORD is incomparable with what the prophets proclaimed about the gods, he does, nevertheless, fulfil many of the functions which the heathen attributed to the gods. It must be stressed, however, that he fulfils only those functions which are com-patible with his own nature.

But this attitude of the prophets and apostles is often lacking in theology. There is a tendency to link up uncritically with what certain Greek philosophers taught about God without: (a) clearly distinguishing between the *true* God and the god of the Greek philosophers, who is not as they say he is since God is incomparable; and without (b) measuring what they accept from Greek philosophy against the Scriptures. How difficult this critical evaluation was, and still is, is illustrated by a reaction of E. P. Meijering to a comment made by H. Berkhof. In connection with the influence of Greek thought on the development of early Christian doctrine Berkhof remarks that by using the language of Greek philosophy the church wished to give expression in a contemporary idiom to what it had heard in the Bible about God's transcendence; this also enabled the church to declare to a searching Hellenism that the God of Israel was the fulfilment of their quest.[45] Meijering reacts to this by suggesting that Berkhof could have given a finer nuance to his words, since the formula-tion he had chosen might give the impression that the Platonic concept of

God was something that the early Christians could have freely decided to adopt or reject, whereas in fact this concept was an unavoidable part of their cultural background, even as was the knowledge of the God of Israel. He then proposes that Berkhof should rather have said that as children of their times the early theologians read the Bible from the perspective of their own philosophical presuppositions about God.[46]

To throw a little more light on this problem it will be helpful to consider more fully an exceptionally illuminating article by W. Pannenberg on the appropriation of the philosophical concept of God as a dogmatic problem in early Christian theology.[47]

In this article Pannenberg achieves three things. First of all he shows that it is possible to speak of a single (Greek) philosophical doctrine of God, as well as indicating some of its chief features. Then he explains why early Christian theology had to associate itself with this philosophical theology, and by what norms. Finally he examines the way in which the apologists linked up with this philosophical concept of God.

First of all then, the philosophical concept of God. According to Pannenberg this was dominated by the idea of 'origin' or 'cause' from the beginning. To Greek thought God was the origin of common things which constantly recur. The extraordinary plays a minor role in their concept of God. For this reason the Greek gods (and here the Olympian deities and the philosophical concept of god were at one) were immanent, ordinary, and in a certain sense, unnecessary. Many of the things done by the Homeric gods could quite easily be done by people. (124 footnote 15.) This method of enquiring into the origin of things in terms of the existing ordinary phenomena is common to all Greek thought about God. Existing reality must be explained through God.

They were also unanimous about the unity of God. This 'origin' must be singular since more than one origin (God) would mean differences between these origins, and every difference would then require a further origin.

Finally, Pannenberg mentions the otherness and unknowability of God. Precisely because the things that must be explained are many and transient, their origin must be different, single and incorruptible. There can therefore be no analogy between existing reality and its origin. God's otherness is seen especially in contrast to the physical and visible things, and as a result, the origin of all things is interpreted more readily as spirit or mind (or reason). What was determinative for all Greek philosophy and later philosophical views of God was the line of thought leading from existing reality to its cause: 'God'.

In pursuing further the fact that the apologists had to use this philosophical concept of God, and the norms that this association of thought required, Pannenberg shows first of all the meaning (and advantages)· that this had for the church. In order to declare to the heathen that the God of Israel was the universal and only true God, who therefore had a claim on all men, the church made use of the Greek concept of the one origin of all things and explained that the God of Israel was this origin. This opened the door to taking over certain terms from the philosophical concept of God, as Paul had already done in Romans 1:19 f. (God is *in*visible, *im*mortal – thus beginning the later prediliction for speaking of God in negative terms). Then too, missionaries made use of the monotheistic concept of neo-Platonism in order to convey their message of the one true God.

The real question is whether the apologists distinguished carefully enough between the God of Israel and the God of the Greek philosophers. The first and perhaps most important difference is that the philosophical concept of God is tied to the quest for the origin of all existing things. While the message concerning the God of Israel can of course link up with this enquiry, and in fact does so in the doctrine of God the Creator, Pannenberg is sure that God is more than the 'origin' of all things because he is free, free to do more than he already has done, free to do unheard of new things. (Cf. e.g. Isa. 43:18–19 – indeed the whole treatment of the mocking of the gods in Deutero-Isaiah – as an illustration of one of the essential differences between God and the gods: that he can do new things, and announce them in advance.) When enquiring into the emphases in the respective concepts of God, one could say that the Greek philosophical God serves as the explanation of the origin of existing reality, whereas the God of Israel (in addition to this) does new things through which the course of history is determined and eventually reaches its goal. Together with this, one should observe that the philosophical God-concept does not provide for that personal revelation of God which leads to a special relationship and fellowship between God and man, God and his people, God and the world.

This all means, that on the one hand, the philosophical God-concept can be taken up into the message concerning the Father of Jesus Christ, but that, on the other hand, it needs to be radically transformed. All philosophical concepts which are taken over must be refashioned in the light of the freedom of the biblical God to fashion history. It is not acceptable merely to append certain truths of revelation to the philosophical God-concept. All mere syntheses are superficial.

In the third section Pannenberg uses certain examples to investigate more closely the extent to which early Christian theology transformed this philosophical God-concept in order to genuinely adapt it to the message concerning the God of Israel. (He chooses, *inter alia*, the relationship between monotheism and creation, the otherness of God, his unchangeableness, his uniqueness and his lack of attributes). His conclusions are interesting. On the one hand he repudiates Harnack's radical contention that the early Christian doctrine of God was deeply Hellenized and that it was this which opened the way for the Hellenization of all early Christian theology. It seems that Pannenberg really does succeed in showing that the church (in particular the Apologists) did not simply take over the philosophical concept of God in an uncritical way.

Thus, the early Christian doctrine of *creatio ex nihilo* (creation from nothing) broke through the Platonic doctrine of the eternity of matter (145). In this way early Christian theology enabled Greek philosophy to come to a consistent monotheism, since with eternal matter alongside God there is no real monotheism (146). And even though the Christians took over the unbiblical concept of the unchangeableness of God from Greek philosophy, they nevertheless succeeded thereby to emphasise that God does not simply arise and then perish. To the extent that arising and perishing is tied up with changeableness, God as the origin of the world cannot be changeable in that the existence of all things is grounded in him (329). Similarly with regard to the appropriation of the idea of the simplicity of God (the fact that he is not a composite being), Pannenberg shows that the apologists never went so far as to conclude that God was a being without attributes – as, for example, Philo attempted to do. (Cf. ch. 2.)

At the same time Pannenberg shows equally convincingly that the greatest lack of critical evaluation is shown with regard to the conclusion which they drew from the philosophical God-concept. By accepting the epistemological principle that one can begin theoretically with existing reality as a consequence of something and then proceed to a conclusion concerning its origin or cause, early Christian theology adopted uncritically certain decisive presuppositions underlying the philosophical God-concept which touch on the being of God (157f). This philosophical conclusion did not originally have the sole function of proving the existence of God, but was intended to illuminate the being of God himself – that which makes God God. As a result, this conclusion served in the early church as something self-evident with regard to certain aspects of the being of God, which means that these aspects could be directly specified, independently of the historical revelation. In this way the biblical witness to God was constricted, especially in relation to God's personal freedom. Thus, it is something entirely different to conclude from the persistence of existing matter that there is an unchangeable ground or cause of all things, than to argue from the faithfulness of God (his free acts) to the fulfilment of his purposes in history.

Pannenberg concludes quite rightly that the philosophical concept of God as world principle or origin, and the biblical message of God as the free Lord of history persisted largely unreconciled with each other. (And, in the minds of many believers remain unreconciled to this day. A.K.). The insight into the genuine otherness of God will only come into its own if theology introduces the otherness of the free Lord 'as not only the incomprehensibility of the (Greek) world ground but as the otherness of the freedom of God precisely in his acts, which cut across and surpass all expectations and planning' (181). Thus Pannenberg's article.

From all this it is clear that one can judge neither entirely positively, nor entirely negatively, the use that the Apologists made of the philosophical concept of God. From one point of view it is not true that they used everything indiscriminately. Yet from another, it is true that they did not test everything thoroughly in terms of the question as to what is really appropriate to the LORD.

In fact, this judgment is still too vague. But in order to come to a concrete position it is necessary to enquire into what it is exactly, according to the Old Testament, that consistutes God's incomparableness, and what it is that distinguishes him in a substantial way from the gods.

God speaks

The first basic point in which God cannot be compared with the gods is in the fact of his speech. Repeatedly in the mocking of the gods we hear that they cannot speak (Ps. 115:5; 135:6; Isa. 46:7; Jer. 10:5); indeed, that they are dumb (Hab. 2:18; 1 Cor. 12:2). Even when they are urgently invited to speak, they remain as silent as the grave (Isa. 41:21–23, 26, 28. Cf. all the court actions between God and the gods).

To understand what is meant by the LORD's speech it may be helpful to consider first what is meant by the silence of the gods. It seems unlikely that this simply means that they cannot talk. Such a point of view would be as remote from the actual issue as the idea that the gods do not (ontologically) exist. The uncertainty regarding the existence (Exod. 20:3; Judg. 11:24) or non-existence (Isa. 41:24, 29; 43:10, 11; 45:5; 46:9 etc) of the gods results from an ontological rather than a theological approach. When Deutero-Isaiah declares that the gods are nothing, he means that they are not God, i.e. that they cannot do what is appropriate to God, but by no means does he imply that they do not exist. There is only one true God, and when the heathen claim that their gods really are gods, they are wrong, not because their gods do not exist, but because they are not really gods (God!). A. Deissler says that for the Easterner *existence* means primarily *act*, in the sense of *effectiveness*.[48] Ontologically they do in fact exist, and for this reason they can be called demons (Deut. 32:16, 17; Ps. 106:36–7; 1 Cor. 10:20–21). And it seems that the question as to whether they exist above and beyond their images is answered here as well.[49] The identification of a god with its image – which is so strongly radicalised in Deutero-Isaiah – is an intensive form of the mockery which stresses even more strongly the powerlessness of the god.[50] This identification takes place on theological grounds, after it has already been established that the gods can neither help nor save, nor stand against the LORD.

It is in this way that the speechlessness of the gods must be understood. The issue is not the ability to speak as such. If they can be called demons, and if they can be challenged to a court action, then the silent assumption is that they can indeed speak. But they are unable to speak *relevantly*. What a God should say, they cannot say. This is beautifully expressed in Isaiah 46:7, 'If one cries to it, it does not answer or save him from his trouble.' If it could save it would also answer. To be able to answer, the god would have to be a counsellor (Isa. 41:28), and this it cannot be. The silence of the gods is essentially related to the incapacity to save, to help, to rescue from trouble (Jer. 2:27–28). Indeed this is illustrated in an arresting way in 1 Kings 18. The priests of Baal must call upon their god, and Elijah will call on the LORD. 'And the God who answers *by fire*, he is God' (v. 24). To answer then means to do that which is relevant: in this case, to give fire. This Baal cannot do (v. 26–29), whereas the LORD can (v. 37–38).

What this triumph of the LORD over Baal makes even more arresting is the fact that the LORD does not challenge Baal on his weakest point. On the contrary, the contest in 1 Kings 18 turns on his two strong features. Baal was primarily the god of fire, and is often portrayed with lightening in his hands. And secondly, he was the god responsible for drought and rain (Hos. 2:4, 7, 8; Jer. 14:22 – a disguised play on the belief that Baal gives rain).[51] So in 1 Kings 18 the LORD challenges Baal on his two strongest points: fire (v. 23–38) and rain (17:1; 18:41–46). And what transpires is not merely that the LORD is stronger than Baal on both points (El was also stronger than the 'ordinary' gods), but is incomparable, in that he actually controls both fire and rain while Baal can do nothing.

To answer means then to say and to do what is relevant. The question is not whether on occasion the gods might be able to mutter or squeak (which could be an interpretation of Isa. 8:19)[52] but whether they can give an answer befitting a God and not a mouse!

This contrast brings out very clearly the meaning of the LORD's speech.

It is well-known that the word of the LORD in the Old Testament does not have a mere neotic, explanatory significance, but that through his word the LORD *does* something, his words have certain consequences, indeed that it is, above all, his words that determine the course of history.[53]

By speaking the LORD *made* the heavens and the earth. 'And God *said*, Let there be light! *And there was light.*' (Gen. 1:3; also v. 3 f, 9, 11, 14 etc.). 'By the word of the LORD the heavens were made, and all their host by the breath of his mouth...For he spoke and it came to be; he commanded and it stood forth.' (Ps. 33:6,9). Deutero-Isaiah especially introduced creation by the word of the LORD as a theme in his preaching (Isa. 40:26; 48:13; 50:2).

Against this background one can understand better the expression that the LORD's word is not 'empty' or 'trifling' (Isa. 55:11; Deut. 32:47). His word will 'accomplish that which I purpose, and prosper in the thing for which I sent it'. This means that not only creation, but history too is seen as the work of the LORD's word. When he speaks something happens. In Amos his word of judgment is likened to the terrifying roar of a lion, and what his word does is therefore frightening. 'The pastures of the shepherds mourn...' (rather: are scorched – the pastures are essential to the life of the flocks, and therefore to the shepherds also!); 'and the top of Carmel withers' – on Carmel there were the forests that were the pride of Palestine.

The power of God's word features strongly in the call of Jeremiah. He is appointed 'over nations and over kingdoms, to pluck up and to break down, to destroy and to overthrow, to build and to plant' (Jer. 1:10). But the question is, how could one person destroy nations and kingdoms? It is possible, because in the preceding verse the LORD had said to him: 'Behold, I have put my words in your mouth.' Elsewhere we hear: 'I am making my words in your mouth a fire, and this people wood, and the fire shall devour them' (Jer. 5:14; 23:29). And again: 'Is not my word like a fire says the LORD, and like a hammer which breaks the rock in pieces?' The power of the word of the LORD is also seen in the case where Pelatiah fell dead while Ezekiel was prophesying (Ezek. 11:13).

The comprehensive nature of the word of the LORD and its power to fashion history is very explicit in Deutero-Isaiah (Isa. 40–55). Deliberately following a conscious pattern, these prophecies begin and end with the power of the word of the LORD. Isaiah 40:6–8 considers the power of his word over against the powerlessness of 'all flesh', apparently the nations, and in particular, Babylon. Isaiah 55:10–11 is concerned with the mighty word which, like the rain and snow which cause the plants to grow and make a harvest possible, shall do what the LORD sends it to do. Within this framework reference is then made to the earlier exodus from Egypt, the exile and the 'second exodus' which was about to happen, and which would be incomparably more wonderful than the first (Isa. 43: 18–19). And in contrast to the gods that cannot answer and save when anyone calls on them (Isa. 46:7), the LORD stands and calls a bird of prey from the East (Cyrus the Persian) to break the power of Babylon and to return Israel to Jerusalem (v. 11). Repeatedly, the release of the people and their return from captivity is described as something which the LORD is doing through his words. 'I will say to the north, Give up, and to the south, Do not withhold; bring my sons from afar, and my daughters from the end of the earth' (43:6). Isaiah 40:3–5 also speaks of the power of the LORD's word. All that has been spoken of shall take place 'because the mouth of the LORD has spoken it' (40:5).

So that when later on in the New Testament John speaks of Jesus as 'the Word', it is not surprising that he immediately explains: 'all things were made through him' (John 1:1–3). As Word, Jesus is the power, the working, the act of God – or rather, God-in-action, for this is what the word of the LORD is. And furthermore, it is not strange that Jesus, as the revelation of God, comes to *do* something. As revelation he does not merely come to impart knowledge, but to *do* the will of God. In the same sense Peter confesses his allegiance to Jesus Christ with the words: 'Lord, to whom shall we go? You have the words of eternal life' – that is, the words that give eternal life (John 6:68; see also TEV). And in John 15:3 we hear from the lips of Jesus: 'You are already clean through the word which I have spoken to you.' His word does something: it cleanses.

This is the point of substantial contrast between God and the gods (as also between Jesus and the forces of evil): the gods cannot speak, and this means that they cannot save, and that their words (even if they could literally speak) have no power. In contrast to them is the LORD who 'will slay (his enemy) with the breath of his mouth' (2 Thess. 2:8) because 'from his mouth issues a sharp sword with which to smite the nations' (Rev. 19:15).

So we have here an essential difference between God and the gods. They are on this point incomparable; God is the wholly Other, the absolutely Exalted One. And precisely because God's word is not empty or vain, but does something and can be indicated in history, we can and must speak of proofs of God. This will be considered in detail in chapter 3.

Closely linked with God's speech, we must consider in greater detail a second difference between God and the gods: God acts.

God acts

In speaking of God's word we have already spoken of his deeds. And rightly so, because God is not a composite being consisting of separate compartments which can be independently examined. God is *one*, a person who in all that he is and does remains himself and is always totally present. Hence it is completely fitting that his words imply his actions, and that we have been forced to touch indirectly on his acts in speaking of his words.

In this connection we come to know the gods as 'nothing' (Isa. 41:24). The Living Bible is even more radical: 'You are less than nothing.' The NEB gives another possibility: 'You are sprung from nothing.' If they come from nothing they can hardly be more than their origins!

Important in connection with the acts of the gods is the question of their existence (or non-existence): 'Behold, you are nothing, and your work is nought.' Verse 29 similarly: 'Behold, they are all a delusion; their works are nothing.' They are in fact so powerless that they are challenged to something – anything at all. This is the meaning of verse 23: 'do good, or do harm'. Jeremiah 10:5 says something similar: 'Be not afraid of them, for they cannot do evil, neither is it in them to do good.'

Far from being able to save their supporters (Isa. 46:7), the gods cannot even save themselves from a tumble in the dust if the wagon on which they are loaded bumps over a rut (v. 1–2). In contrast to this the LORD carries his children from their mothers' womb, and will do so into the furthest future – and to 'carry' is to 'save' (v. 3–4).

This contrast recurs frequently in the history of Israel. In Judges 6:25–31 Gideon is ordered to go and break down the altar of Baal, together with the sacred grove, and then to build an altar to the LORD and to sacrifice a bull on it. There was a violent reaction to his action, but it was not Baal's. He did nothing. It was only his worshippers who were able to take up his cause. And this gave Gideon's father the lead to mock them: 'Will you contend for Baal? Or will you defend his cause?...If he is a god let him contend for himself, because his altar has been pulled down' (v. 31).

In contrast to this we read in 2 Chronicles 20:15: 'Fear not, and be not dismayed at this great multitude; for the battle is not yours but God's.'

Against this background one can detect the razor-sharp mockery in 1 Samuel 5:1–5. After the Philistines had defeated Israel and had taken the ark of the covenant as booty, they naturally wanted to approach their god and thank him for the victory. The ark was deposited alongside Dagon – that was his share of the booty. Actually this was not merely an 'it', but the LORD himself, for the Philistines were just as sure as Israel that with this ark the LORD himself had entered Israel's camp (1 Sam. 4:7). The defeated God was therefore required to come and pay his respects to the conquering god, Dagon.

But the following morning, 'Dagon had fallen face downward on the ground before the ark of the LORD'! (5:3). 'Lying (with his face) on the ground' or 'fallen down' are expressions denoting reverence (Gen. 44:14; 1 Sam. 17:49; 2 Sam. 14:4). In this case the 'major' god is thus honouring the 'minor' (defeated) God. And it happens against his will, since he had fallen (cf. other translations). The mockery is further refined by the account of how he had to be lifted up and restored to his place. He was not even able to rise! (Isa. 46:7).

And all this reached a second climax the following day (for the Philistines and Dagon an anticlimax!). Once again Dagon had fallen before the ark of the LORD, but this time he lost his head and his hands. He was accordingly totally powerless before the LORD, being able neither to hear nor speak, nor in fact to do anything at all. That 'hand' here should imply *doing* is evident from the fact that directly afterwards there are three references to the hand of the LORD (v. 6, 7, 9, 11) which indicate his actions against the Philistines. He is able to do something!

There are aspects of this story that call for our attention. First of all, the previous chapter ended with the painful words, 'The glory has departed from Israel'. But the chapter following recounts the opposite. Without a single priest or soldier to help, the LORD alone fought against the gods of the Philistines, while Dagon had to be picked up by his supporters. The LORD took care of himself!

Then further, the Philistines themselves acknowledged the supremacy of the LORD, and that his plagues were too severe for them and Dagon their god (v. 7). And after things had proceeded in this way in Gath there is again biting mockery in the outcry from Ekron that they saw no possibility of receiving the ark – the very ark which was for them the sign of their victory over Israel.

The LORD alone was able to confuse and destroy the entire Philistine power without the help, or even the presence of a single Israelite. Even the great Dagon, one of the greatest gods of the ancient east, could not remain standing before him.[54]

In the light of this supremacy of the God who acts, it is as well to look again at the court actions between the LORD and the gods. The battle of the gods was a familiar feature of ancient eastern religion. Bloody battles

were fought, with the outcome often suspended for a long time in the
balance. Greek mythology is also familiar with such battles. The Bible,
however, knows nothing of battles between God and the gods, in this
sense. There are occasions when they confront one another directly, as in
1 Samuel 5:1–5 and 1 Kings 18, but even these, which would have
provided wonderful opportunities for bloody conflicts, do not result in
hand to hand struggles, but in a proof of the absolute supremacy of God
without a fight.

Elsewhere in the Old Testament, especially in Deutero-Isaiah, a lawsuit
takes the place of these battles. Psalm 82 is another example of this. Cf.
further Isaiah 41:1–5, 21–9; 43:8–15; 44:6–8; 45:20–5. One of the
strongest elements of mockery in these court actions is either that the
gods were not even present – not even being mentioned – or that they
could not answer the questions and demands addressed to them (Ps.
82:5; Isa. 41:21–4, 26, 28; 43:9; 44:7; 45:21). The reason why the fights
between the gods are replaced with court actions (where the gods do not
even react) rests in the absolute exaltation and radical otherness of the
LORD. He is not a God among other gods. He is not even the most
powerful God. He is the only God.

Precisely for this reason it does not really matter how many Israelites
take the field against the enemy and his gods. Sometimes the LORD used
many, even the whole army of Israel, and sometimes few – even as few as
300 against an army 'like locusts for multitude' (Judg. 7:12). In fact, in
this case the numbers did count – they were too many and had to be
drastically reduced 'lest Israel vaunt themselves... saying, "My own
hand has delivered me".'

This discussion has brought two of the most important characteristics
of the LORD to the fore, that is, his words and deeds. The Bible is full of
them. In them God is completely Other, incomparable, exalted above all
other beings that could be called gods. His words and his deeds, in purely
mathematical terms, constitute the greater part of the content of the
Bible. Through them we learn to know him.

In contrast to this there is the Greek philosophical doctrine of the
being of God as the cause or origin of all that is. The early church adopted
a part of heathenism when it followed the emphasis of the Greeks rather
than that of the apostles and prophets. The objection is not that God is
presented as being and origin, and in this way the answer to the deepest
questions of philosophy. In itself this was an evangelistic necessity. That
which exists, at least in its good aspects, did not have an origin other than
the one true God. The 'origin' of sin, pain, injustice will come under
discussion later.

The objection to the Apologists and the later developments in theology
is that they allowed themselves to be misled by the way in which
philosophy posed the question, and so shifted the emphasis in the
doctrine of God. This meant that the words and acts of God, or better,
the speaking and acting God, did not come into their own. The Greek

concept of God as the ground-of-all-that-is would only have been critically refashioned and sanctified if it had been proclaimed in terms of God's biblical uniqueness, as the One who acts, who does things that are new (and does not merely sanction and explain that which is), and who is accordingly a personal Lord. Pannenberg has rightly said that the real difference and incomparableness of God rests in his *deeds*[55] (his words are of course also deeds).

The role of Exodus 3:14 in all this is symptomatic of the wrong emphasis in the history of the doctrine of God. The fact that a Hebrew verb was replaced with a Greek participle used as a noun,[56] meant that the direct, compelling link that God wished to form between himself and his deeds, had to give way to the Greek concept of 'being', which is in many respects the opposite of the living, working God. Preuss comments somewhere that our knowledge of God does not proceed from a resting being, but from the active intervention of God in history, and in this we see God's being. The objective that God has in mind with his acts is that we should know him. For this reason his deeds are always directed towards man. The LORD's wish is that our knowledge of him should include confession and trust, so that those that learn to know him will surrender themselves to him on their way with him into the future.[57]

There are two attributes of God that must be considered in relation to the concept of the acting and speaking God – namely, God as 'the living God' and 'the Almighty'. However, since these have such a close bearing on the relationship between God and history, they will be considered in chapter 3.

The purpose of the mocking of the gods

At this stage it is necessary to consider the purpose of the mocking of the gods, since this contributes to the meaning of the greatness, exaltedness and incomparableness of the LORD.

While there are many examples of the mocking of the gods throughout the Bible, it cannot be regarded as an independent literary form either stylistically or materially – i.e. in terms of content. Preuss rightly observes that the gods are not so important as to occupy an independent place in the Old Testament. The mocking of the gods emphasises precisely their unimportance. This is a significant point. It is possible to give so much attention to insignificant, wrong, and negative matters, even with the commendable purpose of warning against them or eliminating them, that they are emphasised out of all proportion and acquire an unwarranted importance. Barth said in his time that he would not write a book on the devil because the Bible is concerned with the *gospel*. The prophets and apostles did not preach 'on demons' or hold independent discourses on the gods. The mocking of the gods is always part of a greater whole, and is never aimed merely at the gods themselves or even the mockery of the gods. A good example of this is in Isaiah 40:18 f. The purpose of this long parody on the Babylonian gods is found in verses 27–31. According to v.27, the people had begun to say, 'My way is hid from the LORD...' (cf. Isa. 49:14). After having been in captivity in Babylon for nearly half a century, doubt began to eat at the soul of the people. Is the LORD really stronger than the gods of Babylon? Why then do the Babylonians hold them so long in captivity? Would it not be better to begin to serve their gods? If they are able to oppress the LORD's people for so long, and in such a way, might it not be more reasonable to expect deliverance from their gods?

Into this situation the prophet came with his parody of the gods. He addresses Israel, who had already begun to make comparisons between the LORD and the other gods and to express their doubts about the LORD. By mocking the gods he aims to bring them back to the LORD. He wants to convince them that the LORD is the only true God, and that it is just not worth the effort to serve the Babylonian gods (cf. Isa. 46).

To state the matter somewhat more comprehensively, one could point to the following objectives: The first would be to emphasise the uniqueness and otherness of the LORD. In contrast to the gods that cannot answer or do anything, there is the LORD, who is the speaking, acting, living God. By proclaiming him thus in his incomparableness, the prophets aimed to comfort those who were standing firm in their faith, to recall those who were doubting, and, as Hosea especially wished to do, to show those who had fallen away from the LORD that the LORD's judgment on them was legitimate in that there had never been any justification for their turning to other gods.[58]

So one could suggest that the aim of the process of mocking the gods was pastoral, and was accordingly directed mainly to Israel. There are only a few occasions when one might assume that there could have been heathen in the audience (Isa. 44:9–20?),[59] but even in these instances the concern is basically with Israel. It is therefore clear that the mockery cannot be regarded as a missionary method. Never did prophets and apostles go to the heathen and begin by mocking their gods in the hope that in this way they might persuade them to turn to the true God. Paul's approach in Acts 17 is entirely different when he takes the heathen deities and poets as his point of contact. This could be one of the reasons why the mocking of the gods features so much less in the New Testament than in the Old, since the New is written for the greater part in a mission situation.

'God is love'

All that has been said so far is in a certain sense too formal. That God is incomparable in relation to the gods, that he can speak and act, that he is not mere being but is a personal God, that he is the living God, and is great and important are genuine biblical insights which have recieved inadequate emphasis in the history of theology – Reformed theology included. Of decisive importance, however, is the fact that the prophets did not limit themselves to proclaiming these formal facts, but dwelt also on his involvement in concrete history by proclaiming *what* God did, what he *meant* by his actions, and *who* he is.

Utterances which draw distinctions between God and the gods immediately come to our attention. Deuteronomy 4:7: 'What great nation is there that has a god *so near to it as the* LORD *our God is* to us, whenever we call on him?' 1 Kings 8:23: 'O LORD, God of Israel, there is no God like thee, in heaven above or on earth beneath, *keeping covenant and showing steadfast love* to thy servants who walk before thee with all their heart.' Micah 7:18: 'Who is a God like thee, *pardoning iniquity* and passing over transgression for the remnant of his inheritance? He does not retain his anger for ever because he delights in steadfast love.' Consider again the portions in italics.

Other parts of the Old Testament which do not deal with the relationship between God and the gods, also yield utterances that emphasise the goodness, love and faithfulness of the LORD. One well-known statement is in Exodus 34:6: 'The LORD, the LORD, a God merciful and gracious, slow to anger and abounding in steadfast love and faithfulness.' Indeed, this song of praise to the LORD became, with minor variations, a standing expression in Israel's penitential liturgy. Cf. also Nehemiah 9:17; Psalms 86:15; 103:8; 145:8; Joel 2:13 and especially Jonah 4:2. This last text suggests that for Jonah it was already a foregone conclusion that the LORD would show himself in this way.

In an unrivalled way, Barth has examined most of these concepts separately, but here I wish to point to their inter-relatedness.[60] It is possible that by concentrating separately on the various attributes of God one might fail to grasp the whole, the One who has (or is!) all these attributes. Though this is certainly no criticism of Barth's theology.

A careful reading of the above-mentioned texts shows immediately that what they proclaim can be summarised in one expression: God is love. It is not true that we encounter this for the first time in the New Testament. It is not even correct to say that Hosea was the first to bring this message. While the *word* love does not feature prominently in the exodus story, the exodus remains a great testimony to the LORD's love for Israel. Besides Exodus 34:6, which appears to be a very old utterance,[61] Deuteronomy 4:7 means quite explicitly that it was *in love* that God heard his people in Egypt (Exod. 3:7, 9, 17) in their misery, and led them out. Even the nature of his love was strikingly illustrated in this history, for in the exodus the people involved were a small, oppressed and unimportant nation.[62] That the LORD chose them is a miracle of his love (Deut. 7:7–8).

Quite rightly it has been observed that God's love is unique and may be regarded as an element in the exclusively biblical message.[63] This is one of the most profound differences between God and the gods – and in particular the Platonic concept of God. The god who is sufficient-unto-himself cannot love, since, according to Greek philosophy one could only love on account of a need or a lack in oneself. Who in the world desires what he already has? I have deliberately used the word 'desire' instead of love. For love in the Greek concept of God meant: to love on account of the value of that which is loved. A god, sufficient-unto-himself has need of nothing outside of himself. So, while it would be possible to call people to love God, it would be senseless to say that God loves people. He already has in himself everything of value. For this reason Plato also taught that God had no dealings with man.[64]

This illustrates beautifully the difference between a principle (or idea, or a conceived God) on the one hand, and the history (or reality) of the revealed God on the other. Theoretically the Platonic concept is unassailable. A being sufficient-unto-himself does indeed have no need of anything or anyone. For such a god love would be in conflict with his being. But reality is different, and in two respects. First of all, the true God has shown that he does love people. The exodus, the extended history of Israel, Bethlehem, Golgotha, Easter, Pentecost! Against these facts, against history, a theory must surrender. And yet it is one of the most disturbing aspects of the development of the doctrine of God that this love has indeed been suppressed (and at times scarcely found a place in the doctrine of God) on the grounds of the idea that God is sufficient-unto-himself.[65] And, truth to tell, this did not only happen *outside* Reformed theology!

Reality differs from the Greek idea in a second respect. In the history that God has created it is made apparent that God's love is not desire, and that the object of his love is *not* in fact desirable. Even in his created universe as such there was nothing desirable in the sense that it met a need or lack in him. Even in his communion with his good creation there was nothing that he did not already have and enjoy within himself. And in the sinful creation there were elements that were anything but desirable. Indeed, anyone with a 'sense of value' would have expected John 3:16–17 to read in this way: 'God became so tired of the world that he sent his only begotten Son to make an end of it. For God sent not his Son into the world to save the world, but that through him the world might be condemned.' How much disappointment, how much unhappiness the world (and his people) caused him will be more fully discussed in chapter 2, but this much is already clear, that throughout the long history of Israel and the church, God poured out his love on people who were not worthy of it. Love *gives*. This is the second difference from Platonic thinking. For Plato, love was the desire for something that had value (for yourself). But the love of God is a love that goes out to a worthless object, giving it value. Plato is in a certain sense right. God does not love the world in the sense that he desires something that he does not have and can only get from man. His love for the world is a love that gives, a love that enriches the lives of mankind and only in this way enriches his own. That the last point also needs to be made will become clear in chapter 2.

The love of God, or rather the God of love, sustains and controls all history. It is not correct to say that 'God is love' in 1 John 4:8, 16 is the climax to the biblical message about God. It is rather a conclusion to be

drawn from the whole of salvation-history. In the exodus, in the life of his
people in Canaan, in the exile and the return, in the coming of Jesus
Christ and the Holy Spirit, it is the God of love who is acting; the God,
who, unlike the gods, cares for his people, loves his creation, and is
prepared to make the highest sacrifice, to give himself for the need and
for the preservation of humanity.

It will be helpful to consider one or two aspects of the expression 'God
is love'. First of all a question: can the statement be reversed to say 'Love
is God'? The answer must be both yes and no. No, because *we* do not
know what love is. If love were what Plato thought it to be, and love was
God, then we would be lost, for God would have had no interest in us.
Because we have no private knowledge of the nature of love, as John
understood it, the statement cannot be turned around. If we did, everyone
would have his own god, fashioned according to his own idea of the
nature of love. On the other hand, it is just as true and important to say
that John does give to love a particular *content*. In 1 John 4:8–10 John
declares: 'God is love' and follows this immediately with: '*In this* the love
of God was made manifest among us, that God sent his only Son into the
world...' And as though it were still not clear what love is, he continues:
'In this is love, not that we loved God but that he loved us and sent his
Son to be the expiation for our sins.'

Deliberately and unmistakeably the love of God is thus linked with an
act, with a concrete, known history: that he sent his Son to give his life as
an atonement for our sins. Jesus Christ explains the love of God. This
does not mean merely that Jesus Christ gives God's love form and clarity.
It means that he is the climax of God's history of love with the world,
because here his love cost him the dearest and humbled him the deepest.
'God is love' is not the epitome of the message about God, for the whole of
history is borne along on his deeds of love. But Jesus Christ is the climax
and final explanation of 'God is love'. The history which he made is the
history in which God's love (or rather the God of love) could be known
radically and completely, so that the entire history prior to Christ must
be interpreted in the light of this deed of love.

But now, when we know what God's love is (or what the God of love is
like), namely Jesus Christ, we can reverse the expression and say 'Love is
God'.[66] This history which Jesus Christ has made, makes, and will yet
make is the history of God. This is how God is, and this is what he intends
for his creation. Indeed, 'Love (i.e. Jesus Christ) is God'.

That this is what John meant is evident from the identification between
'love' and 'God' in the same context. In 1 John 4:16 we read a second
time, 'God is love', and John follows this up immediately with: 'and he
who abides in love abides in God, and God abides in him'. To 'abide in
love' can be regarded as John's equivalent to Paul's 'abide in Christ'.

This seems to me to be the deepest meaning of the doctrine of Christ's
divinity. Even when theologians attempt today to divest this doctrine of
its Greek ontological character and interpret it more functionally (*inter*

alia Berkhof and Schoonenberg) this at least is clear: when the apostles and the later church said, 'Christ is truly God' they meant: in this history God becomes visible. Here we learn to understand his heart, his intention with creation.[67] Anyone who wants to know God cannot bypass Jesus Christ. That the church originally expressed this in terms of Greek philosophy ought to surprise no one. The church is called to express the gospel in the language of its times. Similarly it is not surprising that the church is struggling to use another, modern terminology to express the gospel in these days. But the norm for all such attempts remains the apostolic message that God is known in his being and in his fulness in the history of Jesus Christ. In passing, I am convinced that the matter is still adequately expressed in the Christological *vere Deus* (that Christ is truly God).[68]

That we come to know God as the God of love through Jesus Christ can be approached from several angles. Most frequently it is approached Christologically with a concentration on the radical self-surrender, humiliation and sacrifice of Jesus Christ. Via the Christological *vere Deus* the church rightly set out to know God through this sacrifice.

But what happened in the process, both in New Testament theology and in Systematic Theology, was that the Father, as we know him in the gospels and in the letters, receded into the background. Few New Testament theologies have a meaningful paragraph on 'God the Father'. This is a deficiency. Through Jesus' preaching, and likewise through the apostles' preaching, we learn to know the Father too as the God of love. Because a fuller treatment of this is often neglected, we will consider briefly Jesus' message about God the Father in the parables.

Jeremias has rightly shown that Jesus did not present the gospel to the 'tax-gatherers and sinners' in the form of parables. For them he used another method: he forgave their sins directly; he invited them to sit at table with him and summoned them to follow him. The parables containing the good news, the so-called 'gospel parables', were addressed to his opponents, to the Pharisees and the lawyers who condemned Jesus' association with sinners and took offence at his relationship with them. To them Jesus described in parables the boundless goodness of God the Father. The purpose of these parables was apologetic – to explain and to justify his attitude towards the outcasts in the light of the God of love.[69]

Parables that belong in this category are the three in Luke 15 (the lost sheep, the lost coin, and the prodigal son); the parable of the workmen employed at various times throughout the day (Matt. 20:1–16); the parable of the Pharisee and the tax-gatherer (Luke 18:9–14); the parable of the creditor and two debtors (Luke 7:41–43); and perhaps also the picture of the father and the child (Matt. 7:9–11).

Can it be that our deficient attention to God the Father is apparent even in the titles we give to the parables? Jeremias prefers 'The parable of the love of the Father' to the traditional 'Parable of the prodigal son'. (Indeed, 'The Father of love', or 'the loving Father' would possibly be better.)[70] And rather than 'Parable of the labourers hired at various hours', perhaps, 'Parable of the benevolent (or generous) farmer'.

In fact, the central figure in Luke 15:11–32 is not the lost son – which of the two sons *is* the *lost* son? – but the father who acts in remarkable love towards both of them. See what he gives his profligate son: the best robe – clothing for a guest of honour; a ring – this probably denotes the seal ring of the Old Testament, indicating a transference of authority to his son; shoes – slaves went barefoot, shoes were a luxury used by freemen; the fatted calf – a celebration in which the erstwhile prodigal was drawn once more into the fellowship of the table (intimate communion). While one ought not to go to great lengths in identifying the father in the parable with God the Father, yet it is clear that in the action of this father God is being proclaimed as the Father who is good, gracious, full of compassion towards one who did not deserve it, overflowing with love for a son who deserved to be rejected in that he had dragged his father's name through the mud.

And yet after this comes the second, and perhaps the most important aspect of the parable. Jesus continues his story on account of the concrete situation, namely, the objections of the Pharisees to his actions towards the tax-gatherers and sinners. It is true that the elder son had never run away, but through his most unpleasant reaction to the loving welcome which the runaway son received on his return, he showed that his heart had never been at one with the father's and that he had never found his life's joy in fellowship with the father, but had always sought his pleasure elsewhere – and was in fact not all that different from his brother, except in one respect: he had concealed his true character! And what was the father's (the Father's) reaction to him? He *entreated* him to come in and join the festivities. This is God's attitude to the indifferent, even hostile, Pharisees. Even in a matter that ought to have been self-evident (v. 32) Jesus pleads with them: be glad that the lost, the tax-gatherers and sinners are saved. And in doing so he pleads with them for their own salvation.

As in the two preceding parables (Luke 15:1–10) the concern is with God's care for the lost, and his persistence in going after them for their salvation. The fact that this chapter ends without a decision on the part of the elder son, testifies to the fact that Jesus persisted in pleading with the reluctant and even the antagonistic. God is like this!

In Matthew 20:1–16 Jesus tells of labourers who were engaged at different times, so that the last had worked only an hour. These were paid the same wages as those that had sweated through the heat of the day. Why? 'I choose to give to this last as I give to you. Am I not allowed to do what I choose with what belongs to me? Or do you begrudge my generosity?' (Or, The Living Bible: 'Should you be angry because I am good?') (20:14–15). Why does the farmer give so much to the latecomers? Simply because he wished to, without there being any grounds for it in either their willingness or special eagerness. God is like this!

This passage becomes clearer when it is compared with a similar rabbinical parable found in the Talmud which was told at the grave of a young, especially zealous rabbi. The parable tells of a king who one day employed a number of labourers to work on his fields. When two hours after they had begun he went to inspect their progress, he noticed that one of them had done so much that he stood out head and shoulders above the others. The king took him by the hand and for the rest of the day walked about with him in conversation. In the evening the labourers were paid, and the one outstanding received as much as the others even though he had worked only two hours. The others protested immediately that he had worked only two hours while they had worked the entire day. However, the king's response was: I do you no wrong, because by his energy and efficiency he did as much in two hours as any of the rest of you did in the whole day. The application was then made that the young rabbi, who had died so early, had in his twenty-eight years done as much as many rabbis would do in a hundred years.

But the difference is striking! In this case the king defends his action on the grounds that the labourer who had worked only two hours had in fact done just as much work as those that had worked the whole day. The reason thus lay with the labourer. But in Matthew 20 the reason lies with the farmer paying the wages. Because he (God) is good, and wishes to give as much to the undeserving as to the deserving, he does so. This is what God is like! Good, generous, indifferent to calculations. Love does not calculate (cf. 1 Cor. 13:5) – and God is love. 'God gives to all men generously without reproaching' (Jas. 1:5). Indeed, this contrast reveals a profound difference between the message of Jesus and the Pharisees – in their understanding of God. It is not 'merely' that the Pharisees could not accept Jesus as the Messiah while in every other respect agreeing with his message concerning the Old Testament and the God of Israel. There is between them a radical and decisive difference in their view of God.[71]

While considering the concept of God in late Judaism (the view shared by the Pharisees), it should be remembered that they did indeed know about the goodness of God, and even that God forgave sinners (i.e. people who did not know and keep the law in accordance with their extended interpretation of it). But in practice this knowledge was overshadowed by the doctrine of merits, according to which man is basically good and that by keeping the law he can build up merit before God. When a person's keeping of the law surpassed his transgressions, he was in favour with God. The law was thus a way of salvation open to all. In the context of their thinking, the idea that God could accept and forgive a sinner implied that if he was able to do *this*, how much more would he not reward the works of a *just* man!

Consequently, for them, sinners fell into a completely different category of people. They were the untouchables with whom one had no social contact – particularly at table – since this defiled one (Luke 5:27–32; 7:34–39). The greatest reason why they separated themselves so completely from sinners was that they were convinced that God did so, and that they were called to follow him in this respect (Luke 7:39). Indeed the law teaches: 'Consecrate yourselves therefore and be holy, for I am holy...you shall therefore be holy for I am holy' (Lev. 11:44–45). The 'gospel' of the Pharisees was that if these sinners would begin keeping the law, they would be rewarded since they would in this way become righteous.

Consequently when Jesus identified in a special way with the 'sinners', that is, with the rejected and despised, showing them in particular his love, and when he justified this behaviour on the grounds that this is what God does, and that through him God was visiting the lost, because it was his will to love them and to forgive all their filthy, offensive sins, Jesus really was a rock of offence and a stumbling block to the Pharisees, an *'Umwerter aller Werte'* (reverser of all values). The Pharisee dedicated himself to keeping the law (God's law) and more than the law (Luke 18:9–12), and he justified himself precisely on the grounds that he was *other* (better) than the tax-gatherers. The Pharisee could perhaps accept the possibility, as a great expectation, that a tax-gatherer could go home justified by merely calling on God for mercy, especially if it were an acquittal 'on probation' (conditional on his proceeding to earn the favour of God through keeping the law). But if so, the logical conclusion would be: how much more then would God congratulate the already righteous Pharisee! But if Jesus sent the tax-gatherer home justified and *not* the Pharisee, then Jesus became a blasphemer. 'This man (the tax collector) and not the other (the Pharisee), was in the right with God.'[72]

This short-circuit between Jesus and the Pharisees lay in the fact that they were able to speak of the goodness and love of God in a periphal way, but did not see the love of God as his very being. Furthermore they did not perceive that even the righteous would gain entry to the kingdom of God only through the goodness of God.

We will now consider more closely the first aspect of this misunderstanding. The essence of God, that which makes God God, that which characterises God, his deity (or however one wishes to express it), is his *free love*. If we learn to know God in Jesus; if God dwells in Jesus in his fulness; if the one who has seen Jesus has seen the Father; if Jesus does nothing of himself, but only that which he sees the Father doing, so that everything that the Father does, the Son does in the same way (John 5:19) – if all this is true, then Schierse is correct when he says that God unveils his deepest being as the compassionate, forgiving Father. The tax collectors, sinners, prostitutes, fishermen and farmers of Galilee to whom Jesus preached this good news, met God in an entirely personal way, as the one who forgave their sins and took them into his fellowship.[73] Jesus *preached* that God is good, and Jesus *showed* that God is good. Remove from the preaching of Jesus the loving, seeking, compassionate Father, and the heart of his message about God is gone. And remove from Jesus' actions his love for people in need, his readiness for sacrifice, his invitation to them to live in fellowship with him, and an empty shell remains.

Anyone who describes God's being in terms of disengagement, remoteness and self-sufficiency, the ground or origin of all that is, has listened wrongly to the biblical message in general and the preaching of Jesus in particular. That these aspects do also enter the picture, and that these concepts may well indeed express biblical truths if they are radically reinterpreted from the perspective of the God of Israel, is completely true. But they are periphal concepts, subsidiary matters which do not belong to the discussion of the being of God.

But again it must be emphasised that we do not learn about the God of love for the first time from Jesus and the apostles. Jesus is the culmination of the history of the interpretation of 'God is love', but the message is heard throughout the Old Testament. That Jesus is the high point of God's love implies, among other things, the following. In the Old Testament, with Israel, we hear and see that God is love (the exodus, Hosea, the return from exile, Jonah – to mention only a few examples); but in Jesus we see what God's love actually *costs* him, and the lengths to which he is prepared to go to restore to creation the value that it had lost. And precisely for this reason, the Christological *vere Deus* is indispensable. With this concept the church wished to say (what the apostles had already implied) that God in giving his Son gave nothing less than *himself*.

One could lay stress on the 'giving' as such, and thus on the more formal aspect of his love. It is striking how God's love (which is Christ's love) and the words 'give' and 'lay down' are spoken of together, with the latter being an interpretation of the former (e.g. John 3:16; 15:13; Gal. 2:20; Eph. 5:2, 25). In his love God gives. Even in this respect his love differs radically from that of a Greek god. The gods desired something, and because mankind had nothing that they did not already have, they could not love them; indeed, in Greek philosophy it would be meaningless to say that God loves mankind. Such radical differences should warn those who wish to use Greek concepts in their doctrine of God to exercise great care. Greek concepts of God must be radically reinterpreted if the God of Israel is to be correctly proclaimed.

However one should not linger too long over this formal difference. The actual issue in God's love (or rather the God of love) is not merely that he gives, but that he gives *himself*. How absurd this would appear in Plato's system. And yet this is the essence of God's love. By giving himself, God creates fellowship between himself and mankind. This fellowship is embodied in the covenant. And this again confronts us with the radical difference between God and the gods. It is quite impossible to speak of a covenant between the gods and their adherents – least of all in the Greek system. One often encounters the fact that what is essential to the God of Israel is absent in the gods.

Jesus Christ is both the consummation and the explicative history of 'God is love'. This means first and foremost that the action of God in the Old Testament must be interpreted as God's giving of himself to Israel, that God himself is involved in the history that he makes with his people Israel, that it affects him (anthropomorphisms!), that he cares (the jealousy of God). This will be considered in greater detail in chapter 2.

Jesus Christ being the consummation and the explicative history of 'God is love' means further that the covenant must be interpreted as a universal covenant, and that the history which God makes in the Old Testament with Israel must be seen as an 'exemplary' history of God with the world. A Christian cannot interpret the history of the Old Testament in a particularist way, recognising only an occasional universalist breakthrough.

But the most important aspect of the love of God that appears from the life of Jesus, is that God's love is not kept in check by other attributes.[74] In this connection closer attention should be given to the wrath and judgment of God. This is done in chapter 2 however, in connection with the pathos of God. Nevertheless, here we can anticipate the conclusions arrived at there. It will be seen that God's wrath does not belong to his essence, or at least not in the same way as his love; and that there would never have been any mention of his wrath if there were no creature that had sinned and in his sin had persisted against the grace of God; that there is thus in God's life of fellowship which he has in himself as Father, Son and Holy Spirit, never any mention of wrath as there is of love; and that wrath is therefore an entirely historical matter, a reaction of God to the rejection of his grace. Should anyone wish to argue that this would involve God in the processes of change, introducing a new element (wrath) into his being, and, finding this possibility of change unacceptable, attempt to re-introduce God's wrath into his *essence* (no matter how), he would have bowed the knee again to the Platonic concept of God according to which God is a principle, a ground, an explanation of what exists, rather than the personal, living God of history. That God necessarily always had to be everything that he is and will yet be, makes of God a thing that can only do, impart or become what was (potentially at least) always present in him. In contrast to this is the God of Israel, who, as the *living* God does *new* things, enters into new relationships and only at the consummation will be 'all in all' (1 Cor. 15:28).[75]

Even with all that has been said so far about 'God is love', no adequate content has yet been given to it. 1 John 4 shows that love is no mere idea, but a concrete history, the history of the coming, life, death and resurrection of Jesus Christ. This is the meaning of 'love' in the expression, 'God is love'.

Yet something more needs to be said. What is the content of this history, and with it, that of the entire history which God makes with Israel and the world? This, of course, is that most profound question with which we will grapple in chapter 3, but, in a sense an answer must be given here as well because it is relevant to the discussion of the relationship between God and the gods.

Earlier in this chapter consideration was given to the mocking of the gods in Psalm 82 because it throws light on the relationship between the LORD and El. It became apparent there that Yahweh's condemnation of the gods arose from their unjust judgments and their partiality to the godless (v. 2), and that they had not done right to the weak and the orphaned, and had not given justice to the poor and the wretched (v. 3). Nor had they saved the weak and needy, nor delivered them from the hand of the godless (v. 4). This then was the reason why the gods (and at this point it does not matter whether they were gods or judges) were deposed and condemned. And in contrast to them stands the LORD who gives justice on earth (v. 8). It became clear that *špṭ* should be translated 'does right' or 'gives justice' rather than 'judges'. This translation is based on its usage in verse 3 as well as on the structure of the Psalm, which consists in a confrontation between God and the gods by means of which the prophet-psalmist wished to call the people back to the worship of the only true God from the worship of other gods (and threatening polytheism). This he did shortly before the reforms under Josiah[76] in order to show that only the LORD actually performed what was to be expected of a God, and what was appropriate to him. So in verse 8 the LORD is called upon by the cultus community to do what the gods should have done, but did not do. 'Do right' in verse 8 (which is also used first in verse 3: 'give judgment' of NEB) is thus the comprehensive concept which embraces all that is demanded in verses 3–4. All that is expected of the gods in verses 3–4, is asked of the LORD in one word, in verse 8. This explanation is usually missed by translators and commentators – and as a result the point of the psalm is lost.

But what is of greater importance is that the LORD finds the gods guilty of the charge against them, and deposes them. It is therefore a serious charge. Labuschagne has rightly suggested that here the gods are summoned to do what is actually characteristic of the LORD.[77] To do right and to give justice are pre-eminently what are of concern to the LORD in the Old Testament. And this was so not merely from the days of the great prophets or psalmists, but since he revealed himself for the first time to Israel and took them to be his people. In the following words we find the reasons why the LORD had mercy on Israel in Egypt. 'And the people of Israel groaned under their bondage, and cried out for help... And God heard their groaning...and God saw the people of Israel...' (Exod. 2:23–25). The story of the burning bush follows immediately, and there again we hear: 'I have seen the affliction of my people who are in Egypt, and have heard their cry because of their taskmasters; I know their sufferings' (Exod. 3:7); also 3:9, 16, 17; 4:31 6:4 f). The 'cry' of 2:23 means the loud cry for help addressed to the judge by a victim of injustice.

Throughout the Old Testament the exodus is looked back on as an act of *God's justice;* i.e. an act through which he liberated the oppressed people from their oppressors (Pss. 106:106:10; 22:5–6; 81:7–8). Strikingly (and perhaps even a little strangely) it is said that this injustice and the plundering of Israel were in part remedied in the exodus, when Israel in turn plundered the Egyptians (Exod. 12:35–36).

It is against this background that the identification of God's righteousness and his acts of liberation must be seen in the Old Testament. His righteousness means, *inter alia*, that he brings about justice. As he did this in the past by intervening in the Egyptian situation, liberating the oppressed and robbed people, so he continues to do this throughout history. Psalm 71 is an arresting example of this. The well-known cry of God's incomparableness: 'O God, who is like thee?' (v. 19) is preceded by mention of 'thy righteous acts' and 'thy deeds of salvation' (parallel utterances v. 15), 'mighty deeds' and 'righteousness' (again parallels v. 16). Once again in the same context, mention is made of the LORD's righteousness, his might, and the great things that he had done (v. 18–19). In this, that is, in his righteousness, which is expressed in his deliverance from injustice, God is incomparable to the gods who had failed to do just this (Ps. 82). Verse 2 becomes understandable in this light: '*In thy righteousness* deliver me.' (Read v. 4 in this light also and compare with Pss. 31:2b; 89:17; Dan. 9:16).

Furthermore, the Old Testament makes it very clear that not only was it God's intention to liberate his people from their oppressors, but that within his people he would identify himself with the poor, the wretched, the widows and orphans, and intervene on their behalf. The book of Psalms especially constitutes an anthology on this theme. 'The LORD is a stronghold for the oppressed' (9:9). 'Because the poor are despoiled, because the needy groan, I will now arise, says the LORD. I will place him in the safety for which he longs' (12:5). The deliverance from Egypt is clearly in the background in this verse, as it is in the next: 'For thou dost deliver a humble people; but the haughty eyes thou dost bring down' (18:27 – see also v. 17 and 48). 'All my bones shall say, O LORD, who is like thee, thou who deliverest the weak from him who is too strong for him, the weak and needy from him who despoils him?' (35:10). The Psalms offer many more examples: 68:6 f; 103:6; 107:41; 113:7; 140:13; 142:7; 146:7–9; 149:4; and 1 Samuel 2:4–8; Isaiah 25:4; Jeremiah 31:11 as well.

Strangers, widows and orphans are the special concern of the LORD because in Israel's society they were (almost) without rights or opportunities. Because the woman played such a confined role in society, she, and her children, easily became the victims of exploitation and injustice (2 Kgs. 4:1 f). Likewise with the stranger. For this reason the list of appalling sins for which Jerusalem was to be devastated included the fact that her princes had treated the strangers with violence, and had oppressed the orphans and the widows (Ezek. 22:7). In contrast to this Israel is commanded to allow the stranger who lived among them and had begotten children there to inherit the land along with them (Ezek. 47:22–23).

When Heschel deals with the wrath of God and argues that this is not what God is like at heart, he then asks what God is like. He then refers to

Jeremiah 9:24: '...that I am the LORD who practices kindness, justice, and righteousness in the earth; for in these things I delight, says the LORD.'[78] It is in complete harmony with this that the LORD sends Amos to declare the final judgment on Israel (the Northern kingdom), on the grounds that they had oppressed the poor, robbed the wretched, and deprived the weak of their rights (2:6–8; 3:9–10; 5:7, 10–12; 8:4–6). This serves to emphasise how important justice and righteousness are to God. The people in fact tried to smother this injustice with zealous religion – so zealous that they even brought an excess of freewill offerings, over and above the obligatory sacrifices (4:5), and certain 'tithes' that were only required every three years they brought every three days (4:4).[79] Such religion was, however, detestable to the LORD (5:21–23) as long as justice and righteousness did not fill the land (5:24). God will not permit himself to be served in this way. He accepts no consecration to himself if no place is created in society for the less privileged. It was for this reason that forty years later (722 BC) he allowed the Northern kingdom to be carried away, never again to return! And it was not only those who were actively involved that came under this judgment, but those too who did not actively resist (6:7 'who...are not grieved over the ruin of Joseph').

According to the gospels, Jesus had compassion particularly for the tax collectors and sinners, and told parables in which the poor, the lame, the cripples and the blind were invited to the feast (i.e. those who were outcasts in the society of his times. These parables have already been touched on in connection with the love of God). In his prophetic discourse, the division between those who will be saved and those who will be lost is made on the basis of love for the destitute (Matt. 25:31–46). The importance of this pericope in its wider context is seldom realised. In Matthew 24–25 Jesus is dealing with his second coming and the end of the age. In subsequent parables he admonishes his disciples to watch and be ready because his return will be unexpected (24:42, 44; 25:13). But in none of these parables does he indicate *what* the disciples should *do* to be ready. In all three main parables (24:45–51; 25:1–12; 25:14–30) he simply repeats with great emphasis the necessity of being ready when he returns. And then only in the last section of chapter 25 does he clearly indicate *what* his disciples should do to be ready for this great day: they should feed the hungry, give the thirsty a drink, welcome strangers, clothe the naked, etc. This means that concern for the underprivileged is of paramount importance for Jesus, who is the one who reveals God's heart to man.

The fact that this aspect receives comparatively little attention in the letters of the New Testament must partly be explained by the fact that the earliest congregations consisted of small groups who were for the greater part the poor and underprivileged. Social structures could not be a priority in admonitions to them because they had no dominant role in society – a situation entirely different from that in which the prophets worked among the people of God, and in which the structures of society could very well come under the critique of God's word. The same applies to the problem of slavery. Amos brings slavery totally under the judgment of God, while Paul does not. Amos was able to address society, while Paul addressed small groups of believers as the people of God. So then, where the church constitutes a significant portion of society, and especially a significant proportion of its leadership, the Old Testament idea of a theocratic social structure (van Ruler; theocracy means that God rules) becomes more applicable than in the situation of the first Christian congregations. Indeed where the situation was appropriate, we have had radical statements on these matters from the apostles as well. James 2:1–9 (TEV) says: 'My brothers in your life as believers in our Lord Jesus Christ, the Lord of glory, you must never treat people in different ways because of their outward appearance. Suppose a rich man wearing a gold ring and fine clothes comes in to your meeting, and a poor man in ragged clothes also comes in. If you show more respect to the well-dressed man and say to him, "Have this best seat here", but say to the poor man, "Stand, or sit down here on the floor by my feet" then you are guilty of creating distinctions among yourselves and making judgments based on evil motives. Listen, my dear brothers! God chose the poor people of this world to be rich in faith and to possess the kingdom which he promised to those who love him. But you dishonour the poor! ... You will be doing the right thing if you obey the law of the Kingdom, which is found in the scripture, "Love your neighbour as yourself". But if you treat people according to their outward appearance, you are guilty of sin, and the Law condemns you as a lawbreaker.'

And as though these sharp words were not enough, James comes back to the same matter in a different context, in James 5:1–6 (TEV): 'And now, you rich people, listen to me! Weep and wail over the miseries that are coming upon you! Your riches have rotted away, and your clothes have been eaten by moths. Your gold and silver are covered with rust, and this rust will be a witness against you, and eat up your flesh like fire. You have piled up riches in these last days. You have not paid the wages to the men who work in your fields. Hear their complaints! And the cries of those who gather in your crops have reached the ears of God, the Lord Almighty! Your life here on earth has been full of luxury and pleasure. You have made yourselves fat for the day of slaughter. You have condemned and murdered the innocent man, and he does not resist you.'

Truly God's care and concern for the poor and underprivileged, the oppressed and the victims of injustice are just as prominent in the New Testament as they are in the Old. What is less in evidence in the New Testament is the task of the government. This is understandable in the light of the differences already mentioned.

The role of the king in bringing about justice and righteousness in the Old Testament is very important in this connection. G. von Rad calls him the guardian and guarantor of law and justice. As the representative of

God, as his anointed, he had to represent the attitude of the LORD towards, and undertake positive care for, the poor. Of him we read in Psalm 72:4: 'May he defend the cause of the poor of the people, give deliverance to the needy, and crush the oppressor.' And further: 'For he delivers the needy when he calls, the poor and him who has no helper. He has pity on the weak and the needy, and saves the lives of the needy. From oppression and violence he redeems their life, and precious is their blood in his sight' (v. 12–14).

Because the king was in this way the representative of God and the personification of government and had this special responsibility to provide justice to the poor, Amos radically pronounced God's judgment on the government and specifically on the king of Samaria (Amos 6:1–7; 7:9, 11). The government should have seen to it that the rich did not acquire the lands of the poor, thus depriving them of the possibility of making up their arrears in a good year. And the government should have seen to it that they were not forced into slave labour by the rich – and sometimes on their own land. Because these things are so close to the heart of God (Jer. 9:24), because he has judged and deposed the gods that did not attend to these things (Ps. 82), justice and righteousness are of the utmost importance for the church and also for the government, especially if the members of the government are members of the church. It is clear that the government has a special responsibility towards the less-privileged in society. Laws should as far as possible prevent the exploitation and deprivation of these groups. And in a democracy it is also very important that these underprivileged have effective voice or vote. In such a situation texts such as Isaiah 5:8 become applicable: 'Woe to those who join house to house, who add field to field, until there is no more room, and you are left to dwell alone in the land' (see NEB).

Against this background it is understandable that there is frequent reference these days to political theology in which God is spoken of as a political God. In a situation where politics is so frequently described as 'dirty' this sounds, of course, like blasphemy. However, it all depends on the meaning given to 'political'. In an essay entitled *Politiek is een heilige zaak (Politics is an holy business)*, van Ruler suggests that politics is first and foremost a sacred matter, because it is concerned with the way in which a society is ordered, and because, van Ruler argues, the life of the people should be lived as a service to God. This is true of the life of a nation in the broadest sense of the word. It holds for culture in all its expressions, its institutions and its forms, in art and in science, in radio broadcasts and in sport, in education and in entertainment. It must be emphasised most strongly that the living God is concerned with these and similar historical-cultural phenomena in which his name may dwell in this world.[81] A couple of pages further on van Ruler adds that the national culture is the place where God is served, and that we may not withdraw into the isolation of a separate Christian culture.

Anyone who understands the Old Testament and perceives the

dominant role played by the exodus from Egypt in prophetic preaching, and who accepts God's atonement from all our sins in Jesus Christ – including our political sins, and the sins that are entrenched by particular structures – cannot help but realise that God intends to be involved politically, precisely because he is not like the gods – a personified natural power with responsibility merely for one facet of life – but is the God of Israel, the Creator and Sustainer of heaven and earth. In *this sense*, the exodus is undoubtedly a political event in which God leads out his oppressed people, liberating them from their oppressors, and punishing the oppressors in the process. And it was not only to Israel that God did these political deeds. The prophetic preaching, which was so often directed towards alien nations, condemning the injustice of one heathen nation towards another (Amos 2:1 f; Isa. 46–51), shows that God wished to sanctify their politics as well, and establish justice and righteousness among them too.

In this connection three matters are of importance. First of all, the question concerning the full compass of justice and righteousness. On the one hand it is certainly true to say that the government has a special responsibility for the underdog (van Ruler).[82] He must be legally protected against exploitation. A truly human existence is more than food and clothes: it is the possibility of joyful living. A. A. van Ruler says, in the essay already referred to, that the goal of all socio-economic politics of government and industry must not merely be to provide for the possibility or even the certainty of existence, but must provide scope for joy in life both in body and spirit. Social injustice and ostracism are not merely the harming of people, but what is worse, the harming of the salvation of the LORD, through the sacrifice of Jesus Christ which is penetrating the whole of society. For this reason the rule of law pertaining to work has a divine sanction when seen from the perspective of the prophetic Word.[83]

On the other hand, God's righteousness is not only concerned with the underdog, the poor and the oppressed. Righteousness is concerned with all men, ruler and subject, employer and employee. Quite rightly van Ruler describes as secretarian the tendency to give attention to one aspect only, because politics that intends to order itself according to the demands of biblical righteousness must give equal attention to all aspects and dimensions of society. Van Ruler asserts that Marxism is a secretarian perversion of the Christian faith.[84]

The second problem concerns a democratically elected government that wishes to correct certain things in society. Such a government cannot do more than its electorate will accept or it will 'govern' itself out of office. Consequently, when the corrections envisaged have direct or indirect associations with the gospel, it is the church that must take the initiative in forming public opinion through its preaching, in order that the public will come to accept the changes. The church must therefore give the lead, clearing the way so that the government can follow. Even when the government is not prepared to make the necessary corrections, the task of the church, of course, remains the same. This does not mean that the church must 'preach politics' – the church may not do this. But it does mean that the church not only may, but must, test political matters in the light of the gospel, and in the process will have to touch on concrete issues. God is indeed the Creator of the earth, and God has given to us a cultural mandate. God has instituted government, and he is therefore involved in society directly. It is our task as believers to do his will, and to see that his will is done in society too.

The third aspect relates to global problems such as the pollution of the environment, population growth, nuclear weapons, provision of food, rich and poor nations. Apart from the immediate importance of some of these problems, recent investigations have indicated that there is a possibility that growth on earth could shortly reach its limits, after which the entire structure could collapse.[85] It is obviously extremely important that attention should be given to the problem. The continued existence of man on earth is at stake. But it cannot be regarded as a purely secular, cultural, or political matter. It must be seen first, and foremost, as a problem that concerns God, with which he is immediately involved, because it is his world and we are his creatures with whom he wishes to live in joy on earth. The matter therefore affects believers, the church, directly. We may not permit God's creation to be abused and devastated. The church will have to proclaim with new zeal: 'The *earth* is the LORD's and the fullness thereof, the world and those who dwell therein' (Ps. 24:1). The church will have to move public opinion to give urgent attention to these global problems, from the perspective of the will of God for his creation. Isaiah 45:18, written specifically against the gods, reads: 'For thus says the LORD, who...formed the earth and made it...for a place to dwell in'. Consequently it is disappointing that the church has given so little attention to these issues in its preaching.

There are also those who will see in these global problems and their threat to the very existence of humanity, a sign that the end of time is drawing near, and that the judgment of God will shortly be executed. Yet with such an attitude, one would of course make no attempt to tackle and solve the problems, but would welcome them as clear signs of the imminent return of Christ in judgment. This attitude is at least correct in the sense that the church should always discern in the things happening around it the signs that point to the return of Christ. It would accordingly be encouraging if these problems were to move the church to a new dedication to the Lord, and a correspondingly more urgent proclamation of the imminent return of Christ. But this does *not* mean that his return is near only now for the first time, and that we are now beginning for the first time to enter the last days. Nor does it mean that the signs of the times have provided us with a means of calculating when (or even approximately when) the Lord's coming will occur. All such thinking is unbiblical, in that the church has lived in the last days ever since Pentecost (Acts 2:17); because the signs of the times are not given for the purpose of calculating the date of Christ's coming, but rather as a reminder *that* his coming is near, and has been near since the days of the apostles; and because *still today* a day is with the Lord as a thousand years, and a thousand years as a day. This means that the church must proclaim that the coming of the Lord can take place at any moment, even today. (This is what the church should have been doing for the past nineteen centuries, though it has often failed to do it because of a mistaken notion of the last days.) On the other hand this does not exclude the possibility that we may continue for another thousand or more years on this unrenewed earth before the Lord comes. This leaves us with a responsibility for safeguarding the conditions necessary for life and for ensuring that God's creation is not frittered away.[86]

The following would seem to be the neglected task of the church that must be taken up in these decades: to think through and proclaim the biblical understanding of the will of God for, and his involvement with the entire world community. That history will blossom eventually into the *new* (renewed) *earth* is of the greatest importance for the way in which we deal with this world *now*, and with the people in it.

GODS IN OUR DAY

This short discussion of the political and social implications of the biblical message about God, has brought us incidentally to the question concerning the identity of the gods in our modern society.

In the time of the Old Testament the gods were fairly readily identifiable. In most cases they were either supernatural powers which imposed themselves upon particular nations, or they were forces of nature that were thought to be spiritual powers. Greater diversification occurs in the New Testament, so that alongside of Satan, reference is made to the demons (apparently the gods of the Old Testament), powers (which can be classified in various ways, e.g. Colossians 1:16 – so that one is not always sure whether they are good or evil powers), and evil spirits. But then the diversity of God's opponents is extended further and includes, among others, mammon (Matt. 6:24), the belly (Luke 12:19 f, and Phil. 3:19), the 'first principles' (Gal. 4:8 f), the local government (Acts 4:19; 5:29), or the emperor in Rome (Mark 12:17).[87]

The work of men such as the Blumhardts[88] and K. Koch[89] has shown convincingly that certain people are still in our own days being possessed and controlled by demons or evil spirits, and need to be liberated by the power of Jesus Christ. This ought to be a normal part of the task of the church, in the situation where the Holy Spirit imparts a special gift to believers for this purpose. It is a mistake to lay down as a condition, as is sometimes done, that the church must first attain theoretical clarity about the many problems which (do indeed) arise concerning special spiritual gifts and their exercise (particularly apart from the established churches). The church did not begin to function and proclaim the gospel only after the message had been theoretically explored and refined and formulated in creeds! The Lord lives and works in and through the church that received the gospel from the apostles, and in pursuing this task problems do arise which must then be theoretically resolved. Theological reflection is essentially a follower, not a leader. In fact, how can a matter be reflected on theoretically if it has not been carried out and experienced in practice? The gospel, after all, is not a philosophical system. It is a practical message which gives a new form to the life of mankind. For this reason the church is the sphere in which the Spirit distributes and directs the exercise of special gifts. Only after that must the church look for theoretical clarifications.

Powers and evil spirits can assume forms other than the demonic with its consequent need for exorcism. Especially in Hitler's time, but also later, a great deal of thought was given to greater and more comprehensive forms of the demonic. Paul's message concerning the powers was investigated in this connection. Berkhof has shown that these powers are not restricted to angels or personal beings[90] (cf. the diversity of divisive factors in Rom. 8:38–9), but relate also to what would today more generally be called social structures. These powers are created by God in order to find their deepest meaning and goal in Christ ('to him' in Col. 1:16 probably means directed to Christ, or moving towards Christ). After these, reference is also made to 'the first principles (of the world)' (Col. 2:8; Gal. 4:9), which acquire their form through traditions ('according to human tradition'). Astrology was one way in which the heathen localized these powers, that is, by connecting them with celestial bodies. The Jews, conversely, sought to do this by obeying the law of Moses. Such powers that control society outside of Christ and prevent total chaos from developing are, *inter alia*, time ('things present and things to come' – actually the present and the future), space ('heights and depths'), life and death, politics and philosophy, public opinion and the Jewish law, pious traditions (and even the fateful positions of the stars!). These structures are the framework through which God wishes to save society from disintegration and to preserve it from chaos. Berkhof likens them to the (Dutch) dykes. They have been erected against the chaotic floods that would overflow the world, and they are indispensable to the preservation of the world outside of Christ. They are powers which give cohesion to society, and which mark out a viable road for the individual and the community. Berkhof refers, among other things, to the clan or tribe among primitive people, the respect for parents and forebears among the Chinese especially, the polis, or city-state among the Greeks, and the Roman empire of the entire known world of its times. These provided an immense amount of order, possibilities for a full life, and room to live in.

When Christ appears on the scene, both in his earthly life and in the subsequent preaching, it is repeatedly apparent that these powers overstep the limits of their God-given task and purpose, rise up in rebellion against Christ and in this way take on the characteristics of idols. This gives rise to an inevitable 'either... or' choice for Christ (and the church) or the world (and the powers). So although these powers can continue to have a protective function in a society (for example, in communist states there appears to be less immorality and drug-addiction than in the western 'Christian' states), they become anti-Christian and must first be radically subdued to the sole sovereignty of Christ before they can again have a positive meaning – even for the church. It is fairly generally agreed that Hitler provides the classic example of how these powers can rise in opposition to Christ. In this case, it was not only the powers of the people, the pure Aryan race, and the state that were involved, but even 'Providence' was yoked in to the Nazi cause, which prompts Weber to point to the alarming possibility that even God can be made into an idol.[91] Weber shows that any 'divine' structure, or power, or anything, that becomes a guarantor for man, for his state organisation, his spiritual or cultural values, is an idol. In South Africa the concept of *apartheid* has for some people evidently become such an independent entity over against Christ, to the extent that even the communion of saints, the unity of the church, must suffer under it, and genuine Christian values such as the love of neighbour, and adequate opportunities in life for others, often suffer under this power. Where apartheid hinders Christian unity and loving mutual service, it is idolatrous. And wherever it results in people (and, in South Africa these will be the black people) remaining permanently subordinate with fewer opportunities than others it is likewise demonic. The concept of 'law and order' also, which is again a protective power in society, tends in some circles to become a value in itself, instead of functioning in the service of the God of justice and righteousness. How striking is Barth's statement that no person can break the hold of these powers once they have begun to acquire idolatrous characteristics, and that the only hope for mankind lies in Jesus Christ, who has already dethroned these powers![92]

FALLING AWAY FROM GOD – WHY?

After so much has been said about God, and his wonderful incomparableness in relation to the gods has become apparent in so many ways, in his deeds, his power, his love, his compassion for the unfortunate, one comes up against the disturbing phenomenon in both the Old and the New Testaments of people falling away from God. Earlier in this chapter it was shown that the mocking of the gods in any real sense is confined to the Bible (on account of the nature of the true God). Similarly, falling away from God is also a biblical phenomenon, precisely because he is the only true God. The followers of other religions are free to take on other gods according to their needs, and gods have frequently been exchanged for others. But those who worship the God of Israel and serve him, must serve him alone. Should another god beside him be honoured, this is apostasy from him. He is everything in our lives – or we serve other gods.

From all that has been said, it has become progressively clearer that this demand is not unreasonable. If God is the only true God, the only Helper and Deliverer, the God who is good, who in his essence is love, and gives love, then it is folly to worship another god, or even to give attention to any other god beside him. If God has undertaken responsibility for the entire life of his people, there can be no single need, nor any valid reason, which would justify them turning to the service of other gods. Anyone who reads the chapters from Deutero-Isaiah or from the Psalms dealing with the mocking of the gods, cannot but help accept it as virtually self-evident that no person in full possession of his faculties would exchange the true God for these powerless idols. Against gods that cannot talk or move or do anything at all, stands the God who has borne his people along from the time of their birth (Egypt!). Over against gods that tumble over, stands the true God who makes the future known in advance, and then causes it to happen accordingly. Against the gods to whom children must be sacrificed, stands the true God, 'who did not spare his own Son, but gave him up for us all' (Rom. 8:32).

How is it conceivable after Egypt, Carmel and Golgotha that given a choice the people might decide against the LORD and for the gods?

And yet the disturbing fact remains that time and again the people turned their back on the LORD and sought after strange gods. How often the LORD pleaded with them through the prophets, and warned them against idolatry. How poignant are the words of the LORD through Isaiah: 'Even the animals – the donkey and the ox – know their owner and appreciate his care for them, but not my people Israel. No matter what I do for them, they still don't care.' (Living Bible, Isa. 1:3) And how shocking is the word through Jeremiah: 'Look around you and see if you can find another nation anywhere that has traded in its old gods for new ones – even though their gods are nothing. Send to the west, to the island of Cyprus; send to the east, to the deserts of Kedar. See if anyone there has ever heard so strange a thing as this. And yet my people have given up their glorious God for silly idols!' (Jer. 2:10–11 in the Living Bible).

How is this possible? How can it be understood that Judah had as many gods (rather: idol shrines) as cities (Jer. 2:28), that they went 'whoring' after strange gods under every green tree and on every green hill (Jer. 2:20)?

Various attempts have been made to answer this question. A. Deissler approaches it by suggesting that the LORD is the transcendent God, who is very much more difficult to grasp for the person who has not learned to think philosophically, than the immanent gods (present within the world) who are so much easier to accept.[93] I have considerable doubts about this. It does not seem correct to me to suggest that it was more difficult in principle for the easterner to believe in the LORD than in the gods. Others have suggested that the gods offered a 'gratis religion' and that their worshippers had no obligations, whereas the LORD had, by virtue of the covenant, given his people the law in order to create a pattern of behaviour for their life. This involved them in definite obligations. Such an explanation might have had validity in certain religious situations, but for Israel the law with its demands held the promise of life and joy for the people (Deut. 28). And in fact, certain gods did lay claim to costly sacrifices, and even asked the sacrifice of children (Moloch). Offerings were also brought to the queen of heaven (Jer. 7:18). Possibly the circumstances were much more complex, and varied so much from situation to situation, that a single general explanation is impossible. The one case in which the Jews do respond to the LORD's charge with an explanation as to why they had turned to the service of an idol (and intended to continue with it!) is very arresting (Jer. 44). In this case the LORD turns sharply on the Jews in Egypt who had taken up the worship of the queen of heaven. In verses 1–6 the prophet reminds the people that it was because of their idolatry and that of their fathers that the LORD's judgment had come on Judah and Jerusalem. In verses 7–14 the prophet announces God's judgment on them because they had not repented of these sins, but on the contrary, continued to 'burn incense to other gods' (v. 8). In verses 15–19 there follows a rare and shocking reaction from the Jews. They bluntly declare that they will not listen to Jeremiah's admonition. 'But we will do everything that we have vowed, burn incense to the queen of heaven and pour out libations to her, as we did, both we and our fathers, in the cities of Judah and in the streets of Jerusalem; for then we had plenty of food, and prospered, and saw no evil. But since we left off burning incense to the queen of heaven and pouring out libations to her, we have lacked everything and have been consumed by the sword and by famine' (v. 17–18).

Jeremiah was confronted here with a radical situation. The prophetic message that God revealed himself in history (dealt with in chapter 3), and that he would bless his people when they were obedient to him and would punish their disobedience, was well known. this was Jeremiah's interpretation of their flight from Jerusalem and Judah: because they had persisted in their idolatry the LORD's patience had come to an end and he had punished them. Through their disobedience they were now suffering want and hardship. But in contrast to this was the interpretation of history as seen by the people. It was because they had ceased their service to the queen of heaven that they had had to flee from Judah and Jerusalem. So long as they offered their sacrifices to her all had gone well. For this reason they would continue with their offerings to her, so that they might prosper once more. Many details of events preceding and attending the reformation under Josiah are raised here, but the real issue concerns the opposing interpretations of history. Jeremiah declared that they were sojourning as strangers in Egypt under the LORD's judgment because they had served the queen of heaven; they said that it was because they had (temporarily) stopped serving her that she had punished them. In this way they made out a strong case for persisting in their idolatrous religion, adding that they had every intention of doing so.

The prosperity which they had enjoyed while serving the queen of heaven (end of v. 17) seems to have been the long and peaceful reign of Manasseh (696–642 BC). During this time alien religions were tolerated in Judah.

In his answer to their reaction, Jeremiah suggests that they had misunderstood the state of affairs. The long years of prosperity under Manasseh were due to the patience of God, who tolerated their idolatry (v. 22). The subsequent disasters which overtook Jerusalem were the LORD's punishment for their idolatry – 'therefore your land has become a desolation and a waste and a curse, without inhabitant, as it is this day' (v. 22).

Here we have two interpretations of the same history posed in contrast to each other. Jeremiah in the last two verses gives two proofs that it is God's work (firstly, that all but a small remnant of the Jews in Egypt will be killed; and, secondly, that the king of Egypt, Hophra, will be killed). Yet this evidence still lay in the future, so that the decision regarding whose was the correct interpretation of history remained very difficult. One thing is clear from this, as must be maintained in chapter 3 as well, and that is that the proofs of God – i.e. God's self-demonstration in history (exodus, return from Babylon etc.) – are not conclusive proofs outside of the realm of faith. In Jeremiah 44 as elsewhere, the Jews should have accepted Jeremiah's interpretation of history – which was based on God's patience – by submitting completely to the word of the LORD, but this they did not do.

We are confronted with a variety of reasons for the apostasy of the people to alien gods. Some of these reasons might seem very convincing to unbelievers, but for those who trust in the LORD there is only one possible decision: the LORD alone is worthy to be served. This reminds one irresistibly of Hebrews 11:6: 'But without faith it is impossible to please him.'

Just as all sin is inexplicable, so also the people's apostasy cannot be explained. In the light of faith it can only be condemned and confessed.[94] Indeed, were it possible to really explain their apostasy (by means of various explanations from the realm of the history of religions, psychology or environmental factors) it would become almost impossible to condemn the people for it. Were one to accept the 'explanation' given by the Jews in Egypt as the reason for their apostasy and idolatry (Jer. 44) the right of the prophet to express God's judgment and to direct them onto the right way would be surrendered.

2

God and man

The comparableness of God

INTRODUCTION

In chapter 1 it was noted that there are also possible points of comparison between God and the gods. A brief study was also made of this comparability, for example, in respect of the 'appropriations' from the gods in the Old Testament. The main emphasis, however, fell on God's incomparableness in relation to the gods, since this is the main emphasis in the biblical message about this relationship.

The position is reversed when we come to the relationship between God and man. One must of course also speak of incomparability here, and in the history of the doctrine of God this aspect has received the greater emphasis. Yet I am convinced that this is not correct. Beside the incomparability, which will in due course receive closer attention, this chapter will stress the fact that there is a particular and important comparability between God and man. Reference will be made in this connection to the anthropomorphisms (speaking of God in human terms) which are used for God, and the theomorphisms which are used in speaking of man. Both phenomena touch upon the same issue, that is, the fact that God made man in his own image. Consideration will also be given to the meaning of the covenant as the essential structure of the relationship between God and man, and to the incarnation as the crowning point of all the anthropomorphisms and consequently of the covenant. Then too the word 'like' as it appears in so many of the exhortative passages in the New Testament will have to be touched on, especially in those exhortations which urge believers to be or behave 'like God' or 'as God' ('like Christ' or 'as Christ').

The investigation will show that God and man are much closer than is often contended in the doctrine of God. The view that presents God in a one-sided and formalistic way as an unknowable entity, linked with an equally formalistic and depreciatory view of the littleness of man, and the inevitability of tension between God and man because man is a creature, will be rejected on the grounds that it is dishonouring to God and does not do justice to his express intention of making man in his image and of living in covenant fellowship with him. It will be shown that the idea of the transcendence of God has not been completely freed from its Greek philosophical origin and actually obscures the Christian understanding of God.

ANTHROPOMORPHISM IN HISTORY

This phenomenon attracted attention from earliest times. On the whole the early church passed a negative judgment on the human ways in which the Bible speaks of God. But that was nothing exceptional in the world in which the church lived. The Jew, Philo of Alexandria, maintained that anthropomorphism, although it was used by God on account of man's weakness, was in itself improper. It was a divine accommodation to our incapacity to understand God as he really is.[1] Before Philo the Septuagint[2] exhibited anti-anthropomorphic tendencies.[3] Indeed, criticisms of the anthropomorphic presentation of the Homeric gods began with Xenophones, and his influence is clearly evident in the theology of the early church. The Christian reaction against anthropomorphisms was thus inspired by a general trend in a particular cultural period, that of the late Hellenistic philosophy of religion.[4]

But there is a growing recognition that speaking of God in human ways is universal in the Bible. In earlier times attempts were made to show that this was confined to the Old Testament, and that it therefore belonged to a period in the development of the portrayal of God (or his progressive revelation) that has been superseded, and, for this reason, it does not occur in the New Testament. However, these older attempts have been abandoned because it is now recognised that the New Testament is the continuation of the Old Testament and therefore it contains no anti-anthropomorphic tendencies, as are found, for example, in the Septuagint.

So far as the Old Testament is concerned, the anthropomorphisms can be divided into three groups. First those that speak of God's form, then those that speak of his feelings, and finally those that refer to his actions.

Concerning *God's form*, we read, i.a., the following: his face (countless times); his eyes (Deut. 11:12; 1 Kgs. 8:29; Ps. 11:4 etc.); his mouth (Num. 12:8; Isa. 1:20 etc.); his ears (2 Kgs. 19:16; Isa. 59:1 etc.); his nose (Exod. 4:14; 15:8; Ps. 18:15 etc.); his lips and tongue (Isa. 30:27); his arms, hands and feet (innumerable times). Mention is also made of God's heart (Gen. 6:6; 8:21; 1 Sam. 2:35); and of his soul (Lev. 26:11, 30; Judg. 10:16).

About the *feelings* of God, we read things such as the following: he loves (Deut. 7:8; 10:15; Isa. 43:4; Hos. 11:1 etc.); he repents (Gen. 6:6, 7; Num. 23:19; 1 Sam. 15:11, 35; Jer. 4:28 etc.); he has (no) pleasure in (Isa. 1:11; 65:12 etc.); he laughs (Ps. 2:4; 37:13; 59:9 etc.); he is glad (Deut. 28:63; 30:9 etc.); he is jealous (Exod. 20:5; 34:14 etc.); he is angry (often) and hates (Amos 5:21; Lev. 26:30 etc.).

About God's *actions* we read things like these: God sees (Gen. 16:13, 14; 31:42; Exod. 3:4 etc.); he hears (Gen. 16:11; 2 Sam. 22:7; 1 Kgs. 8:30 etc.); he speaks (very often); he whistles (Isa. 5:26; 7:18); he rests and is refreshed (Gen. 2:2, 3; Exod. 31:17 etc.); he descends (Gen. 11:5, 7); he smells (Gen. 8:21 etc.); he strolls or walks (Gen. 3:8 etc.).

On the grounds of these anthropomorphisms W. Eichrodt concluded that in the Old Testament God is presented in terms of human personality, and G. von Rad asserted that Israel had indeed conceived of God in human form.[5]

The New Testament continues Old Testament usage. There are many anthropomorphisms both in quotations from the Old Testament and in independent expressions.

Concerning God's *form* we read about his eyes (Heb. 4:13; 1 Pet. 3:12); his ears (Jas. 5:4); his hand (John 10:29; Acts 4:28, 30; Rom. 10:21; Heb. 1:10; 2:7; 10:31); his face (Matt. 18:10; 1 Cor. 13:12; Heb. 9:24; Rev. 6:16); his voice (Mark 1:11; 9:7; John 12:28); his heart (Acts 13:22); his blood (Acts 20:28); his feet (Matt. 5:35).

Concerning his *feelings*: he takes pleasure, and can be pleased (Mark 1:11; Luke 2:14; Rom. 8:8; 1 Cor. 7:32; 1 Thess. 2:15); he loves (John 3:16, 35; 10:17; 14:21, 23, 31; 15:9; 16:27; 17:23–26; Rom. 8:37; 2 Cor. 9:7); he rejoices and is glad (Matt. 25:21, 23; Luke 15:7, 10, 11); he is merciful (Luke 1:72); he has inward compassion (Luke 1:78); he feels sad (Eph. 4:30); he becomes angry (Rom. 1:18; 9:22).

About God's *actions* we read things like: God sees (Matt. 6:4, 6, 18); he notices (Acts 4:29); he hears (John 11:41–42); he speaks (Mark 1:11; 9:7; John 12:28); he searches (John 4:23); he works (John 5:17); he sits on his throne (Rev. 4:2; 5:1); he is also seen by the angels (Matt. 18:10); and by the Son (John 5:19); and by the pure in heart (Matt. 5:8); and by believers (1 John 3:2); in fact, by every eye (Rev. 1:7).

There are certain minor differences here between the Old and New Testaments. Not all Old Testament anthropomorphisms occur in the New Testament, e.g. that the 'anger of the LORD was *kindled*' (Exod. 4:14; 22:24 etc.). Nevertheless the picture of 'fiery judgment' (2 Thess. 1:8), and perishing in flames is essentially comparable. On the other hand, the love of God, while being found in the Old Testament (chapter 1), reaches its peak in the New. Then too there are Paul's expressions about 'the foolishness of God' and the 'weakness of God' (1 Cor. 1:25; cf. modern translations), which are even more radical than many expressions found in the Old Testament.

So then, in spite of minor differences, the Old and New Testaments are similar in that anthropomorphic expressions about God occur throughout them, without hesitation or any impression of unnaturalness or unreality.

It is now necessary to give some consideration to the overwhelmingly negative attitude towards anthropomorphisms in the early church. Hempel has rightly said that the history of anthropomorphism in the church is a passion story.[6] Several considerations must be kept in mind in trying to understand this negative attitude.

First of all, there are the differences between the anthropomorphisms of the Bible and those of Greek mythology. The fact that the Greek philosophers took an early stand against the anthropomorphisms of the Homeric gods springs from at least two considerations. First there was the unworthy behaviour of many of these Greek gods, and, secondly, the nature of the concept of god that was developed by the philosophers.

At an early stage the Greek philosophers stressed that the gods were depicted in an entirely unworthy way in the old myths. Dishonesty, deceit, theft, violence, immorality abounded in the tales of the gods. Greek mythology was, of course, not unique in this respect. The gods of Israel's neighbours were frequently presented in immoral ways. As a result anthropomorphism acquired connotations of what was offensive, destructive of morals, and a bad example to the children.[7]

Then, secondly, there was the god-concept developed by the philosophers to counter these ideas. Brief reference has already been made to this in chapter 1. Amid all the changes taking place around them, amid all the visible things that come and go, that become and perish, they sought for firm ground, the origin, the explanation of all things. Before Plato this was sought in one way or another in some aspect of visible reality. This Plato denied, using his well-known concept of the second, ideal, real, invisible reality beyond the visible. That is the realm of true being, eternal, self-consistent, unchangeable, and therefore accessible only to human reason. This makes god into a predicative concept. Not: God is true being; but, true being is god. Something is held to be god, because it is divine, because it conforms to certain standards that have been formulated as relevant to divinity. This is in radical contrast to the biblical message, in which the true God is subject and not predicate, where the LORD is the true God and decides for himself how he is and how he shall be. In other words, the Scriptures do not first of all outline certain requirements for divinity, and then search for something (someone) to fill them. In the Scriptures the LORD and he alone, is the true God, and we discover the truth about him and his being from his revelation.

The Greek philosophers, however, did not know the LORD, and compiled a list of requirements for the 'divine'. Because he was the cause and ground of all that is, he also had to be other than it all. In contrast to the movement and change in all visible things, the divine would therefore have to be immoveable and unchangeable. Against the dependence of all visible things, the divine would have to be independent and self-sufficient. Aristotle took this idea to the limit at which no movement from god to man would be conceivable and any relationship between god and man would be excluded. God might well think, but by definition he could think only of himself. He is the unmoved mover, pure form, eternal *actus purus*, immoveable, unchangeable, self-sufficient and totally separate. Having no need of anything or anyone, he would therefore need no friend, and indeed, did not have one. All pathos, all feeling (emotion) would be precluded from this god. He knows no involvement in history, or with anything external to himself. He stands entirely apart from everything and everyone. He influences visible things only in the sense that these things have need of him, and that he has a magnetic attraction for them. But in himself he is pure thought, and thinks only of himself. Precisely because emotion (pathos) is the cause of so much instability and unhappiness among men, this god is apathetic, without feeling or involvement.[8]

As already indicated in chapter 1, some of the Apologists and fathers linked up too uncritically with this Greek philosophical god-concept. The idea that the 'divine' possessed certain necessary characteristics was gradually accepted by the early church, even though these attributes were clearly borrowed from the general philosophical trends of the times. Consequently, the anti-anthropomorphic image of God became a prominent feature of the early church's theology. Reference was frequently made to the *dignum Deo*, that which is appropriate to God. According to Kuitert, Origen summarised the *dignum Deo* in three points. First of all, it was opposed to any corporeal idea of God. It was in his view essentially unchristian to portray God as having a body. Then, in addition, the *dignum Deo* excluded any thought of emotions or excitement from God. God is apathetic, and therefore knows no emotions, and thus neither anger nor anguish. Thirdly, the *dignum Deo* would counter any suggestion of change in God, for example, the idea that God might repent. According to his concept of the being of God, God was unchangeable not only in his inward being, but also in relation to external matters. Therefore God would not move either. Since God is not to be thought of in physical terms, he could not be thought of as being in a particular place.

The incorporeal nature of God had a further consequence for Origen. It meant that God was in his essence spirit. He did not belong to the world of the material and visible creation, but to the sphere of the invisible, the spiritual. And it was just at this point that Origen was able to conceive a possible interrelatedness between God and man, for man has a spirit, an incorporeal, invisible part. Between God as spirit and the spirit of man, there is indeed a relationship. Man was, after all, made in the image of God, and Origen found this image in the human spirit.

This has an immense importance for anthropomorphism. Man as physical being cannot be compared with God, whereas man as spiritual being can. Origen therefore repudiated (or rather, reinterpreted) those anthropomorphisms that referred to man's physical being, but not those that had a bearing on man as a spiritual being.[9]

Everyone knows that Philo had a strong influence on Origen and the other Alexandrian theologians, and through them on the whole subsequent development of the doctrine of God. It is therefore necessary to look briefly at Philo's thinking on the matter.

Philo (an Alexandrian Jew, more or less contemporary with Jesus), believed that there were in the Torah (the five books ascribed to Moses) two opposing principles. The first is formulated in Numbers 23:19, and in the Septuagint it reads: 'God is not like a man'. The other principle is not formulated quite so clearly in the Old Testament but finds form

through the various anthropomorphisms used, and is expressed by Philo
in the words: God is like man. In his view the entire Word of God is
characterised by this contradiction: on the one hand, God is proclaimed
as the absolutely transcendent one, and on the other God is presented in
fully human terms. And yet Philo is never for a moment uncertain as to
which principle is correct. It is clear that God is not like a man. The other
principle is too vulnerable to misunderstanding, is inappropriate and is
therefore dangerous. No one can believe that God could repent. All the
sins of preceding generations were nothing in comparison with the sin of
those who thought that the eternally unchangeable God could change.
To Philo it was nothing less than blasphemy to understand the anthropomorphic texts in a literal way. He virtually equated with atheism any
tendency to think of God in terms of human form and human feelings.

Of course, neither Philo nor any of those following him could ignore
the anthropomorphisms. They had to give them some meaning. Philo
explained them in terms of divine accommodation. Because we would
not be able to grasp it if God were to reveal himself to us as he really is, he
revealed himself in human modes. But the spiritual person must move
beyond this phase as quickly as possible. God is, after all, not only
non-human, he is even without attributes!

All of this can be summarised in three points: First and foremost, God
is completely unchangeable. If he is to be the origin and ground of all that
exists, he must be other than it all. Against the continuously changing
order of all visible things, the invisible origin of all things must be beyond
all change. Indeed, the philosophers had already shown that in order to
be happy a person must live as equably and consistently as possible. It
should therefore be self-evident that God is absolutely equable, in which
case anything like repentance is impossible to him.

Secondly, God's unchangeableness and disengagement were pushed
so far that God was conceived to be entirely without attributes – pure
being. The highest insight attainable to man is that God *is*. To enquire
further into the being of God and his attributes merely exposes one's lack
of insight. Indeed, God has unveiled his being to no one. We actually
know very little about this, so little in fact that Philo even says that it is
not clear whether God has a bodily form or not. And for this reason we
have to speak of him in negative terms. God is inconceivable, unnameable,
invisible, indescribable, incomparable. And consequently Philo prefers
to use neutral expressions in speaking of God, such as 'cause' or 'essence'.

God is not only without attributes, but in Philo's view, he exists in no
relationships. As the one who is eternally-sufficient-in-himself he stands
in no relationship to anyone or anything. Even such a fundamental
biblical expression as 'I am the LORD *your* God', is, strictly speaking, a
misuse of language, because pure being as such is beyond all relationships.
Indeed, according to Aristotle every relationship brings a corresponding
involvement and dependence. God however cannot possibly be dependent
on created things since such a dependence would involve him in the

changeableness of the world. The absolute self-sufficiency of God there-fore demands that he stand outside of all relationships.

Before considering a few examples of Philo's exegesis of Scripture, it will be helpful to ponder for a moment his view of God. It is immediately apparent that he is totally under the influence of the concept of God current in Greek philosophy. It is also beyond doubt that his exegesis of Scripture is governed by the Greek concept of *natura Dei* or *dignum Deo*. It is disturbing to see that the Greek heritage was so dominant in him that even the most fundamental element in the biblical message, that God is the covenant God, ('I will be to you a God...'), has to be declared impossible and a misuse of language. One must be completely clear on the fact that Philo took data from outside of Scripture and gave it decisive significance in his exegesis of Scripture. What a paticular text said, Philo did not ascertain from the text but from his preconceived notion of what God was. This method of approach has exercised an almost magical influence in some circles till this very day, especially on the doctrine of God. As a result those biblical texts which speak of God in anthropomor-phic terms have to this day not been able to say what they want to say. Almost without exception they are interpreted by means of information gathered from sources external to them, and the obvious meaning of the text is regarded as an unreal meaning.

As an example we might look at Philo's exegesis of Genesis 6:5–7. Philo follows the Septuagint, which had consciously tried to eliminate all anthropomorphisms. Verse 6, according to the Hebrew, means: 'The LORD *was sorry* that he had made man on earth, and it *grieved* him to his heart'. In the Septuagint it is translated: 'And the LORD *took to heart* the fact that he had made man on earth and he *reflected* on this.' Philo accepted this translation as correct because God could not feel sorry, or repent (a conviction which he acquired from *outside* the text and imported into the text, thus preventing the text from saying what it clearly intended). This would indeed mean that God had changed, and what greater godlessness could there be than to suggest such a thing? To justify his interpretation Philo argued in the same way that Origen did later on in the same connection – even the philosopher must elevate himself above all the changeableness of his moods. How much more will God be above such things? Furthermore, God's knowledge is complete, as distinct from man's. It includes foreknowledge so that from all eternity he would know everything. He lives in an eternal present without a future or a past, and therefore never needs to review a decision. All this he says in connection with the words: 'The Lord was sorry'; grief is dismissed in the same way. Grief is as impossible to him as anger. It suggests movement of heart and even anguish. And one surely cannot suggest these things of God. As little as one can say that God has limbs can it be said that God has irrational waves of emotion.

Genesis 11:5 yields a similar approach. Here we read that God came down to see the city and the tower. But it is impossible for God to move;

this would be contradictory to the most elementary knowledge of the being of God. The text must therefore not be taken literally, but figuratively. God can know no change of place (movement) because by his very nature he already fills everything and is present everywhere. One can say with equal accuracy that God is everywhere and nowhere![10]

Philo's concept of God and his method of argument will not be altogether strange to most of us. A fair amount of it is often unconsciously part of the church's way of thinking about God (including the Reformed tradition). We too do not allow the anthropomorphistic texts to say what they mean, but interpret them from other convictions. Because some of these convictions do lay claim to be biblical, we will first of all have to test this appeal to Scripture and afterwards ask what these anthropomorphic expressions of God are actually trying to say about him.[11]

The most important texts that are quoted when it is argued that God is unchangeable and therefore cannot repent are: (in the order in which they will be discussed) Numbers 23:19; 1 Samuel 15:29; Exodus 3:14; Psalm 102:25-28; (Heb. 1:11, 12); Psalm 77:11; Malachi 3:6; James 1:17; Hebrews 13:8.

Numbers 23:19 and *1 Samuel 15:29*.[12] It is strange that the many texts which indicate quite clearly that God does repent (and there are about forty)[13] should be robbed of their meaning by just two utterances that point to the contrary. It is even more strange when it is realised that these two texts have a very restricted meaning. In Numbers 23:19 'repent' is used synonymously with 'lie'. In *this* sense God cannot repent; i.e. he does not arbitrarily and in an indeterminate way change his decisions. Where reference is made to his repenting it is never in the sense of lying or arbitrary action, and therefore it has a different meaning. In 1 Samuel 15:29 the situation is the same. Repentance and lying are explicitly used together synonymously ('Also the Glory of Israel will not lie or repent'). What is even more striking is that twice in the same chapter it is in fact stated that God repented (v. 11 and 35). This writer surely did not contradict himself twice in the same chapter! When he spoke of God's repentance he meant something other than the kind of repentance equated with lying, which is certainly foreign to God. It is clear that one cannot use Numbers 23:19 and 1 Samuel 15:29 to give the texts that do refer to God's repentance a meaning other than the obvious one that they do have. Two different matters are at stake.

The other texts which are used to deny that God repents (i.a. Ps. 110:4; Jer. 4:28; Ezek. 24:14; Zech. 8:14), actually presuppose that the LORD can repent, and therefore emphasise that under certain circumstances he will not repent. Jeremiah 4:28 stresses that the LORD has taken a decision which he will not go back on, and about which he will not repent. But, apart from the fact that this occurs in Jeremiah where there are repeated references to the LORD's repentance, this assurance presupposes that there may well be decisions which he can go back on and over which he might repent. Thus, Zechariah 8:14-15 declares on the one hand that God had once taken a decision involving evil against the fathers and did not repent of it, but that on the other hand he now was deciding differently, and would show favour to Jerusalem. The question concerning the meaning of the repentance of God will be discussed again later under his unchangeableness.

Exodus 3:14.[14] When Moses asks the Name of God, the answer he receives is: 'I am who I am'. The fact that the word 'am' is a verb in the Hebrew, and was rendered in the Septuagint with a participle with the function of a noun, is of tremendous historical significance. Via the Septuagint this text found its way into history, and provided the basis for Philo, Origen and their countless followers to link up with Greek thought and to speak of God as the eternal, unchangeable, and self-sufficient being. Indeed, the Septuagint translation (*ho ōn*) was a well-known term for God in Greek philosophy – meaning 'Being'. The church fathers were so unaware of the Greek god-concept which had coloured all their thinking about anthropomorphisms, that many of them were even convinced that Plato must have known the Old Testament (especially Exod. 3:14), or he would not have been able to write so 'biblically' about God![15] Today we know that the Hebrew 'I am what I am' means something very different from the Greek-inspired translation of the Septuagint – 'Being'. Boman has reminded us that the little word 'is' is not used in Hebrew sentences such as 'The Lord our God (is) one Lord'. Where the word 'is' (or 'am') is used in Hebrew its verbal significance is stressed. With reference to the Lord the verb is used when he does something, when he acts. It is striking that when the Lord addresses a message to a person it is introduced with this word 'is' in Hebrew, and is translated into English with 'came to'. 'The word of the Lord *came to...*' (Gen. 15:1; 1 Sam. 15:10; 2 Sam. 7:4; 1 Kgs. 18:1, 31; 2 Kgs. 20:4; Isa. 38:4; Jer. 36:1; 37:6, to mention only a few random examples). So when 'is' is used, something *happens*. This verbal character of the verb 'to be' is underlined further in Isaiah 55:11. When God says 'so shall my word *be*' he goes on to state what it will *do*. Similarly the 'hand of the Lord' is frequently spoken of in terms of 'being' on, or against, someone (1 Sam. 5:9; 7:13). But this is always followed by a statement of the Lord's *action in intervening* in a situation. Boman has shown that this meaning of the verb 'to be' is not in conflict with *being*, but that being and becoming are included within working, doing, acting. So it is not correct to say that the Old Testament does *not* teach the being of God, but only that he happens (H. Braun). Just because 'I am' means: I do things, I am the acting God, it implies and presupposes the being of God – but that must be understood as an active and acting being, involved in history. This is radically opposed to the static, withdrawn, sufficient-unto-himself being of Greek philosophy.[16]

The context of Exodus 3:14 leads one to the same conclusion. Indeed, it has been rightly observed that the traditional exegesis of this verse has not done justice to the context in which it stands. What meaning could the eternal, unchangeable, sufficient-unto-himself being have for the people of Israel who were in such distress under the vicious treatment of the Egyptians? Taken in its context the meaning is completely different. In verse 12 the LORD promises Moses, 'I will be with you'. In verses 6, 15 and 16 it is emphatically declared that the God speaking to Moses is the God of the past, the God of Abraham, of Isaac and of Jacob. And for them he did something! The people are therefore to think of him in terms of this covenant meaning. The LORD stresses this in verse 15: 'This (i.e. the God of Abraham, the God of Isaac, the God of Jacob) is my name forever, and thus I am to be remembered throughout all generations.' In the immediate context of the declaration of his name as the 'I am', he explains it in terms of its historical links with, and his care for the patriarchs. The matter is emphasised again in verse 16: 'The LORD, the God of your fathers, the God of Abraham, of Isaac and of Jacob, has appeared to me, saying "I have observed you and what has been done to you in Egypt".' The God therefore who was involved with Abraham and his descendants, the God who had chosen them and cared for them, knew of their need. If in this context he gives his name in the form of a verb which implies 'happening', then the meaning of 'I am that I am' must be somewhat as follows: 'I shall be (do), what I was (did)'. Or, more briefly, 'I am faithful'; that is, 'as your fathers came to know me, so you too shall learn to know me'. I am in full accord with the paraphrase by Maas: 'I am the God who remains constantly faithful'.[17] It is the word 'faithful' that provides the key to unlock the biblical meaning of the unchangeableness of God. We shall return to this later. For the present it is clear that Exodus 3:14 provides no link with the god-concept of Greek philosophy, and in fact teaches the opposite. God is described by means of a verb, and a verb that is particularly used in the Old Testament to point to something happening. By means of telling them his name, God seems to say to his oppressed people: 'You may depend on me; I will intervene in your history; I am the same still as the One who intervened in your history; I am the same still as the One who intervened for Abraham; Isaac and Jacob.' In this sense God is unchangeable – unchangeably faithful.

Psalm 102:25–28. These verses present a contrast between the heavens and the earth on the one hand and the LORD on the other. 'They will perish but thou dost endure' (v. 26). Here that which is perishable is set over against the eternal. It is strange that this text should have played a role in the debate on the unchangeableness of God, whereas it is clearly concerned with his incorruptibility and eternity – not only in verse 26, but in 27 as well: 'Thou art the same and thy years have no end', in contrast to the heavens and earth which do end ('pass away' v. 26). The translation of verse 27a ('Thou art the same') might have led to this misuse of the text. But there are only two words in the Hebrew: 'Thou (art) he'. This the well-known identification formula of Deutero-Isaiah (41:4; 43:10, 13; 46:4; 48:12) and twice it is translated there with the words: '... I am the same' (41:4; 46:4), although what is meant is merely that the speaker ('I') or the one addressed ('Thou') is the LORD,[18] and at the most indicates the uniqueness and incomparability of the LORD.[19] But this verse has nothing at all in common with the Greek philosophical idea of unchangeability – as is clear also from verse 17, where it is said that the LORD would 'regard (turn himself to) the prayer of the destitute...'. This is a strong word which unquestionably implies a turning, a movement or change on the part of the LORD. Hebrews 1:11–12 applies Psalm 102:25–27 to Jesus Christ, but there too it is related to his eternity, and not to a rigid unchangeability.

Psalm 77:10. Reference must be made to this verse, not only because it is often quoted in this connection, but because it might create the impression that change is impossible to God. 'And I say, "It is my grief that the right hand of the Most High has changed."' There are many questions concerning what was written in the original text, and many different readings have been proposed to try to clarify its meaning. Kraus has shown that the meaning proposed for the text depends very much on whether it is taken together with the preceding verses or those that follow. The fact is however that the psalmist is not concerned with a metaphysical unchangeability in God, but is struggling with the question: 'Will the Lord spurn for ever...?' (v. 7). 'Has God forgotten to be gracious?' (v. 9). 'Has his steadfast love for ever ceased?' (v. 8). These questions can only make sense if there is indeed the possibility that God might spurn forever and allow his mercy to cease. Accordingly, some translations put verse 10 into the past tense. (See above: instead of 'that the right hand of the LORD changes'.) This translation views verse 10 as the conclusion to the preceding tribulations that had given rise to the questions asked. But anyone struggling in this kind of turmoil knows nothing of a doctrine of unchangeability, as this had developed in Greek philosophy. He takes account of the possibility that the LORD can react to the behaviour of his people, and can reject them – as did happen later.

Malachi 3:6, 'For I the LORD do not change; therefore you, O sons of Jacob, are not consumed.' Here the issue really is God's unchangeability, although when the real meaning of the text in its context is explored, the radical difference between the biblical message about God's unchangeability and that of Greek philosophy becomes very clear.

There are many difficulties attending the exegesis of this text. Verhoef has made an extensive study of possible translations.[20] There are many problems relating to the word translated 'consumed', a word which has something to do with 'cease'. It could mean that Israel has not ceased sinning (v. 7), and because the LORD had not changed (v. 6a), he remained the judge who would exercise judgment on their sins (v. 5). Or it could mean that Israel had not ceased to exist, because the LORD (in spite of their sins) had remained their compassionate covenant God, and in this sense, did not change (v. 6a).

Whichever of these meanings is chosen, verse 7 remains a complaint and a call accompanied by a promise; '...and I will return to you, says the LORD'. This promise, that recurs countless times in the Old Testament, is characteristic of the fact that the LORD reacts to the sins, or repentance of his people. The promise assumes that at the present time the LORD has turned away from his people (or, put differently, has turned towards them in anger on account of their sins), and that he will remain in this attitude if they persist in their sins and do not repent. But against this, the promise also assumes that he will return to them in love if they repent. It is in this context that we hear of his unchangeableness, and, as we have already indicated, he remains unchangeable either in the sense that in spite of their sins he continues to be their faithful covenant God (thus continuing in a positive relationship with them), or that he will continue to punish wrong and because they had not given up their sin he will enter into judgment with them. In either case he is not a one-sided, self-sufficient God, who knows no relationships, but is the living God, who reacts to the life of his people. Naturally, he reacts in accordance with what he has promised; that is, he is faithful. This does not imply remoteness or detachment, but rather the most radical involvement in history.

James 1:17. 'Every good endowment and every perfect gift is from above, coming down from the Father of lights with whom there is no variation or shadow due to change.' The original expression for 'shadow due to change' promises interesting possibilities in the interpretation of this text.[21] It is thought that the reference may be to the daily interchange of day and night, in the sense that the sun changes by its movement and so gives light by day but darkness by night. God is not like this. In fact, the immediate context points to this conclusion as well. There it is stated that God sends neither evil nor temptation. The positive aspect is given in verse 17: God gives only the good. That is, he is not like the lights (the sun and the moon) which are constantly changing, bringing now light, and now darkness. From him come only good gifts.

This unchangeability of God has been touched on in chapter 1 in other terms: his being as love. If he is angry, and condemns, it is his reaction to mankind's stubborn persistence in sin. God gives only love spontaneously. He will never condemn and reject without it being deserved over and over again. But again there can be no question here of the unchangeable God of Greek philosophy, who cannot react, is not involved with his creation, knows no repentance and cannot change his intentions.

We have now considered all the references which are traditionally used to defend the (Greek) unchangeability of God. It has become evident in each case that the concern is with the living, acting, reacting, involved God. It is also clear that the objections to understanding the 'repent' verses (and other anthropomorphic expressions) in their obvious meaning, are not based on Scripture but on a long ecclesiastical tradition that was inspired by Greek philosophy. We can therefore proceed now to a discussion of the meaning of biblical anthropomorphism.

The first question to arise concerns what anthropomorphism is. Or, which texts contain anthropomorphic expressions about God, and which do not? Traditionally regarded as anthropomorphic expressions are those which refer to God's form (limbs etc.), to certain acts of God (that he hears, sees, speaks, whistles etc.), and to certain feeling-experiences (God's repentance, his perplexity, his pain, a change or turn on God's part, and sometimes even to his happiness and joy).

In contrast to these there are two other categories of statements about God which were regarded as non-anthropomorphic, and therefore as exact and literal statements about God.

The first of these two types of utterance were those that were compatible with the god-concept of Greek philosophy: his unchangeableness, his remoteness and detachment; his self-sufficiency and independence (expressions which, as has already been shown, were usually wrongly interpreted). Secondly there were the many statements dealing with God's love, his compassion, his grace, his faithfulness. It must be conceded to the Apologists and later theologians that they applied these quite literally to God and in this respect deviated from the Greek philosophical model which they otherwise followed so loyally. Although expressions such as 'God is love' were seldom if ever used to describe the *being* of God (the Greek influence was too strong for this and the self-sufficiency of God dominated),[22] they nevertheless had a place among the *attributes* of God. Occasionally a theologian would become conscious of the inner tension between these biblical attributes ascribed to God and the Greek philosophical definition of the being of God. However, this tension never resulted in a radical questioning of the validity of the Greek philosophical approach, since it was simply accepted that God, in any case, was exalted above all human understanding.

At the same time, it is strange that an attribute such as love was not classified as an anthropomorphism, while expressions describing joy and happiness were. This is even more curious when one remembers how many of the expressions suggesting God's changeability and repentance are clearly motivated by his love. Think for example of his decision to spare Nineveh. According to Jonah 4:10–11 this sprang from his love for creatures that he had made, and on which he had bestowed great care.

As a result Bavinck was one of the first to see how invalid is the distinction between anthropomorphic expressions (which must be interpreted in a way different from their obvious meaning) and actual or direct utterances (e.g. about the compassion or love of God). Because the revelation of God was directed to people, and therefore had to be understood by them, Bavinck concluded that we do not merely encounter anthropomorphisms here and there in the Bible but that the whole of Scripture is anthropomorphic, because all of revelation is concentrated on the Word (Jesus Christ), and is as it were a single process of incarnation, of God becoming human.[23] Unfortunately Bavinck did not carry this conviction through to its necessary conclusion. When, for example, he deals with the unchangeableness of God, and cites the many texts which speak so clearly of God's involvement in history, the Greek philosophical background wins again and he goes no further than to say that God is, 'as it were' involved in the life of his creatures and especially of his people.[24] This means that even for Bavinck certain anthropomorphic expressions are not allowed to convey their true meaning but acquire an unreal significance.

ANTHROPOMORPHISMS IN THE BIBLE

Rather than attempt to treat a number of isolated anthropomorphisms, we will reflect on the preaching of two prophets (Hosea and Jeremiah). They are classic representatives of a trend which is present throughout the Bible.

Hosea

First of all, some thoughts on the preaching of Hosea.[25] One of the most striking characteristics of the book Hosea is that the LORD speaks continuously in direct speech, without the customary 'Thus saith the LORD'. The reader is confronted without interruption by God as subject – by God himself.

In Hosea 9–14 we have the familiar five reviews given by the LORD of Israel's earlier history – of Israel's origins. (9:10; 9:13; 10:11–13; 11:1–3; 13:4–6.) These reviews all have the same structure: God's joy over their original love; God's care of them at that time; their present apostasy; and finally, the LORD's judgment on the people.

The joy that the original relationship between God and Israel brought to the LORD is presented in the most arresting images. In Hosea 9:10 we read: 'Like grapes in the wilderness I found Israel. Like the first fruit on the fig tree in its first season.' On the basis of C. van Gelderen's exegesis, the verse might be paraphrased as follows: 'Israel was as tasty to me as grapes in the wilderness; indeed, as pleasant a surprise as early figs on a fig-tree in its first season'. Grapes in the wilderness are a rare treat. Anyone thirsty and tired encountering grapes there would be in ecstasy. And ordinary early figs would be a luxury in Palestine, on account of their exceptional juiciness. But the early figs of the first season would not even reach the market to be sold. Anyone finding such a fig would eat it immediately.[26] The LORD uses such images to express the joy and pleasure that Israel's early love meant to him (at the exodus, the wilderness journey, and the entry into Canaan). Hosea 9:13 confirms this joy. The first part of the text can best be translated (with the fewest emendations to the text): 'Ephraim, as I have seen, was like a young palm tree planted in a pleasant environment.' In 10:11 we read that Israel (Ephraim) was in the beginning like a willing young heifer that loved to thresh the corn. It was customary not to place such a heifer under a yoke, but to allow her free run of the threshing floor (which was in itself light and pleasant work) which gave her the freedom to eat the corn as well! But, against this, in the second part of the verse, it is said that now the LORD 'will put

Ephraim to yoke' – even on 'her fair neck' – and she will have to work hard (the exile!). What interests us now is the earlier joy which Israel had in the service of the LORD, and the joy that the LORD had (as the owner) in admiring his young heifer. This joy on the LORD's part is even more strongly expressed in 11:4, where the LORD speaks of himself as an owner who did not chase his beasts about, but led them with a cord, and, what is more, a soft cord, 'cords of compassion'. Moreover, he made it easier for them to eat by removing the yoke (enabling them to bend lower), and further still, he bent down to feed them with fodder. Besides the joy of the owner (the LORD), this text speaks of a second element: his care for his people.

The most powerful expression of God's love, and therefore of his joy too, is found in 11:1–3 where the image of a father is used, as he loves and calls for his son (as the LORD called Israel out of Egypt), and bears him about in his arms. This picture is eloquent with the joy of family love, joy in which the LORD shares, for the concern here is with him. Mauser is right when he says that one thing is clearly apparent from these images: God's delight, his joy, his happiness over the early relationship, when Israel's heart was the LORD's, when the young bride accompanied her husband, in fact followed him (Jer. 2:2). God uses these expressions with the intention of revealing himself to us as he *really* is.

Anyone who speaks in terms of 'but only', or of 'human presentations', expounds the texts by means of criteria drawn from elsewhere.

But it is God's care as well as his joy that is revealed in these moments of recollection. As has just been mentioned, this care is expressed particularly in 11:1–4, but the LORD's words in 13:4–6 speak of it as well. That the LORD was Israel's God 'from the land of Egypt' (v. 4) reminds them forcibly of the misery and oppression from which the LORD had liberated them. That he had 'known' them in the desert (v. 5) means that he had loved them and had therefore cared for them. The reference to 'the land of drought' only magnifies the miracle of his care – think only of the water from the rock, manna, quails. The NEB links 5b with 6a and reads: 'I cared for you in the wilderness, in a land of burning heat, as if you were in pasture.' The LORD cared for them in such a way that they had enough. He was concerned about them. There was no lack in his caring. If they now have turned their back on him to follow other gods, the cause of their action could not be found in his want of love, or in his failure to be involved in their experiences of life.

For this reason, their apostasy to heathen fertility cults was all the more terrible. Various verses mention the beginning of their apostasy (6:7; 9:9, 10; 10:9). That the LORD then speaks of his judgment on the people is not surprising – it is to be expected. Each of the glances back into the past concludes with such a proclamation of judgment (9:11; 9:13; 10:14; 11:5; 13:7). Because the LORD loved them so dearly and cared for them so assiduously, his judgment is correspondingly radical. Instead of the joy of grapes in the wilderness, there is a barren people

(9:11). Instead of a beautiful palm, murdered sons (9:13). Instead of a young heifer enjoying the lightest of work, captivity and the destruction of mothers and children (10:14). And instead of the liberation from Egypt, comes the opposite: a new captivity, and oppression under two enemies, Egypt and Assyria (11:5).

This is all very gripping, but is still not the actual issue at stake in Hosea. In the midst of these pronouncements of destruction there recurs another theme in Hosea: that of the LORD struggling with himself about whether he will execute judgment (which the people have deserved a thousand times over). Side by side with radical announcements of judgment (4:6; 5:10; 9:15 – as well as those to which reference has already been made), there are astonishing promises of salvation (e.g. 11:9; 14:6 f; etc.). And then in between come the LORD's searching questions, addressed sometimes to Israel, but more profoundly, to himself. 'What shall I do with you O Ephraim? What shall I do with you O Judah?' (6:4). 'How can I give you up, O Ephraim! How can I hand you over, O Israel! How can I make you like Admah! How can I treat you like Zebolim! My heart recoils within me, my compassion grows warm and tender' (11:8). Read especially 2:13–22.

Attempts to divide these threats, this inward strife, and these promises into different periods or phrases have always failed, precisely because Hosea is concerned with the actual involvement on God's part in the history of his people – with exactly the opposite of the god-concept of Greek philosophy. What we learn from Hosea is that the LORD's legitimate anger is awakened, and the people deserve his judgment, but that the LORD cannot bring himself to execute that judgment – because of his love. And, in Hosea, this love is a frustrated love, not as though man were now stronger than God, and God had become powerless before all-powerful man, but because of the nature of the covenant relationship instituted by God, and in which he gave to man a specific freedom and responsibility. To this we will return later in the chapter. It is quite certain that the people misused their responsibility in the covenant in a sinful and therefore culpable way. The result was that the LORD was unable to show them the love that he so eagerly wished to show them. In this sense, the Living Bible is justified in its three paraphrases of Hosea's message that God *wished* to save or forgive, but... (6:11; 7:1, 13).[27] God wished to deliver them but 'could not' on account of their faithlessness (Mark 6:5) and yet he nevertheless hesitated to execute his judgment, because of his love. The most graphic description of this is in 11:9.

To appreciate this verse it must be borne in mind that in the book of Hosea we learn to know God as the God who finds joy in the love of his people; who delights in them, as grapes in the wilderness; who is pained by their faithlessness; who decides to destroy them, but is plunged into inward conflict about the decision. (NB: This conflict arises out of his *love*! – because he does not *want* to give free rein to his legitimate and deserved wrath.) In short, we learn to know God as One who changes in his inward attitude. ('My heart recoils within me' means 'my heart is changed within me' NEB.) It is therefore very significant that in this book we hear it said: For I am God and *not man*' (11:9).

Anyone who uses this expression to declare that everything else that has been heard up to this moment from Hosea about God was 'just' a human way of speaking about God, and that behind this wrestling God of love here is the real God, unchangeable, sufficient-unto-himself who is simply pretending to be so disturbed about the sins of his people, is really speaking blasphemously. These words in 11:9 mean something very different. They give the reason why there is such tension in God, and why he cannot bring himself to execute his judgment on Israel. A man would have executed judgment in such a situation, for Israel deserved it. *But God is not a man*. He is the God of love. He hesitates; he wishes to give further opportunity for repentance; he wants to deliver and preserve. A man would in such a situation have pushed through with his decision and executed his judgment (Jonah!), but God is not a man. He changes!

One of the most important conclusions to be drawn from this is that the anthropomorphisms of the Bible teach that *God differs from man*! In his treatment of the pathos of God, A. J. Heschel writes: 'The idea of the divine pathos combining absolute selflessness with supreme concern for the poor and the exploited can hardly be regarded as the attribution of human characteristics. Where is the man who is endowed with such characteristics? Nowhere in the Bible is man characterized as merciful, gracious, slow to anger, abundant in love and truth, keeping love to the thousandth generation.... Absolute selflessness and mysteriously undeserved love are more akin to the divine than to the human. And if these are characteristics of human nature, then man is endowed with attributes of the divine.... The language the prophets employed to describe that supreme concern was an anthropomorphism to end all anthropomorphisms.'[28] Heschel writes this about God's care for the oppressed, but it must be applied to the whole range of the so-called anthropomorphisms. It is not 'human' to be involved in history, to care about people in need, to be deeply disturbed over Israel's faithlessness. We would have rejected Israel as a contemptible and contentious nation and chosen another, better nation. We can live on restfully and uninvolved in our luxury while other people, even fellow church members, do not have enough food to eat and are often not even treated as human beings in our society. Anthropomorphisms of this kind were indeed applied to the Homeric gods (and more besides: lying, stealing, immorality), and the Greek philosophers rightly repudiated them as being unworthy of the gods. But the biblical anthropomorphisms do not reflect a 'human' way of speaking about God. In specific aspects the biblical anthropomorphisms *distinguish* God from man. We will return to this after we have considered the preaching of Jeremiah.

Jeremiah

It will be useful to consider briefly the anthropomorphism in Jeremiah alongside that in Hosea because at least one new and important facet comes to the fore regarding the changeability of God. But we must look first at the points of agreement between them.

Jeremiah also portrays something of God's inward conflict and distress, particularly as this relates to Judah's apostasy. Some have even spoken of the Lamentations of God in Jeremiah 2–6, in parallel to the Lamentations of Jeremiah. The pathos of God may also be spoken of in this context if we understand by that the LORD's disappointed love, astonishment, distress, and in this sense, his involvement in the history of Israel. Mauser has brought out the striking fact that the apostasy of Judah is not described in prose, but in a lament on the LORD's part. In this way the prophet would seem to suggest that Israel's apostasy from the LORD touches him most deeply. As so often in Hosea, these laments begin with a reminder of the past. The LORD sings of the joy of Israel at the time of the exodus, using the analogy of a bride (2:2). How close they were to his heart is apparent from his care for them (2:3). The meaning of this verse becomes clearer if it is read in the past tense, and if by those who 'devoured' her (i.e. Israel) are understood to be the enemies during the exodus. As in Hosea, here too the LORD charges Israel that they have no single reason for falling away from him (v. 4 f). He cared for them *well*, and gave them success in a *good* land (v. 7).

The distress of verses 10–13 must be understood against this background. Combined with the joy which the LORD himself derived from those happy beginnings, was the care that he exercised over them, which quite legitimately gave him the right to expect a positive reaction from them. In Isaiah 5 the image of a vineyard is used: Israel was a choice vine, which the LORD planted on a very fertile hill which he tended with every possible care, '. . . and he looked for it to yield grapes, but it yielded wild grapes' (v. 2). There too the distressed question from the LORD follows: 'What more was there to do for my vineyard, that I have not done in it?' (v. 4). The remainder of the verse is better translated: 'How is it possible that when I looked for my choice grapes, it yielded wild grapes?' To understand the LORD's distress it should be remembered that wild grapes are bitter, unhealthy and inedible. In Isaiah 5 the LORD makes no secret of his bitter disappointment.

In Jeremiah 2 there is, however, more surprise and astonishment. This is occasioned by the unheard of thing that Israel had done. From the west (Cyprus) to the east (Kedar) the heathen world could be explored and not a single nation would be found that had changed its gods – and their gods are not even gods! (While the heathen frequently adopt new gods, this did not mean the rejection of the old gods – the new ones were simply added.) But Israel, the people with the only true God, the God who bestowed so much loving care on them, 'had changed their glory for that which does not profit'. This means that they had exchanged their glorious God for a worthless one. What an appalling deed! And it is God who expresses this dismay. In verse 12 he calls on the heavens to be appalled – for their hair to stand on end with horror! In the Hebrew there is here a series of sibilants that heightens the impression of dismay and revulsion.[29] What Israel had done was as inexplicable (even to God) as someone exchanging a perennial fountain for a broken tank dependent on Palestine's uncertain rains (v. 13). Or a bride forgetting to put on her wedding dress and jewels (v. 32)! For this reason there is something of the unexpected in all this for the LORD. This is powerfully expressed in 3:19: '*I thought* how I would set you among my sons, and give you a pleasant land, a heritage most beauteous of all nations. And *I thought* you would call me My Father, and would not turn from following me.' (The Living Bible gives an essentially correct paraphrase: 'And I *thought* how wonderful it would be for you to be here among my children. *I planned* to give you part of this beautiful land, the finest in the world. *I looked forward* to your calling me "Father", and *thought* that you would never turn away from me again.' This agrees with the words 'I wanted to' that the Living Bible uses in Hosea 6:11; 7:1, 13 to which reference has already been made.) Israel's reaction has really reached the LORD's heart, and he is deeply touched by it. Just as every sin is essentially irrational, incomprehensible and inexplicable, so even God does not understand Israel's reaction to his love and care.[30] In fact, he had planned things differently from the way in which they were now turning out.

All of this hurt the LORD so deeply because Judah was his beloved (11:5), the beloved of his soul (12:7 – a strong emotional expression). As in Hosea, his dismay flows from his *being* (his love) – and is very far indeed from being a 'merely human way' of talking about him.

Here again we see something of the LORD's inward conflict. It was perfectly clear that Judah was guilty, and no excuse could be advanced which could ward off the LORD's punishment. 'How can I pardon you? Your children have forsaken me, and have sworn by those who are no gods. When I fed them to the full they committed adultery and trooped to the houses of the harlots' (5:7). 'Shall I not punish them for these things?' (5:9, 29). Judah must be punished. They deserve it. But, in the words of Hosea 11:9, God is not a man! He withholds his punishment long after we would have let it fall. In fact, in the form of the utterances cited above (the questions of 5:7, 9, 29) we detect the hesitation. In 31:20 the reason for this hesitation comes out clearly: 'Is Ephraim my dear son? Is he my darling child? For as often as I speak against him, I do remember him still. Therefore my heart yearns for him; I will surely have mercy on him.' (NEB: 'As often as I turn my back on him, I still remember him.') One hears here the words of a deep-rooted, undying fatherly love – cf. 31:3. The Lord's love and faithfulness are once more seen as the reason for his pathos.

Thus far there is agreement between the preaching of Hosea and

Jeremiah. On the other hand, however, it becomes progressively clearer
that the conflict between love and judgment will turn out differently at
least for the generation to whom Jeremiah was preaching. In spite of the
inner conflict it cost the LORD, judgment was not finally passed (e.g.
4:5–6:30; 14:1–15:9). the striking fact is that this change in the attitude
of God towards his people astounded the false prophets and the people
(and perhaps Jeremiah himself.) When the LORD announced his final
judgment (4:5–8), the leaders were in confusion and accused the LORD of
deceit: 'Ah, LORD God, surely thou hast utterly deceived this people and
Jerusalem, saying, "It shall be well with you", whereas the sword has
reached their very life' (4:10).[31] The reason for this misunderstanding
lies in their mistaken view of the LORD and his relationship to the people.
If the LORD had once proclaimed 'peace' to the people, and had promised
it, they regarded it as an eternal truth that could be endlessly repeated. If
the LORD had once said that he would not again wreck his people because
he is God and not man (Hos. 11:9), the false prophets assumed that the
people were not permanently safe, and that they needed only to keep on
repeating this promise of salvation to the people.[32] This is what the false
prophets did, according to Jeremiah 23:17 (cf. Amos 9:10), but the LORD
reacted strongly against them (v. 21). This does not mean that the LORD
had never promised peace to his people, but that it was not *then* the time
to proclaim it, for the situation was different. Verses 18 and 22 indicate
clearly that the LORD's decrees are not fixed and unchanging so that the
prophet may simply proclaim them unaltered throughout history. On
the contrary, the prophet must be continually in the LORD's council to
know what the LORD's word is to his people *now*. Had the false prophets
realised this they would have known that the LORD had now turned
against his people and that it was a time for preaching judgment and
repentance, not 'peace, peace' (v. 22). See also 14:13–16 for the preaching
of the false prophets, and 14:19–15:1 for the way in which the people
were laying claim to old promises of God (v. 19a, 21) without realising
that the situation had changed and God's attitude towards them was
therefore different (15:1).

This change on the LORD's part, this time-relatedness of preaching is
of the greatest importance. It makes us realise again that God is involved
in the history of his people, and that things do not run on according to a
predetermined, unalterable plan. New unexpected situations develop in
which the people cannot simply fall back on promises given in the past,
but must hear a *new* message from God. In such circumstances, anyone
who appeals to God's unchangeability reveals himself as a false prophet.
The idea that the LORD always wills and does exactly the same thing,
independently of the historical situation, was to Jeremiah the sign that
the LORD's word had not been heard (v. 21).[33] We leave the preaching of
Jeremiah at this point.

It was necessary to look a little more fully into two of the books in the
Bible in which anthropomorphisms occupy an important place,

particularly because theological literature often adopts very generalised positions against anthropomorphism. Direct contact with the way in which anthropomorphisms function in prophetic preaching has been necessary to enable us to make a responsible judgment. It is now possible to proceed to a more systematic consideration of the meaning of anthropomorphism.

THE MEANING OF ANTHROPOMORPHISM

First it must be called to mind that the reaction against anthropomorphisms, or their spiritualisation, was not inherent in the early Christian tradition, but was introduced into it from its environment. Just how general this attitude was in the Greek-speaking world is evident, for example, from the clear tendency in the Septuagint to change anthropomorphisms.[34] This bare fact should caution one against negative judgment on them or a spiritualisation of them.

To this must be added the fact that the motive underlying the Greek philosophical reaction against anthropomorphisms is not relevant to the God of Israel. The Greeks were concerned with another god and they worked from a different view of man. Their philosophical god-concept ruled out, by definition, any involvement, movement, or love. Their view of man meant that the mythical gods were endowed with the attributes of *sinful* man, including lying, stealing, immorality, quarrelling and fighting. Both of these aspects have already been touched on. But it must be emphasised again, that the Bible does not apply to God the characteristics of *fallen* man. Repeatedly it is explicitly denied that God is like such a man. 'God is *not man*, that he should *lie*' (Num. 23:29; 'for he is *not a man* that he should repent' (1 Sam. 15:29); 'I will not again destroy Ephraim for I am God and *not man*' (Hos. 11:9).

In the Bible therefore it is emphatically denied that God is like man, when sinful man is taken as the point of comparison. But when the same writers, even in the same chapter (1 Sam. 15:11, 29, 35), proceed to speak over and over in anthropomorphic terms about God, it is obvious that it is in another sense that they refer to God as being like man. Here it is intended that the comparison is between God and man *as the image of God*, and not between God and man as sinner. Heschel has rightly asked (and we have already referred to this): Where is the man that exhibits the human characteristics which are ascribed to God e.g. that he is loving, gracious, prepared to change and forgive (in contrast to Jonah, who was angry about this),[35] one who cannot find it in his heart to destroy the people even when they richly deserve it? In answer to Heschel I would point to *the* man, Jesus Christ. *The anthropomorphisms in the Bible represent the proclamation about God in terms of the person and work of Jesus Christ. This is the most profound reason why they must be judged differently from the anthropomorphisms current in Israel's environment.* Miskotte has rightly observed: 'We miss the mystery altogether if in our explanation of this anthropomorphic language we speak in terms of the inadequacy of human speech, the limitations of human thought, the unavoidability of metaphorical language, the relativity of theophanies.'[36]

In the light of the preceding denial *and* affirmation that God is like man, the attempt to explain that man can only speak about God in anthropomorphic terms because he is man, falls away. This explanation proceeds from the false assumption that there is necessarily an unbridgeable gulf between God and man, that at the deepest level God and man do not belong together (not only because of sin, but because man is created), and that God's revelation is in tension with his being so that he actually cannot reveal himself as he really is but is obliged by man's humanity and creaturehood to reveal himself in an unreal way. This also coheres with the peculiar idea that God is essentially *in*visible and *un*knowable.[37]

In the same way that the Christian reaction against anthropomorphism originated in Greek philosophy, so too did the contrast they made between visible reality and the invisible god, with the result that God was thought of as essentially invisible and unknowable. They did posit a link between the mind (or spirit) of man and God, even as later on in church history the spiritual anthropomorphisms (e.g. the love and grace of God) were more readily accepted than the physical likenesses (hands, eyes, ears etc.).

The real danger here was that the spirituality of God would be influenced by the Greek dualism of matter and spirit, and acquire an alien, unbiblical content. That God is Spirit has, in the Bible, nothing to do with this dualism. In the Old Testament the Spirit of God is either God himself or a power proceeding from him, but it is always presented in a concrete, substantial way.[38] That God is 'spiritual',[39] and therefore identifies more properly with our spirit, or soul, or mind than with our bodies, is an alien thought, comparable with the idea that God's image in man is to be found in his spirit, or soul, or mind rather than in his body. In fact, the formulation of the problem is false, being cast in the mould of a Greek dualistic anthropology which, in contrast to the Bible, sees man as a composite being comprising two or more parts.[40]

The Scriptures however speak of God using anthropomorphisms that refer to physical (visible?) aspects just as freely as those that refer to spiritual (invisible?) aspects. There is no difference between the way in which reference is made to the love or repentance of God and the way in which his hands, or eyes, or ears are spoken of. Indeed, Barth has suggested that our 'human' concepts derive their real meaning from God because he embodies them originally, really and completely. When we use such 'human' concepts for God we do not use them in an unreal way, but actually in their original sense and meaning. Such words are Father, Son, lordship, patience, love, mother, but also concepts such as arm and mouth.[41] One could justifiably say: Because God has hands, we too have hands. Because God has ears, we too have ears. Because God has eyes, we too have eyes. This is surely the ultimate meaning of Psalm 94:9: 'God made our ears – can't he hear? He made our eyes – can't he see?' (TEV). How is it conceivable, in the light of this text and the natural ways in which the biblical writers speak of the hands and eyes and ears of God, to assert that God has neither hand nor eye nor ear? From where do people get this information about God? So far as the Old Testament is concerned it is impossible to see without eyes or to hear without ears!

The way in which some people treat anthropomorphisms in their thinking and preaching raises serious questions. From where do they get the idea that this anthropomorphic way of speaking about God is 'only' a human and therefore invalid mode of expression, whereas God is in fact different and can be described accurately only in Greek philosophical terms? Could not such terms have also been used by the prophets and understood by their hearers? In such a case would anthropomorphism have then been necessary at all?

When speaking of the hand, or eye, or ear of God, it is of course difficult to conceptualise an *uncreated* mouth or eye or ear. These things we know only through experience of a man or animal, thus through created beings. In contrast we would have to speak to God's *un*created mouth, or eye, or hand.[42] And how to present the concept ontologically is of course a very difficult question. Indeed, what 'ontological' means in this context is itself a problem. But this much can be said, without hesitation or explanation, and at the same time declaring God to be different from man: we have to speak of the *un*created reality of these concepts when applied to God. One could of course choose to say that God only peforms what one might describe as the task of the eye, mouth, ear, without really having these limbs himself. But I find no valid theological reason for saying that God cannot have eyes, or ears or hands. Von Rad has said, in connection with Genesis 1:26, that Israel conceived Yahweh (God) as having human form. It is untenable to suggest that he is essentially invisible and that he can only become visible in conflict with his deity (or that he is essentially unknowable and can only become known in tension with his deity). The contrary is true. God's invisibility is a deed – a free decision on his part, for particular reasons and objectives, to be invisible (i.e. to conceal his essential visibility). The same holds for his knowability.

The well-known incident on the mountain involving the LORD and Moses can serve as an example (Exod. 33:18 f). The simple fact that Moses asks to see the LORD[43] and that the LORD replies that he may not see his face ('you cannot see my face; for man shall not see me and live') but will be able to see his back, presupposes that the LORD is not essentially invisible but rather that he keeps himself concealed for the sake of man. In Numbers 12:8 we read that Moses (often?) saw the form of the LORD. It was certainly a special privilege that was granted to him. but it does presuppose that the LORD was visible and deliberately kept himself invisible to the others. There are many other examples in both the Old and the New Testaments of people who saw God. Gideon became

afraid when he saw the angel of the LORD (i.e. the LORD himself), and
then was granted a divine assurance that he would not die (Judg.
6:22–23). Manoah was also afraid that both he and his wife would die 'for
we have seen God' (Judg. 13:22), and Isaiah calls out: 'Woe is me! For I
am lost... for my eyes have seen the King, the LORD of hosts!' (Isa. 6:5).
See also Genesis 32:30; Exodus 3:6; 24:9–10.

But the Scriptures also speak of seeing God without the connotations of
fear, especially in eschatological contexts. 'Blessed are the pure in heart,
for they shall see God' (Matt. 5:8). 'Strive for peace with all men, and the
holiness without which no one will see the Lord' (Heb. 12:14). '...but
we know that when he appears we shall be like him, for we shall see him
as he is' (1 John 3:2). 'And they shall see his face, and his name shall be on
their foreheads' (Rev. 22:4). These texts and various expressions found
in the Old Testament (e.g. Gen. 5:24; Num. 12:8) have to be subjected
to a forced exegesis in order to deny that they imply seeing God.

Accompanying these utterances there are others in the Bible which are
used to support the traditional idea that God is by nature invisible. John
declares. 'No one has ever seen God' (John 1:18), and Paul speaks of God
who 'dwells in unapproachable light, whom no man has ever seen or can
see' (1 Tim. 6:16). He is also spoken of as the 'invisible' God (1 Tim. 1:17).

It is not necessary to juxtapose these two groups of expressions. G. C.
Berkouwer has gone into the matter,[44] and has pointed out the following:
First of all, he sees the witness to the invisibility of God as a denial that
man can adopt the pose of a neutral researcher or observer and make God
a subject for study. God can only be seen when he in freedom approaches
man. And even then there remains in God's appearance and man's seeing
something elusive and supernatural. It is striking for example that when
someone has seen the LORD, he has never given any particulars about the
LORD himself, but only of the accompanying phenomena – e.g. Exodus
24:10; Isaiah 6:1–4. In no sense does God offer himself as a matter of
course to the inquisitive eyes of man. Nowhere is there any mention of
the possibility of studying God in a cool and comprehensive way as one
might consider and study any other subject. He is free to let himself be
seen, or to conceal himself. Kuitert explains:[45] In the measure that *seeing*
implies a degree of intimacy, the LORD deliberately conceals himself, or
does not make himself available to neutral observation, in order to
withdraw himself from an undue familiarity and to maintain a certain
distance between himself and his people. He does this specifically because
he differs from the gods of the heathen, and will not allow his people to
fraternise with him without faith and prayer. This would seem to be the
meaning of the second commandment. God may not be portrayed in
images because he is different from the gods of the heathen, not in the
sense that he is essentially invisible, but in the sense that the heathen took
it as a matter of course that in having the images with them they had their
gods in their possession. (Cf. Israel's sin in 1 Sam. 4:3 f.)

Then there is also a connection between the hiddenness of God as his act (not as his being), and man as a sinner. Israel from the beginning wanted to take their covenant with the LORD for granted and as a result were inclined to presume on his help. But the LORD always opposed any such presumed bond with the people or the land (Amos 3:2!) – and did so by way of his hiddenness. It was precisely in these contexts that the fear of seeing God existed. The dread of seeing God was never related to the creature, as though it were obvious that the creature could not see God. The restful, unproblematic converse between God and man in Genesis 2–3 (up to the fall) and that spoken of in Revelation 21–22 testify against this. The fear or the impossibility of seeing God must be interpreted in terms of man as a sinner. Isaiah was afraid that he might die after he had seen the LORD, because 'I am a man of *unclean* lips' (Isa. 6:5). For this reason we read in the New Testament that 'the pure in heart' will 'see God' (Matt. 5:8), and that 'without holiness' no one shall see God (Heb. 12:14), and that those who looked forward to seeing the LORD as he is 'purify themselves' (1 John 3:2). Augustine was right when he said that it is our sins which make it impossible for us to see God. Berkouwer explains that 'there is only one problem that always arises here, and it is not a theoretical problem of whether or not we can see God, but a problem of the heart'.[46] And Kuitert says that in the Scriptures there is indeed an incongruence between God and man, but not on account of some inherent inability to see or know God that is grounded in man's creatureliness, but on account of man's guilt.[47] There is no tension between the LORD *as God* and man *as man*. Genesis 1–2 recalls that God and man can live together without conflict. The future perspective especially excludes any idea of disparity between God and man, for it is then that God will live with his people. Then his glory (he himself) will fill the new Jerusalem, and then he will himself be the light of the city (Rev. 21:3, 11, 22, 23; 22:5). Kuitert has rightly concluded that the recognition of the remoteness of man from God in both Old and New Testaments is grounded in the awareness of guilt.[48]

The idea that God is essentially unknowable is also an alien Greek concept that has exercised considerable influence over our thinking about and faith in God. This conviction has a great deal to do with the western, Greek theory of knowledge, according to which knowledge presupposes a theoretical relationship between a knowing subject and a known object, a relationship in which the subject analyses the object (in this sense controlling it) and so comes to knowledge. But of course this theory of knowledge is not applied in the Scriptures to the God-man relationship. In the relationship to God, knowledge is not a theoretical matter, but a matter of experience; not a matter of the head, but of the heart. So for example, the Hebrew word for knowing is used for the most intimate relationship between man and woman, sexual intercourse, which is translated: 'He *knew* his wife'. When God declares, in Amos 3:2, 'You only have I *known* of all the families of the earth', he is saying something quite impossible as far as our usual interpretation of the word 'known' is concerned. How could God possibly have known only this one people? Had he not also drawn the Philistines from Caphtor, and the Syrians from Kir? (9:7). This expression only makes sense when 'know' refers to a more intimate relationship, that of love. Indeed, in Genesis 18:19 the same word is translated 'chosen'.

Anyone who persists in saying that God is unknown and unknowable has not read the Bible carefully. Psalm 76:1 says boldly, 'In Judah God is known.' And how much indeed has been written in the Scriptures about God, his will, his being, and his deeds! And because man has been made in his image, it is in no way a diminution of God's deity when he makes himself known to his people and by means of the covenant accompanies them on their way. That we can know God is not alien to his being and a concession on his part, as though he necessarily had to enter a 'strange land' (Barth) when sharing in creatureship and can therefore only be known in an unreal way. That God is in fact unknown in the world belongs to the fact of sin, and is not integral to the Creator-creature relationship. For this reason the knowledge of God coincides with reconciliation to God, and with the community in covenant with God. 'And this is eternal life, that they *know thee*' (John 17:3). And when Jesus Christ appeared on earth, as the reconciliation for our sins, he said: 'If you had known me, you would have known my Father also; henceforth *you know him*' (John 14:7).

It is also clear that God can withdraw himself from us and from our knowledge. Also indisputable is the fact that God's knowledge is more than our knowledge (Rom. 11:34). But these things do not mean that there is some structural impossibility in the creature which prevents him from knowing God – an impossibility that can in turn only be overcome by his becoming something 'unreal'. From the viewpoint of the covenant there is no problem about knowing God, even knowing him well! '*Your iniquities* have made a separation between you and your God, and your sins have hid his face from you so that he does not hear' (Isa. 59:2).

In the light of the discussion on anthropomorphism thus far in this chapter, the following conclusion seems obvious: The anthropomorphisms in the Bible are intentionally used to speak appropriately about God, in contrast to Israel's neighbours. Before proceeding to base the appropriateness of this manner of speech in man as the image of God, it will be helpful to consider together two other matters that always arise in relation to human ways of speaking about God: the immutability (or unchangeableness) of God, and the pathos of God.

THE IMMUTABILITY OF GOD

In considering the revelation of God care must be taken to avoid exaggerations and oversimplifications. We live today in a theological atmosphere in which there has been a strong reaction against the Greek philosophical idea of the unchangeableness of God, and in which the

Apologists have been severely censured for adopting this idea. Such a standpoint is shortsighted, however, and does not take sufficient account of the situation in which the Apologists lived. In Greek philosophy the immutability of God had its background in the denial that God had a beginning, and the resulting conclusion that he has no end. The immutability of God meant to the Greeks that God was not a phenomenon that arose, only to perish again.

The Apologists could not say less than this. Those who protest against such a meaning for immutability forget that the Bible speaks of God in precisely the same terms. Psalms 102:26–28 and 90:2 reflect this mode of thought.

The Greek philosophers used the idea of God's unchangeability to contest the fickleness and arbitrariness of the Homeric gods. Anyone who cannot depend on his gods, lives in total uncertainty. Without the continuity and identity of God, trust in him is impossible, and without trust no real relationship with the God of Israel can develop. In this sense too, the Apologists could not say less than that God is unchangeable, and in this sense the truth of God's immutability must always be confessed in the church. When today so much emphasis is placed on the *new* deeds of God, it remains a great reassurance to know that these are not undertaken at the expense of the former deeds, and that the history which God has already made with the world is taken up in the new things.[49] This is evident, among other things, in the fact that the new man (the justified, or born again man) is not *another* man, but a renewed man; that the new earth is not another earth, but a renewed earth; that Israel's history, and law, are not abrogated or abolished by Jesus Christ, but are fulfilled; that God remains faithful to all eternity and never abandons the work of his hands.

E. P. Meijering in particular has repeatedly stressed these positive aspects of the immutability of God. As early as his study on Athanasius he appealed for an appreciation of the positive meaning that the Platonic ontology had, and continues to have, for the gospel.[50] He starts out from the idea that basic to every person is the need for certainty (security), but that most people attain at best a partial fulfilment of this need. He goes on to show that the immutability of God in Platonic-Christian faith offers an answer to this need. This God can be trusted because he *is*. One cannot be sure that a person will not change – but one can be sure of God. If the heart of the biblical message about God is that he reveals himself in love, then the word love demands an ontological basis. One can only really trust when one is sure that love is genuine and not a pretence. People will often conceal their reality behind their actions, but is it not God's prerogative to *be* as he *does*? Meijering argues that Christian theology could clarify this truth by using Platonic ontology.[51]

Meijering returns to the matter in a later article. Again he gives a positive verdict in favour of the unchangeableness of God, and argues that without it we would not be able to speak of the dependable identity of God – and as a result, not of the living God either.

It is important that someone who can offer such a positive judgment on God's immutability can in the same article be critical of the way in which the idea has actually functioned in the thinking of the church. His main objection is that God's identity cannot be 'objectified'. For this reason he prefers the expression 'the living God' to 'deity' for example, for the word 'living' encloses the dynamic of that changeableness which can occur within the identity of God. By not taking the changeability of God as a matter of course, but as the great marvel to be confessed, the living God is clearly differentiated from fate. But this must not lead to the deification of mutability, and we must confess that the living God can retain his identity and yet change in such a way that we can never make him into an object.[52]

This balanced approach is fairly general today. M. Löhrer sees in the formulations of the Apologists the positive meaning of God's self-determination, in the sense that he is not subject to any external compulsion. In the course of the history of salvation this self-determination acquires the form of his faithfulness, so that he carries through his purpose of salvation in spite of the faithlessness of his covenant partner. The faithfulness of God, however, includes his free relationships with his creatures and is therefore something entirely different from metaphysical immutability. In the light of the incarnation it becomes clear that God, who actually remains unchangeable, *becomes* something (someone) else.[53]

Pannenberg also offers a positive judgment, but then observes quite rightly that the Greek concept of immutability is too impoverished, and says too little. God is more than the unmoved cause or foundation of what exists. He establishes himself in a wealth of new possibilities, and when he does new deeds he demonstrates his freedom. Though having neither beginning nor end, God is not immovable but is the living God. God is faithful, but this too cannot be understood in terms of Greek philosophy because his faithfulness acquires its form in his free, contingent, historical acts. In contrast to this is the idea of God's static immutability which so inhibited theological insight into his historical deeds.[54]

Certain Christological problems, especially the incarnation, played a considerable role in this question. The fact that one theologian after the other in the early church encountered huge problems in trying to reconcile the incarnation of the Word with the immutability of God,[55] speaks volumes about the poverty and inadequacy of their concept of immutability. In spite of clear statements, especially in Paul and John, the *becoming* and *changing* involved in the incarnation were repeatedly weakened. John declares: 'The Word that was with God and was God *became* flesh (man)' (John 1:14), but theology began a long tradition which taught that the Word merely took on a human nature. This idea if consistently applied means eventually, as H. Küng has shown, that the Word *became nothing,* and therefore not man either.[56] Similarly, a statement such as Paul makes in Philippians 2:6–8 has always created complex problems for theology.[57] According to this statement, Jesus Christ emptied himself by taking the form of a servant, he *became like man*, and *humbled* himself.... Anyone who wishes to do justice to these words cannot speak in terms such as: He remained unchanged within himself, and merely took on something – e.g. human nature. According to Paul, he *became* something (someone) other than he was before (while at the same time remaining himself). Indeed, with Luther, one is inclined to search for a new grammar to avoid falling into a major heresy with every word, and to truly interpret what the Scriptures wish to say. But, to say the least, a metaphysical dogma of immutability in this context gets us nowhere.

The link between the incarnation and anthropomorphism has evoked a great deal of thought. The various points of view regarding the matter usually fall between two extremes. The one extreme suggests that here the impossible happens, because the invisible Creator God and the visible creature are essentially incongruent and it is actually impossible for God to reveal himself as a man. As a result his revelation in the man Jesus is usually seen as a simultaneous and obvious concealment, followed by all kinds of speculations about the dialectical relationship between this revelation and this concealment. At the other extreme is the view that nothing new has actually happened here, and that one can proceed directly from the anthropomorphism to the incarnation, and conclude that it was God's intention from the beginning to become man, as the natural development of his 'humanity'.

Neither extreme is acceptable. It has already been argued that revelation does not imply an inevitable diminution of the deity of God, and that the anthropomorphisms represent a fully legitimate, reliable and genuine way of speaking about him. The idea that God is also concealed in Christ cannot be derived from a formal 'incompatability' between 'the divine' and 'the human'. The miracle of the incarnation is not seen in the New Testament as the impossible combination of two incompatible natures, which nevertheless somehow took place! On the basis of the genuineness and naturalness of the way in which the Bible speaks of God in human terms, it must be accepted that there is a connection between the anthropomorphisms and the incarnation, and that both aspects do point to the same reality.

At the same time one cannot go to the other extreme that takes the incarnation as a matter of course, and suggests that it was logically necessary and had to happen. The jubilation and wonder found in the New Testament is too great for this, and it speaks too clearly of the incarnation as a *humiliating* event.

On the one hand it is necessary to speak of a connection between anthropomorphism and the incarnation. Neither is contrary to the being of God. In neither case is God involved in the alien and unreal, making revelation a virtual impossibility. Why not? Because God created man in his own image and there is accordingly a definite analogy between God and man. (Later in this chapter fuller consideration will be given to this aspect as the basis for seeing the anthropomorphisms as real and appropriate ways of speaking about God.)[58]

On the other hand, the incarnation is a radicalising of the anthro-
pomorphisms, and that in a negative, humiliating sense. To *be like* man
on the basis of man as the image of God, is one thing. To *become* man
(even 'flesh', i.e. humbled, despised, fallen man) is another thing entirely.
It has already been shown that the anthropomorphisms never refer to
God in terms of sinful man (stealing, deceit, quarrelsomeness), but now
God becomes this man in Jesus Christ – 'in the *likeness of sinful flesh*'
(Rom. 8:3). To become a creature is humiliating to God because he is
forever more than the creature. But then to become a man 'who was
tempted in all points like as we are' (Heb. 4:15), and 'to be made like his
brethren in every respect' (Heb. 2:17) is an indescribable humiliation.
But God took this upon himself because he wished to fulfil our 'part' in
the covenant as well, having faithfully fulfilled his 'part' while Israel
broke theirs.

This *change* in God, that was in addition a *humiliating* change, means
that one ought not uncritically to accept an ontological identification
between Jesus and God. When later on some thought is given to God and
suffering this will be looked at more closely and the conclusion will be
drawn that we ought not simply to speak of the suffering and death of
Jesus as the suffering and death of God. In Jesus we have the *Mediator
between* God and man. Jesus is (ontologically at least) *more* (naturally not
higher!) than, and *different* from, God. Jesus is God emptied, in the form
of a servant, in the likeness of our sinful flesh! One cannot, therefore,
deduce a doctrine of God directly from Jesus. God is not 'like sinful flesh'
in his being, any more than he is 'wrath' in his essential being. God
became such for our salvation (but does not in the process betray his being
or surrender himself). So anyone who takes this becoming seriously will
remember that Jesus was a unique person who cannot be ontologically
identified with God, but is *more* than God (God *and* man), and *less* than
God (God emptied to become like sinful flesh).

This is the reason why Jesus Christ does not hold a central place in this book.
The true God is the God of Israel who created a history with this world,
and continues to do so, and only a part of this history is his incarnation in
Jesus Christ. It becomes necessary to use the doctrine of the Trinity to
proceed further at this point, because once the incarnation is spoken of, it
has to be explained that the God who became man in Jesus Christ is not
(God) the Father, nor (God) the Holy Ghost, but the Word (*Logos*). But
this causes a certain limitation in the meaning of the word 'God' because
speaking of the incarnate One as God is not speaking of God the Father or
God the Holy Spirit. But no such limitation is involved in using the
concept of the God of Israel. Here we are concerned with the Father *and*
the Son *and* the Holy Ghost – the one, true God.[59]

This 'minimalising' of the meaning of Jesus Christ in the doctrine of
God (*contra* Barth) needs however to be explained further. It does not
mean that God is not revealed in Jesus Christ, or that only a 'tip' of God is

revealed while the greater part of the iceberg remains concealed beneath the waters. God had already revealed himself in the history of Israel, and this revelation reached its climax in Jesus Christ. This has already been described in chapter 1.[60] Nor does it mean that Jesus is not God; on the contrary. But it does mean that we must build a doctrine of God on the foundation of the biblical preaching about the God of Israel who is the Father of Jesus Christ, and Christology (not the doctrine of God) must be built on the biblical preaching concerning Jesus Christ the Son of God. Of course the doctrine of God and Christology will illuminate each other, and even decisively determine each other (which became clear in chapter 1 when we dealt with 'God is love'), but a doctrine of God built upon the proclamation concerning Jesus will eventually be a disguised Christology and not a real doctrine of God in the strict sense of the word, because Christ is the Mediator between God and man.[61]

In this we have the explanation of the remarkable fact that Berkhof on the one hand can deny the deity of Christ, and yet on the other, can develop a doctrine of God with which one is in substantial agreement. [62]

In this light not all of Christ's human experiences can simply be considered as human ways of speaking about God, but at the same time the two natures of Christ will not be so divided that these experiences (e.g. his hunger and thirst, trouble and anxiety, suffering and death) are only applied to his human nature.

What we must derive from the incarnation – and this must be seen as the high point in the anthropomorphic proclamation of the changeability of God – is that we cannot be satisfied here with a metaphysical concept of immutability. In Christ, God became man, and therefore changed, becoming what he was not previously.[63] For this reason the doctrine of God cannot be constructed on the proclamation concerning Jesus Christ. (God became man in Christ, and anyone building up his doctrine of God on Jesus will have to ask himself whether he is not actually denying the 'becoming' on the basis of a metaphysical concept of immutability!) But the incarnation does offer a decisive testimony against a barren view of unchangeability.

The biblical concept of faithfulness (the faithfulness of God) allows us to be confident that even in the change introduced by the incarnation God remains faithful, both to his creatures that had long since ceased to deserve it, and to himself, who through creation became the God of mankind and who does not abandon the work of his hands. All of this is confirmed precisely through his incarnation.

Therefore my preference is for the concept 'faithfulness' as an alternative to 'immutability'. Both the concept of mutability and that of immutability can be used to express an aspect of the truth. The concept of immutability can be used positively, but it is too impoverished – as has already been shown. It does not allow room for God's involvement in history and his reaction to the deeds of men. In contrast to this, the expression 'mutability' carries such a negative connotation that it is quite unable to do justice to the certainty that God offers us, his identity and continuity. And so we must choose a third, genuinely biblical expression, namely the faithfulness of God.

We understand by God's faithfulness the fact that he achieves his purposes, and does not abandon them on account of our unfaithfulness; that even in the face of Israel's unfaithfulness he achieved what he had in mind. We understand therefore that in his faithfulness God keeps his promises, and that we can go into the future with confident expectation, knowing that he will give us the new heavens and the new earth! It also means that the individual can depend on his promises. Since he has promised: 'Him who comes to me I will not cast out' (John 6:37), every sinner who hears the gospel can come. The one who comes is accepted; he who receives Jesus Christ is a child of God.

But God's faithfulness includes faithfulness to himself. Precisely because he is unchangeable in the best sense of the word, and is not controlled by powers outside himself, he remains who he is, or 'shall be what he was' (Exod. 3:14!). This may be illustrated by reference to God's dealings with Nineveh. On the one hand, God really intended to destroy Nineveh, as he commanded Jonah to proclaim. It is a violation of the text to suggest that he 'only' threatened them in order that he might execute the real plan that he had prepared; namely, that they would repent and he would spare them, and that these were the things determined in advance by his unchangeable decree. Anyone interpreting Jonah 3 in this way would have to have access to secret information from elsewhere, in conflict with the meaning of the text.

At the same time he remains true to himself when he reacts to the repentance of the Ninevites and repents of his decision to condemn them, and spares the population. He is faithful in this and true to himself, because this is the kind of God he is, and how he has repeatedly made himself known to his people: 'a gracious God and merciful, slow to anger and abounding in steadfast love, and repentest of evil' (Jonah 4:2). It is impossible to explain this event without using the word 'change' about God. And yet the change does not terminate his faithfulness, but confirms it, *because* he had promised: 'If that nation concerning which I have spoken, turns from its evil, I will repent of the evil that I intended to do to it' (Jer. 18:8). God's faithfulness means that he changes his plans. This does not make him undependable, but the converse. The heathen of Nineveh, on the basis of their experience of their gods, said: 'Who knows God may yet repent and turn from his fierce anger' (Jonah 3:9). But the prophet, who knew the LORD, proclaims: 'I *shall* repent...' (Jer. 18:8).

Finally, God's faithfulness means that he remains true to the way in which he has determined to execute his promises. When he promised the land of Canaan as an eternal possession to Abraham, and later to Israel, he promised it in the covenant relationship, the covenant with the following content: 'I will be your God, and you shall be my people'. He made this promise to Israel *as his people, and he would keep this promise to*

Israel as his people. Therefore when the Jews broke the covenant through their persistent disobedience and were no longer his people, they could no longer lay claim to his faithfulness to keep this promise. In other words, those who do not live by faith can lay claim to none of the promises. God's faithfulness is also a faithfulness to his covenant. Those who stand outside of his covenant cannot call for the fulfilment of his promises. (Likewise a person who is baptized but is not obedient cannot claim any of God's baptismal promises.)

This does not mean that these promises remain unfulfilled. It only means that they are not fulfilled for *the Jews*. Because God often fulfils his promises in a richer way than can be expected from the promises themselves, these promises are fulfilled for the new, true, Israel, the church. But, precisely for this reason, 'the land of Canaan' is broadened to include 'the earth' when Paul applies the fifth commandment to the Christian community (Eph. 6:1–3).

All of this shows that God's faithfulness is not something automatic. As the living God he decides how and where he will fulfil his promises – but not arbitrarily. There is a fixed pattern. This can be read, among many places, in Jeremiah 18:7–10. This is the unchangeableness of God, that he always unchangingly, changes in this way.[64]

THE PATHOS OF GOD

It is fairly generally recognised that A. J. Heschel was the first to write about the pathos of God in a positive sense, and even to call the prophetic preaching a theology of pathos.[65]

The concepts of 'apathy' (feelinglessness) and 'pathos' (involvement) have played an important role in Christian thought. In Christology especially, the biblical comments concerning Christ's suffering (hunger, thirst, weariness, anger, pain, death) were either applied in a one-sided way to his human nature, or were weakened, reduced or interpreted away. The reason for this must be sought in early Christian convictions about the apathy of God. This is an idea which the Apologists took over, almost without alteration, from Plato's doctrine of God: God cannot suffer.[66] Suffering must not be limited here directly to its Christological aspect. Like so many other words, apathy (Gk: *apatheia*) can be used in many senses. Referring to God the Greeks used it particularly to indicate that God was beyond the reach of external influences, that he was independent of the human situation, that he was free, self-sufficient, and without feeling. By pathos they understood: dependence, compulsion, passion, contingency, and the lower emotions.

Given such a choice there could be no doubt which the early Christians would select. They chose the apathetic God because, quite rightly, they believed God to be perfect, independent of man (or other powers) and unable to be pressurised from without. But the doctrine of God in Plato and Aristotle contained a serious shortcoming: on the basis of God's perfection they taught that he neither had, nor needed, any friends. And since one can only know and love one's peers, God being sufficient to himself would know, love and think about himself alone. He could therefore experience, share and suffer nothing. As the one sufficient unto himself he could know no passions such as anger, hatred and jealousy, but by the same reasoning he could not know love, compassion or pity.

This apathy was not only a characterisation of God but, as in Stoicsm, was also presented as an ethical ideal for man. To become like God, a person would need to overcome his needs and passions and live a life free from struggle, fear, anger and love. He would need to be uninfluenced by others. As his highest ideal he would find his rest in God by thinking God's thoughts with him.

It is immediately apparent that this mode of thought is alien to the biblical view of both God and man. Indeed, the distance between these two worlds of thought is so great that it is better to abandon altogether any attempt to reinterpret the concept of apathy (as has been done, for the greater part, in the history of dogma, using concepts such as the aseity of God). One should rather, like Heschel, ask whether the God of the Bible ought not rather to be described as the God of *pathos*, on the grounds that in the Bible other alternatives exist which are different from those posited by the Greeks.

By pathos Heschel does not understand the being of God, but a situation. According to Heschel (and we have already found him to be correct through what we have learnt of Hosea and Jeremiah) the prophets do not proclaim a detached, remote, dispassionate, uninvolved and neutral God, but the God of Israel who was deeply engaged in Israel's joys and sorrows. The fate of the people involved him, and as the living God he lived with them, and among them. Their love and obedience gave him joy; their unfaithfulness pained him; he suffered with them in their captivity and exile.

This is not to say that God was dependent on them and could not manage without them, and that he was influenced and compelled by powers external to himself. God is not robbed of his exaltedness, his freedom and his perfection. But the prophets perceived that God, who was perfect and sufficient in himself, had freely chosen to be Israel's God, had freely decided to love them and to care for them, had freely resolved that he would live in a commitment to them and would find his joy in their love, and pain in their faithlessness. This means that there is no suggestion of powerlessness in the LORD's cry in Hosea 11:8: 'How can I give you up, O Ephraim! How can I hand you over O Israel!' It reflects an exercise of God's freedom in which he freely bound himself to Israel. Such was his decision – made within his sovereign authority: he could not surrender them; he could not destroy them. Were Israel the pride of the earth, one might be misled into thinking that their exceptional worth had overwhelmed and captivated God. This would be pathos in the unacceptable, Greek sense of the word. But it is emphasised most clearly that

Israel was a small, insignificant nation, oppressed by the mighty Egyptians – in fact 'the fewest of all peoples' (Deut. 7:7). That God chooses them, and cannot surrender them, and suffers because of their unfaithfulness, is indeed his free decision.

Heschel understands pathos to be this situation of free involvement of God with Israel's history, and by way of Israel, with the history of mankind. 'It is not a passion, an unreasoned emotion, but an act formed with intention, rooted in decision and determination... its essential meaning is not to be seen in its psychological denotation, as standing for a state of the soul, but in its theological connotation, signifying God as involved in history, as intimately affected by events in history, as living care.'[67]

God is therefore the opposite of the ideal judge. The ideal judge must be neutral, emotionally uninvolved, objective. It must be all the same to him whether he finds the accused guilty or innocent, whether he must condemn or acquit. His judgment must not be influenced by any involvement with either of the parties. God is not like this. The accused are his concern. He is deeply involved with their fate. He wants at all costs to acquit them and give them a new future, because he loves them. This involvement with Israel, and through Israel with the world, is so much the stronger because it was not initiated by Israel. It was not forced upon God by qualities inherent in Israel, and did not arise from a need or lack within himself; but because he who had no need of it, chose it, and freely decided to be involved with them. God himself decided quite freely that his life and history would no longer be separate from the life and history of his people and his world.

This involvement of God in history is so important in the Bible that even concepts that were regarded as beneath the dignity of God, or unworthy of God, acquired a positive meaning for Israel. Two such concepts were the wrath and jealousy of God. Along with these we must also look at the old problem of God and suffering.

Wrath

On the one hand, one hesitates to speak of the wrath of God as a form of his love. In cases where a positive reaction to his anger and judgment is evident, such as when Israel repented, it is easier to suggest that his anger had achieved the objective of his love in bringing Israel back to him. But when his anger and judgment lead eventually to the rejection of Israel and the forsakenness of Christ, and point the way to eternal judgment, it becomes more difficult to see in it a form of his love.

On the other hand it is undoubtedly correct to see a particular relationship between his wrath and his love. Had God not been loving, he would never have been angry. Were God uninvolved and neutral in relation to mankind, both love and wrath would have been excluded. The opposite of love is not wrath; the opposite of both love and wrath is neutrality. Such a neutrality would mean that God had withdrawn himself from the covenant. The fact that he continued to be angry with Israel meant that he was still interested in them and was involved in their weal and woe. His wrath is injured love.[68] For precisely this reason, the wrath of God is proclaimed the most powerfully by the prophets of his love – Hosea and Jeremiah.[69] (See Hos. 5:12, 14 and Jer. 13:12–14).

But the concept of wrath can be used in a variety of meanings. There is a negative meaning. And in this sense it is rejected in the Bible. Jacob condemns the anger of his sons Simeon and Levi (Gen. 47:7); because of its anger, Edom comes under God's judgment (Amos 1:11); anger produces disputes and quarrelling, so the writer of Proverbs tells us (Prov. 30:33); hence the admonitory call: 'Refrain from anger, and forsake wrath! Fret not yourself. It tends only to evil' (Ps. 37:8).

However, when there are repeated references to God's wrath, it is clear that, as with God's repentance, we have to distinguish between various meanings of the word 'wrath'. In a psychological sense, anger means emotional excitement caused by intense dissatisfaction, and implies that the person concerned has lost his self-control, and that his action is directed towards revenge and punishment. One would expect the Scriptures to forbid such an emotion. But when it is applied to God, it is clear that it has a different meaning. The prophets never speak of his wrath as an uncontrolled explosion, unpredictable and irrational. Indeed, his wrath is never spontaneous but is always a reaction, caused or provoked by the behaviour of people. For this reason the prophets always make a great deal of the occasion for his anger – the sin and disobedience of the people – and then show that God's anger is a purposeful action (reaction) by means of which he wishes to express his revulsion and call the people to repentance. That his wrath is an *act*, willed and completely under control, is evident from Exodus 32:10 where God *asks* Moses: '...now therefore let me alone, that my wrath may burn hot against them and I may consume them'. It is therefore not an uncontrollable eruption, but a considered action in favour of which, or against which, the LORD is able to decide.

As has been said, his wrath is a *purposeful* action. There is no wrath for the sake of wrath in God. He has a goal in mind. He wishes to express his revulsion. He wishes to make known what is right and what is wrong, and that he does not connive at wrong – in short, that he is holy. But wrath frequently has the intention of repentance as well. God punishes his people in wrath precisely in order to win them back to his love.

Furthermore, wrath is God's *reaction*. It is not spontaneous; it always has a definite cause. His wrath is never arbitrary and undeserved, but is always more than deserved. How different from his love! His love is always spontaneous. We never deserve his love. He loves us in spite of ourselves and what we are. Where does this difference lie? Quite simply in the fact that we read in the Bible, 'God is love', but never 'God is wrath'. His love flows from his being. He had love within himself before he loved us. From eternity the Father loved the Son and the Son the Father. Even were there no people, God would still be love. Free love is his very being.

But wrath does not belong to his being in the way that love does. His wrath is never spontaneous. Had there never been creatures, he would never have been angry. He *became* angry; but he *is* love. Here we have another situation in which we cannot speak of God without mentioning 'change'. In his dealings with his creatures God became what he was not previously – wrathful. He also became Creator, man, redeemer – but that we mention only in passing. It becomes progressively clearer that the prophets are very serious when they speak of the *living* God. God does not only create our history, but also has his own history. But more of this in chapter 3. In the meantime it has become clear that God's wrath is holy wrath, and is something other than the wrath of man and gods, which can only be rejected, that his wrath is actually something for which we may be glad.[70] Without wrath – as injured love – there could be no love; and without judgment on Christ crucified there could be no deliverance. It is only when we resist the purpose which he has in mind with his wrath that it becomes destructive and disastrous for us.

Jealousy

The jealousy (zeal) of God is another concept that is open to misunderstanding. According to the Greek god-concept jealousy was considered unworthy of a deity. The Homeric gods were usually jealous of people who were happy and did all kinds of reprehensible things to them. According to Herodotus the gods wished no benefits or happiness for anyone else, and often bestowed these things on people only to have the satisfaction of expressing their jealousy by taking them away again.[71]

Once again we have here a good example of the difference between Homeric ways of speaking of the gods and the anthropomorphisms of the Bible. It certainly is unworthy of God to speak in such terms of him! But in the Old Testament the jealousy of God has a totally different meaning, and one might perhaps even say that it has exactly the opposite meaning. Because God knows that his people can only be really happy with him, he is jealous and refuses to allow his people to worship other gods beside him.[72]

Jealousy in this sense is unique to the Bible. The people around Israel knew no such meaning for jealousy. But because the LORD is the only true God, and because he had bound himself to Israel by way of a covenant, Israel were not free to serve other gods, nor were they free to serve him in the way that these other gods were served, through their images. His jealousy assumes an exclusive relationship.[73] Because this is a relationship of love (which is often presented in the figure of marriage), God cares, and Israel's faithfulness or unfaithfulness affect him. Therefore, perhaps the best description of his jealousy is that he is a God who *cares*.

Here we have another example of how radically the El figure was adapted to suit the LORD. A jealous El, in the sense that only he might be worshipped, would be unthinkable in the Canaanite pantheon. And yet in Exodus 34:14 the LORD is spoken of as a jealous El (God).[74]

The LORD is not only jealous, however, but zealous as well. In this case the same Hebrew root is used. His zeal relates especially to his acts in history. He is zealous for his people against their enemies (Ezek. 36:5; 39:25; Joel 2:18; Zech. 1:14). He is also zealous against his people when they refuse to live according to his will (Exod. 20:5; Deut. 6:15; 32:19 f; Ezek. 5:13; 16:42; Zech. 8:2). Preuss had pointed out that when a promise of salvation is sealed with a reference to the zeal of the LORD it means that the LORD guarantees this promise with his whole being.[75]

Suffering

While much has already been said about this, it is nevertheless necessary to consider directly the question as to whether God also suffers. The history of theology has usually proceeded from the Greek *natura Dei* concept involving the *impassibilitas Dei* (God's impassibility – God cannot suffer), thus on the basis of the same concept of God that led to the suspicions concerning anthropomorphism. Suffering was seen as something inappropriate to God. This raised serious problems for Christology,[76] because from a very early time it was confessed that Christ was God. If God cannot suffer, the implication was that Christ could not suffer either. But against this was the New Testament evidence, especially in the gospels, that Christ was hungry and thirsty, that he became tired, suffered and died. Two ways of resolving the problem have been traditionally used. Sometimes the meaning of these utterances has been minimised by a variety of limitations and explanations. But more often, and especially in later times, his sufferings were applied exclusively to his human nature. It is quite customary even today to apply to the humanity of Jesus all kinds of expressions in the gospels that are considered inappropriate to God, e.g. he suffered only as a man; it was only as a man that he prayed that the cup might be taken from him; it was only as a man that 'he offered up prayers and supplications, with loud cries and tears . . . and was heard for his godly fear' (Heb. 5:7) (Living Bible, 'with tears and agony of soul'); it was only as man that he was forsaken by God, and it was only in his humanity that he died.

In passing, however, it is clear that there is as little evidence in the texts for limiting these things to the humanity of Jesus as there were grounds for regarding the other anthropomorphisms as an inappropriate or unreal way of speaking about God. Indeed it is questionable whether it is possible in general to apply statements about Jesus only to his human nature (or only to his divine nature). The reason for this doubt lies in the awareness that Jesus was not in the first place a combination of two natures, but *one* living Person. The doctrine of the two natures was an intellectual construction of later times and was used to confess something concerning this unique Person: the *Word* that *became* man. It is a good confession, and the church has thus far judged that it is the best confession, but we must not turn the apostles into ventriloquist's dolls and pretend that it was they who spoke and thought of Jesus in terms of two natures.

But there is another problem in connection with limiting the sufferings of Jesus to his human nature. We confess that in him two natures were united, but in such a way there was but one Person (one 'I'), so that the *impersonal* human nature was taken on by the Person of the Son (or the personal divine nature). So then, even if we were to project this thought construction back on to the apostles, it would mean that what he experienced, he experienced as a divine person. It is surely unimaginable that an impersonal human nature could experience what the divine person who assumed this nature did not experience.

On the other hand, Berkouwer has argued, against Barth's view of the sufferings of God and Christ, that we cannot proceed simply from the *vere Deus* (Jesus being God) and speak of the sufferings of Christ as the sufferings of God. Barth is convinced that the *vere Deus* enables one to see the history of Jesus Christ as the history of God himself. And for this reason he speaks of Christ's obedience as the obedience of God, Christ's self-surrender as the self-surrender of God. So for Barth, the suffering of Christ can be equated with the suffering of God.

Berkouwer, however, shows that not all the resistance to the idea of *theopaschitism* (God's suffering) comes from a barren god-concept derived from Greek thinking about an immoveable being, but that theologians who fully accept the deity of Christ and the unity of his person hesitate, seemingly intuitively, to speak of the suffering of God (in Christ). Berkouwer is convinced that this hesitation springs from Scripture itself. The Scriptures know definite limits to the proclamation of the impenetrable mystery of the incarnation and the cross, and a consistent theopaschitism oversteps these limits. Scripture recognises a definite relationship between Jesus and the Father, a relationship of subjection, but in theopaschitism this relationship fades into the idea that God himself is suffering in Christ. It is then easily realised why theopaschitism finds its most fruitful soil in some kind of Monophysitism (the view that Christ had only one nature – the divine nature), in which only the divine nature really comes into consideration, with the result that the fullest emphasis is placed on the idea that God himself suffers. The Christological 'God himself' is thus elevated to the point of decisive significance from which the whole life of Christ is to be approached. In contrast to this idea, Berkouwer sees the New Testament emphasis as being on Christ's mediatorial role. Anyone proceeding from the divine nature of Christ directly to God himself cannot do justice to the position of Christ as mediator. If God himself is the One who takes and bears the suffering, the mediatorial role of Christ between God and man is obscured (1 Tim. 2:5). In this connection the relationship between God and Christ in the New Testament is of decisive importance. Christ is subject to the Father, doing the work given him by the Father; Jesus can do nothing of himself, and declares that the Father is greater than he. All this is difficult to accommodate in a consistent theopaschitism, in which there is always a tendency to reduce Christ's dialogue with the Father to a monologue. The subjection of Christ to the Father, grounded in his mediatorship, forbids making the *vere Deus* a point of departure for a series of conclusions in which the idea of 'God himself' serves as an explanation of the incarnation, instead of as an accentuation of the confession concerning the deity of Christ. It is accordingly also striking that the Theopaschites usually exhibit some hesitation, so that while they speak easily of the suffering of God, they are reluctant to apply to God without qualification sayings in which it is declared that Christ became a curse or in which his death is mentioned. Thus far Berkouwer's criticism in *The Triumph of Grace.*

In *A Half-Century of Theology* Berkouwer explains that he did not mean to suggest that there was no connection at all between the suffering of Christ and God.[78] It is even a mistake to proceed from the assumption that Christ did not suffer in his divine nature. In this respect he cites Bavinck who argued that the Scriptures frequently mention Christ's humiliation in relation to his divine nature.[79] He argues that God was indeed involved in the suffering of Christ, but it is clear that he wishes to avoid a theory of passibility or impassibility, and does not wish to speak of seemingly logical conclusions to be drawn from the doctrine of the two natures. Rather, he wishes to emphasise God's concrete involvement in Christ's pathway to suffering, in which he did not spare his own Son, but gave him (and through him, himself) for us all. In this way, and in this place, 'God himself' is visible. At this point Berkouwer finds himself in agreement with Barth and quotes the following ideas: God gave himself over – but did not give himself away, or surrender himself – to his creature, and became a man. Yet, Berkouwer would rather view God's involvement in the sufferings of Christ in terms of the Father who gave his Son, than in terms of the *vere Deus* – but without attempting to preserve the divine nature of Christ from suffering on the grounds of some theory that 'God cannot suffer'!

My personal conviction is that we ought not to approach the question concerning the relationship between God and suffering via the Christological gateway (*vere Deus*), but by way of the preaching about God and in particular the anthropomorphisms of the Old Testament, and by way of the involvement of the Father in the suffering of Christ. It is equally wrong in principle to create a problem (or worse, a position) concerning the death of God via the death of Christ. The unique position of Christ as mediator does not allow us to proceed directly from Christology to the doctrine of God – although, on the other hand, we cannot proceed via the old Greek concept of *a natura Dei* to limit the death of Christ merely to his human nature. An appeal is sometimes made incorrectly to the last sentence of article 19 of the Belgic Confession to substantiate the view that the death of Christ was limited to his human nature alone. This appeal neglects the last words in this sentence which read: 'and (Christ is) very man that *he* (not only his human nature, AK) might die for us...'.

Let us now attempt to discuss the problems of the suffering of God in terms of the biblical doctrine of God, and not via Christology. Our task, as with the anthropomorphisms in general, is not to proceed from certain things that God 'can' or 'cannot' do. We must take to heart Barth's warning that we cannot subject God to a superficial general concept of what 'can' and what 'cannot' be done. Our task is to listen to the witness of the prophets and the apostles to whom he revealed himself, and who therefore knew what he had in fact done and what he had not done. So we work in the doctrine of God, and especially here, not with principles, but with history.

History informs us that God really was involved with Israel's joys and sorrows. We know further that the prophets often use the image of marriage to describe the relationship between God and his people. And we know that a man suffers greatly when his wife whom he loves is unfaithful to him. The conflict in God which we saw in both Hosea and Jeremiah showed that the LORD really suffered under the unfaithfulness of his people (Isa. 5). Other utterances too should be understood in this light: 'In all their affliction (his people's) *he was afflicted*... in his love and in his pity (TEV: compassion, literally: to suffer with) he redeemed them' (Isa. 63:9). 'So they (the people) put away the foreign gods from among them and served the LORD; and he became indignant over the misery of Israel' (Judg. 10:16. NEB translates: 'and he could *endure no longer* to see the plight of Israel). Hosea 11:8 also speaks of God's 'compassion'.

From earliest times Romans 8:32 has been very important in this connection. In his discussion of Origen's negative attitude towards anthropomorphism, Maas[80] has shown that in his homily on this text a glimpse of the living God of the Bible shines through. Origen's thought of God is usually totally dominated by the Platonic tradition. He sees God as immoveable, unchangeable, uninvolved, apathetic and incapable of suffering. But in Romans 8:32 we read that God 'spared not his own Son, but gave him up for us all', and here for a moment the idea of what is 'worthy of God' cannot smother the biblical message about God. Origen explains that this act in which God gave his Son touched him deeply, causing him suffering. He says concerning the act of 'giving' that the Father suffered in that the Son, who was in the form of God, humbled himself and adopted the form of a servant. The Father was affected by this. He who did not spare his own Son, was himself not spared in the process and did not remain untouched.

Once or twice again we hear from Origen that the Father suffered together with those on whom he showed mercy because he is not unfeeling (Gk: *asplanchnos*). When he bends down to mankind, he too suffers in the suffering of love. He suffers with the suffering of man. The Father is therefore able to suffer. Thus far Origen.

These few glimpses are of great importance simply because in other respects Origen is dominated by Greek philosophical thought, and its system of the *nature Dei* and the *dignum Deo*. Consequently, when something contrary does break through in his thinking it must be seen as a triumph for the obvious meaning of the Scripture over the unbiblical system that governed his thought in this respect.

When Berkouwer deals with Romans 8:32 as it functions in various modern discussions (among them Wiersinga's),[81] he points out that a number of other utterances also come into the picture, among them, Romans 8:3; John 3:16; Matthew 21:33 f; Mark 12:6. All of these references mention that God sent his Son. Two aspects are of importance. First of all, almost intuitively, it is always felt that this affected God – as even Origen sensed! A little word in Romans 8:32 leaps to one's eyes: 'own' – and also the implied 'even' in 'God who did not spare (even) his own Son'. This is no neutral, or objective report, but expresses astonishment: Did God do even this? In the parable of the vinedressers, the almost unbelievable moment when the Son was sent is similarly emphasised: 'He had still *one* other, a *beloved* son; *finally* he sent him to them, saying, "They will respect my son"' (Mark 12:6). These and other similar utterances are so full of meaning that there is nothing strange in seeing in them a reference to the involvement and the suffering of the Father. It would be a terrifying, cold being who would be left indifferent after giving up his own son! One would not be able to recognise the LORD in such a being (Jeremiah and Hosea!). When Moltmann treats this text he offers a quotation from Popkes which states, that 'God gave up his Son' is one of the most unheard statements of the New Testament. 'We must understand "deliver up" in its full sense and not water it down to mean "send" or "give". What happened here is what Abraham did not need to do to Isaac; Christ was quite deliberately abandoned by the Father to the fate of death; God made sin, Christ is the accused of God. A theology of the cross cannot be expressed more radically than it is here.' Thus Popkes.[82]

The second matter that is of extraordinary importance in this connection is that no detailed statements are made in these utterances about the nature of the Father's suffering. There is surprise over what he has done, grateful surprise, but not a single attempt to describe how the Father experienced it and what his emotions were. This phenomenon is common to all anthropomorphic expressions in the Scriptures. In a slightly different context reference has already been made to Isaiah 6, where the prophet saw the LORD seated, but gave no description of him but only of his clothing and the heavenly beings around him. Hosea and Jeremiah repeatedly made it clear that the LORD was disappointed, that he was suffering as a result of Israel's unfaithfulness, but nowhere are we given a detailed description of his inner feelings or experiences. Even the statement that is often quoted to support this (Hos. 11:8) actually testifies to the opposite. Here we read: 'How can I give you up, O Ephraim! How can I hand you over, O Israel! How can I make you like Admah! How can

I treat you like Zeboiim! My heart recoils within me, my compassion grows warm and tender.' The word recoils is often quoted to indicate how 'tempestuous' God's feelings are. But this is a wrong interpretation. On the basis of the well-known *parallelismus membrorum* (indicating the same meaning in successive lines or phrases) it is evident that the first phrase of the last sentence is to be interpreted in the light of the last phrase. Now the last phrase indicates something that has happened already. It is a change indeed, a change in accordance with the way in which the Lord changes in his mercy and faithfulness, but this change has already taken place. This then is also the meaning of the first part of the parallelism: 'My heart *is changed* within me' (NEB). Gispen suggests: 'I have changed my mind.'[83] This does not eliminate the anthropomorphism but it becomes clear where the emphasis falls in *this* text, not on the inward tension, or details about how God is emotionally stirred, but on the fact that he has changed his intentions – as he did in Jonah's case.

The same is true of the other important example of anthropomorphism, Jeremiah 31:20: 'Is Ephraim my dear son? Is he my darling child? For as often as I speak against him, I do remember him still. Therefore *my heart yearns for him*; I will surely have mercy on him, says the LORD.' The italicised portion again indicates something that has already happened, a decision already taken, that the LORD had already changed ('as often as') and decided to be gracious to Israel. Hence: 'I will surely have mercy.' The original points to the deepest love and compassion, and not to an 'inward tempest' of emotion and conflict as God struggles with judgment and mercy. Such anthropomorphisms do not occur in the Bible, and we would overstep the bounds of revelation (Berkouwer) were we to interpret the anthropomorphisms in this way.

This limitation indicates a very important function of the anthropomorphisms, namely, that they are not intended to analyse God's inner emotional life and tensions, but have the *practical* goal of admonishing us radically (e.g. by the greatness of his wrath), or of offering us a strong consolation (he will *always* alter his condemnation if the sinner repents), or else to emphasise God's intimate involvement in history with a view to leading his people to repentance and to worship him in gratitude (Rom. 8:32). In this sense it is necessary to speak of the suffering of God. The anthropomorphisms speak of his *fellow-suffering* with *us*, of his involvement in history, but are not independent phenomena intended to depict God's inner life itself in all its details. It would therefore be correct to say that God is in, or enters into, suffering, but not, as Moltmann says, that suffering is in God.[84] Indeed, *The Crucified God* is a good example of an approach that goes further than the Scriptures. It derives too much from the cry of dereliction ('My God, my God, why hast thou forsaken me?') concerning what it cost the Father and what he experienced in it and through it. That this word from the cross suggests a revolution (*stasis*) in God, a 'God against God', enmity in God, and that in this way suffering and death have been taken up into God, is simply to say more than the scriptural data allow us to say.[85] In chapter 3 we will consider the consequences of speaking anthropomorphically about God for the relationship between God and history.

MAN AS THE IMAGE OF GOD

In the traditional treatment of the anthropomorphisms of the Bible and especially the attempts to show their inadequacy and inappropriateness, and to search for their 'actual' meaning, the greatest deficiency has perhaps been in the fact that man as the image of God has been virtually ignored. In itself it is striking that on the one hand, prophets and apostles preach about God in human terms and images in a completely unforced way and without all sorts of explanations, and on the other hand, that man is created in the image of God and is repeatedly summoned to exhibit this image once more. When both these matters are taken seriously, it might seem that God and man, in spite of radical differences (Creator-creature, and all that this implies), suit each other, at least to the degree that it is fitting to speak of God in human terms, *because* man has been created in the image of God.

It is realised that there is seemingly no direct and well-defined content given to the image of God in Genesis 1:26 f. During the course of history various attempts have been made to provide content for the image of God from the immediate context. Attention has been drawn to the link between 'image' and 'rule' in verse 26, and the function of man as ruler has been seen as the image of God. Barth has pointed to the relationship between the image and 'man and woman' (v. 27) and has suggested co-humanity as the image of God. While both of these points of view make sense and contain hints as to the content of the image, there remains the feeling that the intention of these phrases was never to give a comprehensive indication of the meaning of the image of God.

Another important tendency in history has been to exclude the body of man from the image of God, and to limit the image entirely to the soul and/or spirit of man. Later insights into the unity of man and the value of his physical existence have however made this distinction impossible. As has been shown earlier in this chapter, the anthropomorphisms make use of physical features (limbs, form) just as readily and unassumingly as any other facet of man's make-up in speaking about God.[86] According to the Genesis story, *man* – and not some aspect of man – was made in the image of God.

A matter that arises in Genesis 1 and that has received inadequate attention thus far, is the uniqueness of the statement that man was made in the image of God. Frequent reference has been made to the fact that God simply went ahead and made all the other creatures, but with man, there was first the consultation: 'Let us make man...and let them have dominion...' (v. 26). After this he proceeded to the creation of man. It has also been pointed out that it is only man *with whom* God speaks. He speaks *about* the animals and other creatures, but a verbal relationship is confined to man. Man has therefore been rightly spoken of as the crown of creation, and the covenant as the goal of creation. I am persuaded that the content of the covenant was already present in the relationship between God and Adam – I will be your God, and you shall be my people. These are all familiar and valid ideas.

But less well known is the exceptionalness of this communication that man is made in the image of God in its context. Attention was drawn earlier to the nature of Genesis 1 as a kind of disguised mockery of the gods, and a radical de-divinisation of creation.[87] The sun and the moon, regarded as deities by other nations, are here called 'lights', and their names as deities, 'Sun' and 'Moon' are not even mentioned. The earth loses its autonomy and becomes a creation of God, which cannot act on its own but can only respond to God's word. Everything that lay within the experience of the people of those times came within the category of the created. No gods were left – except God. It is in this context that man is spoken of as the image of God.[88] A deliberate and specific relationship between God and man is thus laid down, a relationship which does not apply to the rest of creation. For this reason it is a mistake to look for some form of the image of God in the remainder of creation. To do so is to mistake the intention of Genesis 1. Nothing else in creation stands in this relationship to God – not even the angels, as Calvin thought, on the basis of Matthew 22:30.[89]

The statement that man was made in the image and likeness of God is made even more striking by the fact that Deutero-Isaiah excludes every likeness between God and the gods when he asks: 'To whom then will you liken God, or what likeness compare with him?' (Isa. 40:18; cf. also 40:25; 46:5). Indeed, in chapter 1 it became clear that the prophetic message emphatically proclaimed the incomparability between God and the gods. The gods cannot be compared with the LORD; they are not his 'likeness'. And yet the same concept is used in Genesis 1:26 f to declare that the LORD does in fact have a 'likeness'. That which was disallowed to the gods was not only appropriate to man, but was intended for him – God *must* be compared to man, man *is* his likeness and image.

This must not be wrongly interpreted. It does not abolish the difference between God and man. In this respect as well Genesis 1 could be regarded as a polemic against the surrounding religions. Man is also de-divinised by the creation story. The blood of a conquered god does not flow in his veins, as the Babylonian creation myth would have it; nor did he come into being from the tears of the sun-god, as the Greeks believed. Against this background, Genesis 1 stresses the difference between God and man.[90] God, and only God, is God, or divine. Man is neither God nor divine, and has nothing divine in him. Man is man, creature, and this he remains. Even on the new earth we do not become angels or divine beings, but will serve God as his servants.[91] We neither can nor need to be more than human. To be what God made us to be is the way to achieve the greatest happiness possible.

And yet, according to Genesis 1 man is the image and likeness of God. God cannot be compared with the gods – enough has been said about that in chapter 1 – but he can, and must be compared with man. (This thought underlies of course the sub-titles in chapters 1 and 2.)

To answer the question: In what way, and to what extent can God be compared with man?, we must determine what the content of the image of God is. We do not have full details about this in Genesis 1, although there are one or two hints; but the anthropomorphisms immediately come to mind. It is in the *comprehensiveness* of the anthropomorphisms that we have an indication of the content of the image of God. This is actually the focal point of the whole debate: because man is made in the image of God it is possible to speak of God in human terms, and to do so most appropriately. In contrast, it is inappropriate to speak of God in metaphysical and transcendental terms. But this point of view will not be properly established until we have a clearer demarcation of the image of God.

Explicit attention is given to this in the New Testament. On the one hand, Christ is repeatedly spoken of as the image of God (2 Cor. 4:4; Col. 1:15 and Heb. 1:3), and on the other, the community is called to become the image of God (Col. 3:10). The link that this last text establishes between the image of God and the new man prompts one to think also of Ephesians 4:24 f in terms of the image of God. Elsewhere Paul suggests the same thought, for example, when he expresses his desire that 'Christ be formed in you' (Gal. 4:19). Christ, *the* Man, is the image of God, and comes to show, as the last Adam, what God had intended with the first Adam. He is of course more than this. But he is at least this. Paul speaks of the renewal of man as the ending of the old life (Gal. 2:20; Rom. 6:6), and the rising to a new life in which Christ exercises dominion, or 'takes form'. So when the children of God are called to become the image of God, they are summoned to give Christ the freedom to reign in their lives and so to let him live his life in them.

But this does not take place outside of the realm of the consciousness and responsibility of the believer. He is not only the instrument through which Christ wishes to live, or the uniform in which he wishes to live. By virtue of Christ's dominion in his life, he lives differently, and we have here the most important aspect of the biblical teaching of man as the image of God: he is called to be and to live *like God and like Christ*. The admonitory portions of the New Testament are full of this, and especially the letters of Paul. 'Forbearing one another...and forgiving each other... *as* the Lord has forgiven you, *so* you also must forgive' (Col. 3:13). 'Forgiving one another, *as* God in Christ forgave you' (Eph. 4:32). 'And walk in love, *as* Christ loved us...' (Eph. 5:2). This throws light on the future perspective in John and gives it a deeper meaning. 'But we know that when he appears, *we shall be like him*, for we shall see him as he is' (1 John 3:2). Immediately after this he says: 'And everyone who thus hopes in him purifies himself *as he is pure*' (1 John 3:3). The letter of Peter is also familiar with this 'as': 'But *as* he ... is holy, be holy yourselves in all your conduct, since it is written, "You shall be holy, for I am holy"' (1 Pet. 1:15–16). In the gospels we hear: 'Be merciful, *even as* your Father is merciful' (Luke 6:36) and: 'You therefore must be perfect as your heavenly Father is perfect' (Matt. 5:48). This 'as' can be turned around in the same gospel when in prayer we ask God to act *as* we have: 'Forgive us our debts *as* we also have forgiven our debtors' (Matt. 6:12). But God will comply with our request only if we have first acted towards others *as* he has done. The word is also used in the gospels with reference to Christ. '*As* the Father has sent me, so send I you' (John 20:21).

There are many examples. But what we are discovering here is a basic structure of the gospel: there is a certain agreement, analogy, comparability between God and man. Deliberately I do not use only one of these concepts, because all suffer under their own history! But in each of the concepts there is an element of truth. God's children do in some sense 'look like' him, or are made in his likeness. Indeed the summing up of the law that Jesus gives shows a remarkable similarity to what we understand to be the being of God, and here too we need to speak of a 'likeness': '*God is love*' and 'Thou shalt *love* the LORD thy God with *all thy heart* ...and...thy neighbour as thyself'. It seems as though God wished to fashion man into a likeness of himself by means of the law, so that man, for example, was to rest on the sabbath *because* God rested on the sabbath.[92] It is not only the 'as' utterances that point to a particular agreement between God and ourselves, but the entire admonitory (paranetic) wealth of the New Testament. Ephesians 4:24 for example is important, serving as a caption for the list of admonitions that follow. It is generally recognised that this utterance is an allusion to Genesis 1:26. As God created man in his image, so the new man (the new life under the dominion of Christ) 'is created after the likeness of God in true righteousness and holiness', indicating a definite 'agreement with God', and must be seen as Paul's version of the image of God. 'True righteousness and holiness' would then indicate what the image is, and what the agreement between God and man consists of.

What follows after this verse (v. 25 f) is a concrete description of the new man (or the image of God) in terms of the behaviour of God himself. It is not surprising then that the 'as' relating our new life to God (Christ) is explicitly repeated several times (4:32; 5:2). In fact this 'as' is the presupposition of every admonition because we are God's children and must therefore be *as* he himself is.

While the 'as' does not occur as often in the Old Testament, the matter itself does. Here are a few examples chosen at random. In Exodus 22:25–27 the people are called upon not 'to be to him as a creditor', if they have lent money to a poor man. Then too, clothes taken as pledge from a poor man must be given back before evening, lest he become cold during the night. Should the Israelites not do this, and the poor man calls on the LORD, 'I will hear, for I am compassionate'. The Israelite is therefore called to act mercifully towards the poor man because the LORD is compassionate and will help him when he is in need. In Leviticus 11:44; 19:2 and 20:7, 26 there is the familiar call on the people to be holy 'because, I, the LORD your God am holy'. And the entire prophetic message against injustice and violence and oppression (chapter 1)[93] derives its force and sharpness from the fact that God is just and acts righteously, because he is Father to the orphan and husband to the widow. The deepest reason why Israel must be merciful is that God is merciful. When Israel is unfaithful, he reproaches their unfaithfulness. Because he had remained faithful to them, they too should have been faithful to him, as is clear from Jeremiah 2:5: 'Thus says the LORD, "What wrong did your fathers find in me that they went far from me, and went after worthlessness and became worthless?"' Perhaps the most comprehensive 'agreement' between God and man in the Old Testament is in an idea which recurs quite frequently, that people should walk in God's ways (Pss. 81:14; 128:1; cf. also Pss. 25:4; 27:11).

It is therefore not strange that it is difficult to define the content of the image of God. It is reflected in as great a variety of facts as the wealth of paranetic material in the Bible. The entire life of man is covered by the concept. The whole man in his whole life is the image of God, and is called to be the image of God.[94] When the image of God is spoken of in terms of 'righteousness and true holiness' in the answer to question 6 of the Heidelberg Catechism, the reference is of course to Ephesians 4:24, and must be understood in terms of the meaning it has in Ephesians 4, i.e. as a summary, or caption, of the whole of life which is discussed in the subsequent verses. That the Catechism in fact understands it in this way is clear from the description given to the image of God in the rest of the answer to question 6.

This view, that the image of God lies in a particular harmony between God and man, cannot be rejected by way of an appeal to Genesis 3:4 f, and a definition of the essence of sin as the ambition to 'be like God'. Anyone doing this forgets that words do not always have the same meaning. Genesis 3:4 f represents a different form of being 'like God', a disobedient and rebellious form. It teaches us how *not* to be like God, but it in no way contradicts the multitude of instances in which we are clearly called to be like God.

Besides the analogy or agreement or particular similarity between God and man, Berkouwer points out that there is another concept that is often introduced in the discussion of the image of God: *representation*.[95] This concept is not separate from the previous concepts. It is not as if in addition to analogy we also have representation. Rather, *because* there is a certain similarity between God and man, and this similarity is not confined to man's inner life (which was evident from the 'as' admonitions), God becomes *visible* in the life of man, and man must represent God: literally, he must make God present on earth. The word transparent could be used here: man must become transparent so that God can be seen through him, as through a window. Because it is in the believers that the image of God is restored, and where Christ, the image of God, is formed, it is especially their task to make God visible in the world. The command is that we *do* something, so that the Father can become visible, can, so to speak, come into focus. 'Let your light so shine before men that they may see your good works and glorify your Father who is in heaven' (Matt. 5:16). They are *our* good works (even if in the final analysis we receive them as a gift from God – Eph. 2:10), but through them the Father must be glorified. 2 Corinthians 3:18 tells us something similar. 'And because for us there is no veil over the face, we all reflect as in a mirror the splendour of the Lord; thus we are transfigured into his likeness, from splendour to splendour; such is the influence of the Lord who is Spirit' (NEB). There was a veil over Moses' face that concealed its radiance (v. 13), but from our face (life) the glory of the Lord shines. F. Pop comments that this person in whom the Spirit has begun a transformation, begins to exhibit many characteristics which are reminiscent of the virtues of the LORD: his goodness, love, majesty, power, life. God's compassion, grace, faithfulness, stability, patience are embodied in him. He begins to display the signs of the image of God; he begins to reflect the glory of the Lord. And Paul says that this is true of all. It refers to all Christians and stamps their lives. It is their badge of identification. For this reason they are able to be like letters written by the Spirit of the living God, known and read by all men (3:2 f). Thus Pop.[96] So then, the image of God is concerned with the substantial reality and visibility of our entire life, as a life which must draw back the curtain and make God visible to the world, to allow all to see the things that are of concern to him. Of course this is not possible if we look to our own potentiality, but it becomes possible when Jesus Christ, the image of God, takes form in our lives.

The reason why not all human analogies are applied to God in the Bible is also clear from what has been said. In contrast to the religions around Israel and Greek religion, where the most abhorrent sins were committed by the gods, the anthropomorphisms in the Scripture are circumscribed. This limitation is based on the fact that the anthropomorphisms are essentially derived from the theomorphic character of man. Because man is made in God's image, it is possible to speak of God in human terms. But then only in terms of man as God willed and intended him to be, and not in terms of man the sinner.

Kuitert has pointed out other limitations to the anthropomorphisms.[97] While sin relates to something inhuman in man, something that is inappropriate to man, there are two other facets of man's life that are not used in the anthropomorphisms of the Bible. The first is the vital rhythm of life – birth and death. These features, so peculiar to our human life, are never applied to the LORD. He was not born, nor does he die. The other area excluded is that of man's sexuality. While the prophets do use the analogy of marriage, with God as the man and the people as the woman, and the unfaithfulness of the people is likened to adultery or prostitution (especially in Hosea), no sexual functions are ever ascribed to God. These two limitations are of great importance. Firstly because they are so peculiar to our human life that they would without any doubt have been applied to God if God were merely a product (projection) of Israel's thinking and longing (Feuerbach). Secondly, because in the religions around Israel, and indeed in almost all heathen religions, the regular death (or sleep) and resurrection of the gods, as well as their sexual lives, feature prominently.[98] Here then is a further point of radical difference between the true God and the gods. The gods were personified nature powers (chapter 1), and it is accordingly not surprising that such basic aspects of created reality as propagation and birth would have a significant importance for them. But God is different. *He* determines in what sense man is to be his image, and as a result he is free to declare certain aspects of our lives, regardless of how important they may be to us, unsuitable for proclaiming the truth about him.

Earlier in this chapter we indicated a limit to the use of anthropomorphism,[99] and proposed that the real significance of anthropomorphisms is that they lead us to speak of God in terms of the Man, Jesus Christ. Here we now have the reason for saying this. We are not able to speak about God in terms other than those he has given. He made us in his image, and in doing so created in us a certain agreement, likeness, analogy between himself and us. On these grounds we can speak of him in human terms, but not without limits. In his word he has also given us the limits within which we must remain. One cannot therefore say without qualification that it is correct to speak 'anthropomorphically' about God. What we may and must say is that it is correct to speak in anthropomorphic terms about God within the limitations imposed by the Scriptures.

The anthropomorphisms provide us with a suitable, appropriate and indeed a divine way of speaking about God. We do not need to surround them with conditions, but must regard them as a gift from the hand of the LORD. They are supremely the structure of the proclamation of the prophets and apostles, by which the living God is distinguished from the barren god-concept of Greek philosophy. The God of Israel is involved in history, and in his freedom has bound himself irreversibly to his creation. He reacts to the faithfulness and unfaithfulness of his people. This involvement is genuine and real, and such that it actually affects God so that he is delighted and enjoys the obedience of his children. He is glad when they glorify and serve him, and he is shocked, surprised and pained and even experiences frustration when his people, against all expectations and reason, break his covenant, turn their backs on him and serve other gods.

This proclamation in human terms does not have as a primary intention the portrayal of God's emotional life but, like all Scripture, has a practical objective. It aims at convincing us that God cares for us, that we matter to him, that it is dangerous both to our life and eternal destiny to ignore his appeal, but that he loves us; so that with him we are safe. He ensures that we may live near him without fear (in the sense of being anxious about the overwhelming greatness of God), as sheep that follow their shepherd daily,[100] and as a heifer might eat from the kindly hand of a good farmer (Hos. 11:4). The anthropomorphisms above all proclaim the nearness of God, and deliver us from a concept of a God who is different, remote and inaccessible, a concept that would make us into practical deists who think that this little world and our little personal lives are too insignificant to warrant God's attention.

God cares – for us, for our world, and for our history! This is the heart of biblical anthropomorphism.

3

God and history

The first two chapters have dealt with God's involvement in history, albeit at times only indirectly, and the fourth will continue with this theme. That the subject is given further special attention here is due entirely to its exceptional importance. We have no knowledge of God other than in and through his participation in our history. Indeed our history is actually his history with his creation, in which we are granted a share. For this reason the chapter before us must take up specific themes in addition to those dealt with indirectly in other chapters, such as the living God, the covenant, the providence of God, the counsel of God.

While these themes have an unavoidable link with the doctrine of election, this will not be dealt with further here. For, on the one hand, the doctrine of election is such a comprehensive subject that it ought not to be treated as a subordinate issue in a single chapter. And on the other hand, so many of the problems surrounding and accompanying the doctrine of election arise directly from our view of God that is necessary first of all to engage in a reasonably comprehensive study of the biblical doctrine of God before undertaking a formulation of the doctrine of election. A static immoveable God patterned on the god-concept of Greek philosophy yields a concept of election very different from that which comes from the doctrine of the true God who is living and active in history.[1]

Although the subject of God and history has been a burning issue in the theology of recent decades, it is far from self-evident that there is a positive relationship between God and history. In the concrete historical circumstances in which we find ourselves, it has become an enormous problem to believe in God and to see a meaningful direction and purpose in history. The sudden rise of the God-is-dead theology was a sign of this. The actual course of history, and especially the development of certain of the natural sciences and technology, led some theologians to conclude that there was no longer any room for God in history, and they declared that God was dead.

THE GOD-IS-DEAD THEOLOGY

While the expression 'God is dead' goes back as far as Friedrich Nietzsche, the atheistic philosopher, it was in the sixties of this century that it was first used by theologians to indicate a certain line of thought within the church.[2]

To understand what these theologians meant it is important to remember the time when these trends came to the fore, namely, in the nineteen-sixties. It was a time of unequalled development in the natural sciences and technology. Space exploration had begun, the first heart-transplants were performed, increased rainfall began to be successfully achieved – to mention only a few of the spectacular advances.

And God? Where was he? In the midst of all these achievements did man still need him? In this connection D. Sölle said that in earlier years when we were sick, we said a prayer and therefore needed the Lord, whereas today we ring the doctor; previously we expected rain from God, today we make it ourselves; in earlier years we thought of the heavens (e.g. the moon) as God's domain prohibited to us, but today the moon is but the first stage on our journey into space.

What has happened? In this view, God has lost his functions one by one. Gradually we have begun to provide for ourselves those things that previously we asked from him. In this way he has gradually disappeared from our world of experience and has been displaced by our scientific advances from the things that concern us. Consequently more and more people in the 'Christian' west live through their days and nights without a thought of God, and seem to be none the worse for it. Even those who remain Christians in the formal sense might devote a couple of minutes a day to reading the Bible and saying a prayer, but for the rest of the day they live much like the rest. And seemingly, western man today has a more certain, safer, and more prosperous life than ever before. Sölle then comes to the conclusion that man himself has taken over the functions previously ascribed to God, and performs them better than he! Since God is 'dead', i.e. has vanished from man's world of concern, man seems to be better off than ever before![3]

Besides this process in which God has lost his 'functions' in our community life, there have been colossal disasters in this century which have also played their part in the rise of God-is-dead theology. There have of course always been terrible disasters on earth, but improved communications have made us more aware of how many there are, and how much pain is caused by them. In 1755 there was the Lisbon earthquake; some years back there was the tidal-wave disaster in Pakistan. Where was God then? the theologians ask. And what of the two horrifying world wars? And what of nuclear weapons? What of Hiroshima, and Auschwitz (where it is estimated that 6 million Jews died)? And what of the indescribable suffering in Vietnam? Where was God then? If he was there, if he is alive, if he is love, how could these things have happened?

Here then we have two important aspects of the background to the God-is-dead theology: the miseries of the world, and man's phenomenal technological advances. The God-is-dead theologians were convinced that God was doing nothing in these extraordinary hardships, and furthermore that we hardly needed him any longer for the provision of our daily needs. In this sense they said that God was dead. It should actually be understood figuratively. God no longer functions; he does not do what is expected of him, and we virtually have no further need of him and therefore he disappears from our thinking and wanting. God is accordingly 'dead' in the sense, for example, that a political conviction might be called dead when it ceases to capture the imagination of the people and leaves them indifferent.

We God really dead, various reactions would be possible. One might feel it to be a terrible tragedy and be extremely agitated. But someone like Altizer endeavoured to bring out a more 'positive' meaning. He asserted that God deliberately intended to die. To Altizer this was an essential aspect of the dialectical relationship between God and man, God and creation, God and history. He saw an essential rivalry between God and man, and therefore between concern for God and concern for man and the world. Anyone living for God and loving him with all his heart loses sight of his fellowman and the need of the world. The ascetics, monks, and nuns would be a good example of this. Further examples would be the beautiful cathedrals built 'to the glory of God' while masses of people went hungry, or white church elders in South Africa, piously donning their Sunday suits, while their black labourers receive insufficient wages to maintain themselves and their families in a respectable way of life.

God therefore had to be eliminated, so that man in his need could receive attention. But, because God is love, he wished to disappear so that the living conditions of the masses could be improved. In fact, from the very beginning God has been engaged in a process of self-elimination for the sake of humanity. The most vivid example of this was his incarnation in Jesus of Nazareth. He emptied himself, and in the thought of Altizer and Hamilton, this meant that he terminated his divine existence totally and radically in Jesus. God became Jesus – surrendering his own existence completely.

Since these theologians do not believe that Jesus rose from the dead, a question arises as to what happened to God after the death of Jesus. Their answer is that the incarnation was but the beginning of the process in which God identifies himself with, and surrenders himself to, world history. The incarnation continues through the Holy Spirit, and God's identification with the world is progressively more intense as he makes all things new. Because God is love, he does not wish to remain aloof (transcendent) from the world, distracting our attention from the need of humanity. He enters the world, filling it with his love, in such a way that the world demands and deserves our full attention, so that God continues his incarnation in us. The distinction between God and man comes to an end. God became man, and in so doing ceased to be God. The world must be saved and preserved, and to this end God surrenders himself. He does this deliberately because God and man (God and the world) are rivals. Either the one or the other receives attention. For our sake and because

of our need God dies and vanishes into a continuing incarnation, in order
that we might live.

We have now reached a point in the history of God's continuing
incarnation at which the incarnation must be radically promoted, so that
the *Jenseits* (the beyond) can be wholly absorbed in the *Diesseits* (this
reality, in which we are). When this is achieved no transcendent Father
God will remain and the 'temporal' reality and history will provide the
only horizons within which everything is to take place. This point is then
called the moment of the 'death' of God.

This whole line of thought is so completely unchristian that it is not
surprising that after a decade and a half it exercises little visible influence,
and in circles such as the World Council of Churches has had no influence
at all.

In criticism of this 'theology' one could observe that the concept of
'salvation' has been severely attenuated. Aspects of it such as the forgiveness of sins, adoption, eternal life vanish completely. Salvation becomes
happiness and prosperity now, on this earth. There is no expectation of
the return of Christ or the gift of a new earth from the hand of God. In
this one-sided view there is of course an element of truth and a legitimate
criticism of earlier views which saw salvation only as the forgiveness of
sins and blessedness in the life hereafter.

And yet an exclusive 'here and now' view of salvation is not actually the
most appropriate answer to an 'exclusive there and then' view. When
reconciliation with God, the forgiveness of sins, the resurrection and
eternal life are excised from salvation, then happiness and prosperity and
opportunities in life here and now also lose their meaning. 'If for this life
only we have hoped in Christ, we are of all men most to be pitied'
(1 Cor. 15:19). Such a one-sided view rests on the unbiblical idea that
God and man are competitors, and that one must *either* love God with all
one's heart *or* one's neighbour as oneself. Of course one must admit that
even though this tension is unbiblical, it does nevertheless occur. It may
be necessary to go even further, and say that almost without exception
there is a tendency both among churches and individual Christians to
align their lives either vertically (towards God) or horizontally (towards
mankind). It is even possible to make a division between the churches.
The more 'evangelical' a church is, the less attention does it give to the
socio-economic needs of people, and conversely, the more a church is
concerned with social problems, the less attention does it appear to give
to reconciliation with God, forgiveness of sins and personal piety.

Why this is so is difficult to determine. The fact is that from a
scriptural perspective such a division is illegitimate and unacceptable.
One could even say that in their extreme forms, 'verticalism' and
'horizontalism' both fail in their intended objective – whether it be God
or man. That is to say, the person who thinks he is serving God but
bypasses the need of his neighbour, or who claims to be concerned about
the reconciliation of his fellow man with God but has no eye for his social

and economic needs, is in fact involved neither with God nor with the needs of his fellow man. Not with God, because God's peace (*shalom*) is promised to his people; and not with his fellow man, because man is not an abstract being who merely has a relationship to God, but is a substantial being in a real life situation (with a stomach, a feeling of respect, and a need for relationships etc.).

And all this must be repeated to those who are horizontally aligned. Anyone who is completely preoccupied with the socio-economic needs of mankind has lost touch with God (Ps. 73 reminds that the eyes of the 'wicked', 'godless', swell out with fatness, but the believer is chastened every morning), and with his fellow men, because man is man-before-God,[4] and therefore anyone wishing to help a person must give attention to his relationship to God.

The either/or aspect of the God-is-dead theology must therefore be firmly rejected. We must however consider this further. The answer to this onesidedness is not merely the finding of a balance between God and man, between the vertical and the horizontal. Anyone trying to find a balance, even with the very best intentions, is continuing with the assumption that God and man are rivals and that the needs of both must be given adequate attention. However if the *covenant* is taken as the point of departure (and we deal with this later), then, because the covenant is concerned with Israel's God as the Creator God, it is impossible to be aligned with God without being involved with man or to be aligned with man without being involved with God. Man is God's man. Man is a creature who finds the meaning and purpose of his life in God and in living before God. And God is no longer God without being the God of man, his Creator, Reconciler and Destiny. There is therefore no essential rivalry between God and man demanding that a careful distribution of time be made between God and man, lest one of the two receive an undue proportion. Anyone rightly related to God is by that very fact rightly concerned about man, and indeed, the whole man and the actualisation of his full *shalom* (peace, salvation). And the person who is concerned with man, with God's man, with man before God, is thereby also concerned with God and with the work and glory of God.

These propositions are not automatically true but are in principle, biblically true. That is to say, things can be done differently, but then they are done wrongly. The church must continually point out this link in its preaching, and repeatedly emphasise the integral connection between love for God and love for man, in the same way that justification cannot in principle be separated from sanctification in the sense that men must continually be called to holiness of life. Yet the fact that this pastoral need is always there, should not detract from the fundamental union and involvement of God and man (and love for God and love for man). In fact various New Testament scholars have pointed out Paul's tendency to summarise the whole of the law in terms of love for one's neighbour. In Romans 13:8–10 love for one's neighbour is mentioned twice as the fulfilling of the law. In Galatians 5:14, he says with emphasis: 'For the whole law is fulfilled in one word, "You shall love your neighbour as yourself".' (NEB and other modern translations read: 'one commandment'.) James too in a particular situation summarises everything in 'the royal law according to the scripture, "You shall love your neighbour as yourself"' (Jas. 2:8). Jesus, in answering the rich young ruler's question about eternal life, also summarises the whole law in terms of love for one's neighbour. The demand that Jesus proceeds to make of him is genuinely 'horizontal' (if one is to persist in thinking in terms of the unbiblical concept of rivalry between God and man): 'Go, sell what you have and give to the poor... and come, follow me' (Mark 10:21).

This 'one-sidedness' in Jesus, Paul and James is actually based on the presupposition, regarded as self-evident, that there is an essential connection between God and man; that man is God's man, and that love for man in obedience to the command of God is a service in love to God. It is possible that when Jesus 'summed up' the law he meant that the second commandment was the same in content as the first, and not merely that it was equally important. Various new translations incline in this direction. The TEV for example: 'The second most important commandment is like it' (Matt. 22:39). The word *homoia* ('like') can indicate an agreement in content here, as elsewhere in Matthew. For example, in 11:16 ('like'). See also: 13:31, 33, 44, 45, 47, 52; 20:1, where in every case there is definitely such an agreement. This approach would then mean that when Jesus answered the lawyer's question concerning the greatest commandment, he was saying that the law and the prophets can be viewed from two angles: either from the perspective of love for God, or of love for man, but that either approach would give a view of the whole law.

It is therefore not a question of a choice between these two commandments, which to obey and which to disregard, for disregarding one means disregarding the other which is *like* it. The whole of God's will is found in these *two* commandments together (Matt. 22:40). It was for this reason that Amos had to tell the people that all their religious fervour was of no value, and in fact had a negative, irritating effect on God, because of their socio-political injustices (Amos 5:21–24). While Amos did not criticise their religious activities, these were obnoxious because of their social wickedness.

In John too (13:34–35) we find a concentration of the entire will of God in love for one's neighbour (focussed in John on brotherly love but by no means confined to this),[5] which should indeed be the mark of the follower of Jesus. When the teachers of false doctrine in the church attempted to separate the 'first commandment' (love for God) from the 'second' (love for one's neighbour), they encountered a vigorous reaction from John: 'If anyone says, "I love God", and hates his brother, he is a liar' (1 John 4:20). God's love achieves its objective in us when we love one another. There is also a striking 'deviating' parallel in John: 'If God so loved us, we also ought to love (not *him* but) one another' (4:11). He laid down his life for us, and therefore we ought to lay down our lives, not for him as we might again have expected, but for the brethren (3:16).

It is because the gospel is an essential unity, and not a collection of separate, equal truths that must be preached simultaneously with equal emphasis, that these 'one-sided emphases' are not one-sided at all, but are the truth for a particular hour and situation. And the church will have to pray continually to be prophetic in this respect, that it may know in what way the will of God must take shape in every concrete situation. If a prophet had to proclaim God's word to the meeting of the World Council of Churches the possibility is not to be excluded that he would have called out, in a variation on Paul's words: 'For the whole law is fulfilled in one word: You shall love the LORD your God with all your heart and all your soul and all your mind. And though you may be concerned about the need of the world, you reflect in this concern nothing that is Christian unless it is the love of Christ that drives you to it.' At the same time it is possible that the same prophet might feel moved to say to us in the Reformed or Evangelical Churches: 'The whole of the law is fulfilled in one commandment: You must love your neighbour as yourself.'

From this inter-relationship between God and man, between love for God and love for man, from this integral unity of the gospel which means that everything repeatedly revolves around a single issue, it is evident that any suggestion of rivalry between God and man is a lamentable misunderstanding of the gospel, a disobedience to the Lord Jesus and, as the principal feature of the God-is-dead theology, is to be totally rejected.

A second criticism, to which passing reference has already been made, must be directed against the view that salvation is to be confined to an adequate life and prosperity here and now. Here too the concepts of vertical and horizontal are used in such a way as to identify the vertical with eternal life, the forgiveness of sins, peace with God, while horizontal would relate to justice in human relationships, a life of adequate opportunity and self-realisation for all men in the here and now. These two facets are just as closely bound to each other, and constitute two aspects of the same thing in the Old Testament, God's peace (*shalom*). This peace embraces all relationships: peace with God ('peace of heart'), peace between nations, in human relationships; it includes good health, prosperity etc. Because God created the whole man, he has good intentions for the whole man. A one-sided concern about the 'soul' is as unbiblical as a one-sided concern about the 'body'. God became man to serve man, to save *people*. Once again, a concern with one aspect is not half the truth. In the biblical view it is all or nothing.[6] A one-sided preaching of the 'gospel' without desiring, and where possible giving a full human life to others, has just as little to do with the true gospel as a one-sided humanistic human rights' campaign without the driving force of Jesus Christ.[7] Although God in his goodness, and as it were through a miracle, has used one-sided approaches (for example, on the one hand, the missionary activity of the nineteenth century pietistic missionary organizations or, contrariwise, the 'social gospel') to the good, yet it must be seen as highly undesirable that one church or group of churches should preach eternal salvation without social justice, while another church or group of churches preaches social justice without eternal salvation. Not only does this lead to great confusion, but is a betrayal of the gospel, a betrayal of the belief that God made the whole man. There is an urgent need for contact between such groups of churches. God is greater than our one-sided emphasis, and his salvation embraces our whole life.

Attention must next be given to one of the most potent driving forces behind the God-is-dead theology, the *absence* of God. Besides his loss of functions, his apparent absence from world catastrophes and cruelties so gripped certain theologians that they could no longer believe that he existed or was involved in these tragedies. Where was he in Vietnam? In Auschwitz? These are questions that were repeatedly asked. If God is a God of love, why should my child be deformed? Why should my wife be murdered? These are questions which all have heard. How many people call on God in their need, and are not helped? These are things that we have all wrestled with at one time or another. The question asked by these theologians are our questions, even if we were not so involved in the Second World War, or Vietnam, or Biafra.

The first mistake these theologians made was to regard these as *modern* problems. Sölle, for example, proceeds from the assumption that God was conceivable to Luther, but that this is not the case today. In reality, the experience of God's absence stretches back to the beginnings of Israel's contact with the LORD.[8] The Psalms especially are full of the problem. How the suffering righteous cry out to God for salvation from their need and wretchedness! And how often God (apparently) does not answer and remains far away, as is clear from Psalm 10:1 'Why dost thou stand afar off, O LORD? Why dost thou hide thyself in times of trouble?' (Read the remainder of the Psalm, as well as the others that follow, from which quotations are taken.) 13:1: 'How long, O LORD? Wilt thou forget me for ever? How long wilt thou hide thy face from me?' 42:9: 'I say to God, my rock; "Why hast thou forgotten me? Why go I mourning because of the oppression of the enemy?"' 88:14: 'O LORD, why dost thou cast me off? Why dost thou hide thy face from me?' Compare also: Lamentations 3:8; Isaiah 45:5; 64:1, and the book of Job![9] It is evident that the absence of God, his apparent inaction when a believer, or his people (his church) are in need, is an experience as old as faith itself. All this means that the God-is-dead theologians have not come up with something modern. We have not only recently stumbled across these problems. Reliable witnesses over the centuries testify to this. But, and this is what is important, there is a radical difference between the way in which the believers in the Bible reacted to the problem and the way in which the God-is-dead theologians reacted. The believers accepted the absence of God not as a fact, a datum on which they should now (after the death of God!) proceed to build a theology. On the contrary, they could not accept it; they rebelled against it; they called on God; they 'wrestled with God' over his absence and inaction.

At times they found the explanation of God's absence in their sins, and God's anger against these. Sin could thus be a cause of God's absence. In Psalm 30:7 the poet expresses it in these words: 'Thou dost hide thy face, I was dismayed,' but in verse 6 he confesses that his pride and self-confidence were the reason why God had acted against him in anger: 'As for me, I said in my prosperity, "I shall never be moved".' Deuteronomy 31:16-17 also indicates that God would forsake his people were they to forsake him and break his covenant. See also Micah 3:4; Ezekiel 39:23, 24; Isaiah 59:1-3.

In contrast to this the God-is-dead theologians take no account of our sin and God's wrath. They accept no connection between the disasters of the world and the wrath of God over man's sins. Naturally we cannot find satisfactory solutions to all problems in this way, but the Scriptures do indicate that through disasters and plagues the LORD calls his people to repentance. Anyone who reckons with the reality of God's anger (which has been deserved) also learns to be thankful for his grace, and stands amazed that he does not destroy the earth.

Those who explain away his wrath at the same time lose the sense of awed gratitude for Golgotha; in fact, they lose God himself. As a result the God-is-dead theologians failed to share the psalmist's experience in which he confessed his guilt and thereafter knew again the overflowing joy of God's presence and fellowship (Ps. 32:1-5).

But on the other hand, believers have not always found an explanation for God's absence and inaction. In the Scriptures a sense of bewilderment over God's absence is more frequent than a clear insight into why he is no longer there.[10] It is in these circumstances that we encounter the struggle, the distress over the fact that God has deprived them of his company – so different from the God-is-dead theologians, who calmly proceeded to construct a theology without God.

It is in the psalms especially that the cry of the person in need is heard. Psalms 44 and 88 are good examples. In Psalm 44 the people are in dire straits. According to verses 9-16 they had been humiliated, defeated, trampled on, scattered abroad and taunted by their enemies. But, and this is the ultimate indignity, the LORD had done it all to them. Notice the repeated 'thou'. This feature which sees the LORD as the actual enemy of the people is found repeatedly in the prophets, and especially in Amos. (Notice the 'I' in Amos 3:14-15; 4:1-12; 8:9-11; 9:1-9.) But then there is a reason for it, for the people had been warned countless times and called to repentance, without responding. They were accordingly ripe for destruction. (Cf. Rom. 9:22 'made for', 'prepared for'.) But Psalm 44 presents a very different situation. The humbled people reverently recall God's mighty acts for their fathers when he brought them out of Egypt and led them into Canaan (v. 1-3), and their trust has been unceasingly in the LORD alone (v. 4-8). On this follows: '*Yet* thou hast cast us off...'

(v.9) and verse 71 ends the description of shame and misery with the words: 'All this has come upon us *though* we have not forgotten thee or been false to thy covenant'. The 'though' contains surprise and pain: How could God do it? In verse 22 some light glimmers through, which is uncertain and yet sometimes helps to answer these most perplexing questions: 'Nay, *for thy sake* (that is, on account of our relationship to you) we are slain all day long', but two facts indicate how uncertain this consolation is. First, that it was the LORD who had handed them over to their enemies. And secondly, the 'explanation' ('for thy sake') is followed by the urgent, almost accusing cry, 'Rouse thyself! Why sleepest thou O LORD?' (v. 23), and the anguished 'Why?' of verse 24 ('Why dost thou hide thy face?'). So, in spite of verse 22 we must accept that the people of the LORD had found no answer to their cry, and that the LORD had not broken his silence or his absence. Yet they kept up their cry, complaining *to God* over his failure to be with them or to do anything.

Psalm 88 is another example of the anxious 'why?' that follows God's failure to respond to a cry for help. This person is in great need (apparently physical illness). But his greatest need arises from God's failure to answer his call for help which he pours out night and day (v. 1). In verse 14 comes the urgent question: 'O LORD, why dost thou cast me off? Why dost thou hide thy face from me?' He receives no answer. He does not know why God is far from him, and no answer is given to his 'Why?'. But he continues to plead with God. And this is the deepest difference between the Psalms and God-is-dead theology. The God-is-dead theologians formulate a proposition about God's absence and then theorise (theologise) about it. The psalmist persists in wrestling *with God* about his absence. Think of Psalm 22:1: '*My* God, *my* God, why hast thou forsaken me?' God's remoteness is not a matter of theological speculation, but rather a totally unacceptable situation about which one can only persist in complaining... to God.

No explanation can be given for this absence on God's part (as distinct from the first case in which it was caused by the worshipper's sin). The most moving example of this took place on the cross when Jesus cried out, 'My God, my God, why hast thou forsaken me?' Anyone who thinks that he has a complete explanation for this, has not perceived how incomprehensible that event was.

But notice that he does not make the Father's absence a point of departure for theological speculation. Rather he clings to the Father and wrestles with him over his intolerable absence: '*My* God, *my* God, why hast thou forsaken me?'

In this prayer he too received no theoretical answer to his 'why', but rather the wonderful experience of being raised from the dead on the third day by the Father. In this way his forsakenness was brought to an end by a new act, and replaced by a renewed relationship.

Many who engaged in prayer in the Old Testament experienced a restoration of fellowship after the experience of God's absence. Read

Psalm 22:24: 'he has heard, when he cried to him'; verses 22–31 are a song of praise to God in which the outcome of the struggle is announced and everyone is summoned to trust in God.

This is the point at which there occurs an irreversible parting of the ways. Those who forsake God, and accept his absence as final, building their theology on this assumption, with a view to living and theologising without him in the future, cannot look forward to the end of God's absence and renewal of fellowship with him. While Sölle leaves the possibility open that God might turn up again some time in the future, it is a theoretical possibility that plays no decisive role in her theology.

Although not all those who pray experience God's re-emergence out of his absence, we have in the Scriptures, and especially in Jesus, examples of how believers should conduct themselves in such circumstances. Furthermore the biblical promises concerning the resurrection from the dead give us the prospect that on the new earth God's absence will be among the old things that have passed away. There God will live among his people on the new earth (Rev. 21–22).

It is by means of these examples, and promises that the LORD sustains us in times when we painfully experience the seeming absence of God. The Old Testament believers teach us how they clung to God by faith, despite and in the midst of their bitter experience of his absence. This is the paradox of their struggle. They doubt God, yet still hold fast to him. They do not make a theoretical problem out of God's absence, but wrestle directly with him about his absence and inactivity. And they do so because in the thick of their glaring injustices and agony they believe in God as the *living* God.

THE LIVING GOD

This is a common description of God in the Bible and appears also in relation to the mocking of the gods. In contrast to the gods which are made by human hands, and which must be secured from falling, with hammer and nails, and which can do neither good nor evil (i.e. nothing), God is called 'the living God and the everlasting King' (Jer. 10:10). H. J. Kraus has shown that the name, the living God, is very old and was applied to the LORD in deliberate contrast to the dying, or dead gods of Israel's neighbours.[11] In contrast to the gods that died annually, and then rose again in the spring, there was the LORD who never 'slumbered nor slept' (Ps. 121:1–3).

Some scholars in the field of the Science of Religion have argued that the Old Testament does accept the idea of gods that die and rise again and expresses it especially in the assertion that God 'sleeps' and 'awakens'. See for example, Psalms 7:7; 9:20; 10:12; 35:23; 44:23; 59:5; Isaiah 51:9 and especially Psalm 78:65. It is wrong, however, to proceed from the mere co-incidence of certain words and concepts (such as 'sleep' or 'awaken') to the conclusion that there is an agreement between the biblical message and its heathen environment. Words derive their meaning from the context in which they are used. Words such as 'sleep' and 'awaken' have a meaning in the Bible different from what they have, for example, in Baal worship. First of all, attention must be paid to those utterances in which it is expressly *denied* that the LORD sleeps: 'He who keeps you will not slumber. Behold he who keeps Israel will neither slumber nor sleep' (Ps. 121:3–4). The antithetical, polemical character of this utterance becomes even clearer when it is read against the background of 1 Kings 18, where Baal was indeed asleep, but the LORD was not!

We can now return to the expression in Psalm 44:23, and note the context: 'Rouse thyself! Why sleepest thou, O LORD? Awake, do not *cast us off* for ever. *Why dost thou hide thy face?* Why dost thou *forget* our affliction and oppression?'

The italicised words and phrases explain clearly the meaning of the words 'awake' and 'sleep': the LORD had *deliberately withdrawn* himself from his people, and had hidden himself from them. This action of hiding himself is expressed in the metaphor of sleep. There can be no suggestion of literal sleep here, any more than a literal 'forgetting' is implied. 'Forget' also refers to a deliberate act, as is clear from Jeremiah 31:34: 'I will *remember* their sin *no more*'.

When one moves in this way from the superficial sound of words to the meaning of the writer, it is clear that, for example, Psalm 18:46 has nothing to do with a 'God' who dies (as nature dies in the autumn) and now lives again. 'The LORD lives' is the call of the believer who has experienced the acts of God in the life of his people (v. 26–50). There is no suggestion of a God who was dead and now is alive again. Habbakuk 1:12 gives a powerful indication to the contrary: 'Art thou not from of old O LORD? My God, the holy, *the immortal*' (NEB – the better translation, rather than the older 'We shall not die'). Such a translation is in perfect harmony with the New Testament witness to the King of kings, 'who alone has immortality' (1 Tim. 6:16). It is in fact very possible that Habbakuk 1:12 is directed against the idea that God is like the Baals that periodically died and came to life again (along with the cycle of nature). (See also 1 Kgs. 18:27.)

Kraus has also drawn attention to the well-known oath formula: 'as the LORD *liveth*', which occurs a good hundred times in this form, and means that the person making the oath calls on the LORD to watch over his oath in the future. It points to the certainty with which Israel accepted the fact that the LORD was alive, and would remain so, a certainty derived from their history as a people and their personal experiences. It is again the exodus that is recalled in this connection, in various places such as Jeremiah 16:14–15 and Jeremiah 23:7–8. According to these references it was a standard formula: 'As the LORD lives, who brought up the people of Israel out of the land of Egypt.' It was through his intervention in their history that they had learned to know him as the living God. However in these verses the prophet says that a new formula will replace this old one: 'As the LORD lives who brought up and led the descendants of the house of Israel out of the north country and out of all the countries where he had driven them' (the return from Babylon). This meant that the prophet was promising them a new intervention by God in their history, in their time of need and oppression, which would convince them even more that the LORD was alive – an intervention which took place a short while afterwards and which resulted in the return of the exiles to Jerusalem.

1 Kings 2:24 provides a second example. Here Solomon uses the oath formula: 'As the LORD lives, who has established me on the throne of David my father...'. This is a reference to 2 Samuel 7:12–16 where the Lord promised that David's son would sit on his throne. Solomon experienced this as a historical event in the life of his people, and saw in the fulfilment of this promise the proof that the LORD was alive.

David himself provides a further example, as he points from time to time to things that the LORD had done in his life, such as delivering him from the hands of his enemies (2 Sam. 4:9: 1 Kgs. 1:29).

That God is the living God has a fundamental and comprehensive significance in the Bible. T. C. Vriezen has said: 'God is a living God. The Old Testament speaks of His activity and His self-revelation, His works in nature and history, of His chastisement and His salvation, of His miracles and His mercy.... This remarkably unsystematic way of speaking about God, this seeing of his revelation in the most different forms, this experience of his intervention in the most divergent situations, all these things indicate that the living Being of God is a fundamental idea in the Hebrew concept of God.'[12]

In chapter 1, under the heading 'God acts', attention has already been given to the deeds of God. It was shown there that he differs from the gods in that he is the God who acts, who *does* things. It is exactly this that is at the heart of the confession that God is the living God. But it has a far more comprehensive significance than simply to proclaim his incomparability to the heathen's gods. This wider meaning lies especially in the relationship between God and history, with which we shall now deal.

That God is the living God renders the Greek philosophical god-concept alien and unsuitable as a way of describing the God of Israel. In a discussion of Exodus 3:14 Preuss shows that the Hebrews verb for 'is' does not mean 'being' or 'that which exists', but rather an act or an event. He then points to the striking expression that is often encountered in the prophets, usually translated, 'And the word of the LORD *came* to...' but which actually uses this Hebrew word for 'is'. One might therefore equally well translate this expression: 'The word of the LORD *happened*', or 'became a reality'. Exodus 3:14 is therefore in opposition to the idea of God as eternal being. On the basis of these words the Israelite found an association between the name 'LORD' and the verb 'happen', or 'do', or 'actualise'. The familiar expression that God would 'be with Israel', implied that Israel would experience, and learn to know God's deity through his *acts*. The being of God is found in his deeds. He would be with them in the future as the God who works, who would lead them by his deeds, who would accompany them until his purpose was achieved.[13] Elsewhere Preuss explains that the knowledge of the LORD is never a revelation of an inactive, immobile God but of God who actively intervenes in history. The LORD's deeds are continually directed towards man. He wishes man to learn to know him so that he will recognise him and (therefore!) entrust his future life to him. So, in this sense, God's deeds are always directed towards a future goal[14] – an aspect that will be developed more fully in chapter 4. Thus far Preuss.

The expression 'the living God' brings us then to the characteristic and unique view of history that is found in the Bible.[15] Israel's view of history as a purposeful unity of events, brought about by the LORD,[16] differs radically from the views of the great ancient cultures surrounding Israel. In Mesopotamia especially, centuries before the rise of Israel, a cyclical view of history had developed. From the rythmic repetition of the seasons and the rotating movement of the stars, it was accepted that world eras succeeded each other in a regular pattern, and that everything moved from order to chaos and then back to order again. Essentially it was a mythical cyclical pattern of thought viewing history as having no specific beginning or consummation, and involving the eternal repetition of all things. Cullmann has shown that this is also true of Greek thought,[17] and that on this point there is no real difference between the Greeks and the people of the ancient Near East.[18]

In contrast to this religiously sanctioned view of the mighty ancient eastern cultures, a radically different view emerged from a small and insignificant nation which saw history as an irreversible progression of events under the sovereign control of the LORD, who began it, accompanied it and would see it through to a definite conclusion.

A clear illustration of this unique view is to be found in Israel's feasts. These derived from the Canaanitic calendar of feasts, and were originally linked with the rotation of the seasons, seed time and harvest. This sequence had direct religious meaning for the Canaanites, as was evident also in their belief in the passing away of the gods with the coming of autumn and their subsequent resurrection in spring.

Israel changed this calendar of feasts, which was linked with nature, into one which was tied to history. The feast of unleavened bread was originally a feast linked with the beginning of the wheat harvest, but Israel changed this into a feast celebrating the exodus from Egypt (Exod. 23:15). The feast of the vintage (originally a nature celebration) became, for Israel, the feast of tabernacles, during which they spent seven days in branch shelters so 'that your generations may know that I made the people of Israel dwell in booths when I brought them out of the land of Egypt' (Lev. 23:43). In this way Israel changed the old agricultural and nature feasts into acts of historical remembrance because they did not base their existence in the periodic changes in nature, but in God's interventions in their history.

Israel's exodus from Egypt played a decisive role in this view of history. It was for them a unique and incomparable act which placed God in a category completely different from the gods, as is clear from Deuteronomy 4:32–35: 'For ask now of the days that are past... since the day that God created man upon the earth... whether such a great thing as this has ever happened... Did any people ever hear the voice of a god speaking out of the midst of a fire, as you have heard, and still live? Or has any god ever attempted to go and take a nation for himself from the midst of another nation, by trials, by signs, by wonders, and by war, by a mighty hand and by an outstretched arm, and by great terrors, according to all that the LORD your God did for you in Egypt before your eyes? To you it was shown that you might know that the LORD is God; there is none other besides him.' This means that no other god even tried to do what the LORD had done.

In this way, through what God had done in history, or rather, through the history that God had made with them, Israel learned to know him. Here there is no question of speculative thinking, philosophical reasoning, human ingenuity or perspicuity. Here there is no question of a universal truth that might be recognised by an astute observer anywhere on earth. The interest here is in specific events that these people had experienced and through which they had discovered *who*, and *what kind* of person the LORD was.

Gradually the people saw history in wider and more comprehensive terms. From the exodus they looked back and saw the hand of the LORD in the call of Abraham, and (later?) traced it back as far as creation itself. And as they moved into their future they experienced every phase of their history as the accomplishing of God's purposes with them: the entry into Canaan, the monarchy, the exile, the return. But always, it was a history which God continued to make with *them*. It was only in the apocalyptic literature of the Old Testament, and Daniel especially, that the whole world was incorporated into this view and it was seen that the consummation of history would occur when God had achieved his goal with all mankind.

A few aspects of Israel's view of history which are of great importance for the doctrine of God may be mentioned. The first concerns the sovereign authority with which the LORD achieved his objectives by using great world powers. One after the other they are taken into his service: Assyria, Nebuchadnezzar king of Babylon, Cyrus the Persian. He speaks of Assyria as 'the rod of my anger' (Isa. 10:5) against the northern kingdom; Nebuchadnezzar is called 'my servant' for the punishment of Judah (Jer. 25:9; 27:6; 43:10); Cyrus is even described as a messiah, or one anointed by the LORD (Isa. 45:1). He has them entirely in his control. He can 'whistle for the fly' at the sources of the streams of Egypt, and 'for the bee which is in the land of Assyria' (Isa. 7:18). While the custom might seem a little strange to us, we do at least know what it means to see a dog obey instantly in response to a whistle! The fact that these ancient kingdoms are only instruments in the LORD's hands is further illustrated by the utterance, that he will use them as a razor to shave bare the head and the feet and the beard of his people (7:20); and these are the greatly feared world powers!

In his supremacy, the LORD is not even bound to use these powers. Although they might be world powers before whom the nations collapse, the LORD is able to use them powerfully at one moment and to punish them at the next (Isa. 10:7–15 against Assyria, and Isa. 47, especially v. 5–7, against Babylon), because they had acted viciously and mercilessly against his people.

In this connection, Von Rad has pointed to the radical difference between the prophets' view of history and ours as Christians.[19] We are completely preoccupied with movements in the foreground – with the super-powers and their treaties and covenants, their armaments and threats, with their destructive activities or peace endeavours. These constitute history for us. Then, somewhere in the 'background' we search diligently for God, and for what he achieves in this confusion. Occasionally we see somewhere on the edge of events some meaning that we then ascribe to God, but for the greater part our view of 'God in history' is completely obscured by the foreground, the great powers. The message of the prophets stands in direct contrast to this. According to them God works directly and immediately in history. His decisions, acts, and purposes control everything and place the great powers completely in the shadows. He does indeed use them, but he and his acts dominate the situation so totally that – to select only one arbitrary example – it is never clear exactly who or what Amos thought would be the instrument by which the LORD would punish the northern kingdom: war, exile, plague or an earthquake? (See Amos 3:14–15; 4:12; 6:8 (war?); 6:9–10 (plague?); 6:11–12 (earthquake?).[20] God himself had become their enemy, and this is the message of Amos; he would intervene in history, using any method to execute his judgment on them.

This supremacy on God's part meant that neither Amos nor the other prophets needed to take prevailing circumstances into consideration nor to search for particular visible causes. When Amos predicted the destructive judgment on the northern kingdom, they were enjoying a period of unusual prosperity and calm, free of threats from without and entirely at ease about their future (3:15; 6:1–6, 13). And from a human point of view, this quiet was not a false calm, but a correct deduction from their actual situation. But because history is determined by God's free action, and he can whistle for a world power as a man might for his dog, the prophet can announce the impending judgment on the people even in the midst of such peace and plenty. The LORD is not dependent on particular international conditions. And the opposite is also true. When the people sat in humiliation and powerlessness in Babylon, and their actual situation said but one thing: 'My way is hid from the LORD, and my right is disregarded by my God' (Isa. 40:27), right there the promise came to them of the great things that the LORD would do for them, greater than ever before; greater even than the unique, incomparable exodus from Egypt (Isa. 43:18 f).[21]

Closely related to the LORD's independence of prevailing circumstances, is the fact the the LORD made known to his people in advance what he intended doing. This fact plays an important role in Deutero-Isaiah in persuading the people about the incomparability of God in relation to the Babylonian gods. It serves as a powerful proof of God, but because it relates so closely to the question of God and the future we will defer discussion until we come to chapter 4.

A further aspect of Israel's history that is of special importance is the fact that while God does achieve his purposes in history and in his sovereign power can use anyone to this end, yet he does not do or occasion *everything* in history. Israel had seen God intervene in decisive moments in history (creation, Abraham, exodus, monarchy, exile, return), but nowhere is it suggested that God does everything, as though history were simply a matter of working out a detailed plan.[22] On the contrary, it is evident that there were times when the LORD intervened precisely when things were going wrong and his will was not being done. He sent Amos with a final warning of judgment to the northern kingdom because they would not listen to him, because in spite of his repeated interventions in their history (4:1–12) they persisted in their social unrighteousness. As a result he executed this judgment in 722 BC because they had not done his will, and because they had not expressed his will in their social life. Similarly when the people of Judah had served decades in exile and were humiliated and discouraged, they were in a worse situation than the LORD wished for them, and had suffered more than was his will. For this reason he declares that he will punish Babylon because it showed no mercy to his people and placed a heavy yoke on the grey-headed old men (Isa. 47:6). Throughout Scripture it is clear that alongside God's history-making interventions, there are also other factors that influence the course of history, which in turn make God's interventions necessary.

This matter has caused many problems in the history of theology, and it will therefore be best to consider it separately.

THE COVENANT

I presuppose that the covenant is the goal of creation and intend to develop this elsewhere.[23] However, at this point the following may be noted. While many examples of covenants can be found among Israel's neighbours, God's covenant with Israel is unique in many respects. In the first instance, it is unique in that it is the central theme of all God's revelation.[24] But furthermore, the relationship between God and Israel is not a natural, matter-of-course affair, but is an historical covenant.[25] This means that it was deliberately entered into at a particular point in time, and that there was no natural relationship, such as family descent, between God and Israel, as in so many heathen religions. Then too the covenant is 'monopluristic', in the sense that it is one-sidedly ('mono'-) established by the LORD, but involves obligations on the part of both the LORD and his people ('pluristic'). Now a few important conclusions must be drawn from these points for our concept of history, and so also for the way in which God is involved in history. One of the great deficiencies in the accepted presentations of the biblical view of history lies in the fact that the covenant is not given its rightful place in them.

Two aspects must be emphasised from the beginning: the 'mono'-aspect (that God established the covenant in his free love, and thus without any compulsion from without, and without any needs or deficiencies in himself);[26] and the 'pluristic' aspect (that in this covenant man really has freedom to live, he has responsibility, a task to fulfil and a contribution to make).

The rest of creation has a 'contribution' to make too. 'The *heavens* (TEV) "sky") tell the glory of God; and the *firmament* proclaims his handiwork' (Ps. 19:1). The sun, moon and stars, waters, sea creatures, the depths, fire, hail, snow and steam, mountains, hills and trees, everyone and everything, must praise the LORD! (Ps. 150; cf. also Ps. 96:11–13). And yet these things do not have responsibilities that can be discharged in freedom. Such responsibility is given only to *man*, and here an aspect of man as the image of God is discernible. Only man is addressed directly by God, and only man is free to answer him. This at least was the freedom in which Adam was created: free to serve God, free to respond to him with the 'yes' that he asked for, free to discharge his responsibilities within the covenant in which he was placed from the very beginning (Gen. 1:26 f). In the past the conclusion drawn from this was often that man was given a freedom of choice; that is, God created man and then gave him the choice of either serving him or not. But this is a mistake, and reflects a secularised, western view of freedom that cannot be found in this form in Scripture.[27] Biblical freedom is primarily a material freedom, free *from* and free *for*. Free from the power of sin and the devil; free for the service of God; free to glorify him.

What actually happened was inconceivable and inexplicable – Adam and Eve misused and so lost the freedom they had been given by paying attention to the serpent. God, however, did not surrender either man or the covenant relationship, but called them back into his fellowship (Gen. 3:8 f), revealing himself immediately as the gracious God (Gen. 3:15, 21), and going with them into the future. Man was free to live in fellowship with God, and in certain cases did so, but repeatedly he did the inconceivable thing by turning his back on God and thereby broke the covenant.[28]

So in actual fact history was formed by a faithful God and an unfaithful nation, in that Israel followed the same path as Adam! Preuss suggests that God has still not achieved his objective because history is formed by both the faithfulness of God and the unfaithfulness of man who is resolved to walk his own way.[29] Pannenberg distinguishes between the earlier view of history in which only the promises of God determined the course of events, and the later development (Deuteronomy) where the promises were linked with a condition, the condition of keeping the law. By thus linking promise and law it is understandable why history has (provisionally! A.K.) developed negatively. This happened because of the steadily growing guilt of the people, which led eventually to Israel having to leave the land that God had promised and given to them. Thus through the law the sin of the people, which had grown steadily, contributed to forming history alongside the promises of God. Thus far Pannenberg.[30]

Seen from the perspective of the structure of the covenant ('pluristic') this means that God, in creating man, had in his sovereign power, placed limits on himself. When man fails to live up to his responsibilities, God reacts, and takes new initiatives in order to achieve his goals in spite of this. Seen in this way the history of God and his people can be summed up as follows. God chooses, accepts, frees and cares for the people, who let him down, disobey him, and serve other gods. God warns them, calls them to turn back to him, and punishes them, in order to restore them to communion with himself and to peace. Initially the people react positively to the LORD's disciplinary measures, thus enjoying prosperity and the new heights of the return from exile to which he leads them. Yet later they become ever more hardened and finally reject the Messiah, thus losing their special place and task in God's history with the world. The Northern Kingdom had in fact already been finally rejected and exiled in 720 BC. God's unique reaction to this was to use the church (composed mainly of members from among the heathen) to make Israel jealous. This was exactly the reverse of the position in the Old Testament, where it was Israel who was to be the light that would entice the surrounding people to Jerusalem, and so to the LORD. So in this way God eventually achieved his objective: to have and to bless both the heathen and Israel as his people. But the way in which he achieved his goal was through many disappointments, interventions, detours and 'new things' (Deutero-Isaiah).

It is of decisive significance that this history reveals the essence of all history, and that this history is genuine *history* (and not some kind of puppet-show), in which two covenant partners each have their own responsibility, allocated to them respectively by God alone, but not executed by God alone. Indeed the idea that everything that happens in history is the will of God can only be sustained in a theoretical atmosphere in which one forgets the millions of murders and adulteries, the glaring injustice and the blatant spurning of God's law which take place every day in the world. Anyone who still tries to find a place for sin (not mere 'sin' in general, but sins such as brutal terrorist attacks, or the killing of hostages – to mention only a couple of arbitrary examples) within the counsel and will of God, makes a mockery of the holiness and grace of God, and a laughing-stock of God's rejection of sin and of the price that he paid to reconcile the sinner with himself. God is against sin and he has no other secret attitude towards it. On the new earth there will be no sin or injustice (2 Pet. 3:13; Rev. 21:27). Here and now we are forbidden therefore to serve other gods, to break our marriage pledge, or to murder. Those who transgress these commandments, transgress the will of God (his actual, only will, and not 'merely' his revealed will).[31] This is not to contradict the good and legitimate motives that have often lain behind these distinctions, but the legitimacy of making these distinctions in the first place. The greater part of history (that of Israel, the church, the world) is in fact a violation of the will of God and has been other than he willed it to be. When the church confesses the omnipotence of God, the church confesses it without being able to prove it in history, and hopes for it as one hopes for that which one does not yet have (Rom. 8:24, 25), and longs for the day when God will be 'all in all' (everything in everyone – 1 Cor. 15:28). This he is not yet. To say that he is this already is to make a mockery of him in the midst of chaos and pain.

It was in his free and soverign will that God chose to accompany this world to his final goal in a way other than would have been the case with a world of wooden dolls. By virtue of the structure of the covenant man has received his own realm of responsibilities from God, responsibilities which at best he fulfils only in part, and at worst, (mostly!) not at all. This is the 'explanation' for the chaos and misery, and for God's disappointment with his creation (Gen. 6:5,6; Matt. 23:37, 38). This was the factor that prompted the incarnation, humiliation, suffering and death of Jesus Christ.

The comfort of the gospel does not lie in the suggestion that nothing happens contrary to the will of God, and that everything that happens to us is his will and that we should let it rest at that. The consolation of the gospel is that, in spite of our unfaithfulness, and the pain and chaos which we have brought into the world through it, God has promised that he will achieve his purposes, that he is faithful and will accordingly keep his promises, and that in history these promises have already been fulfilled in one way, through the fulfilled covenant, that they are being fulfilled at present in another way, thus strengthening our faith that with the return of Christ he will fulfil them in their third and final way.[32] Our comfort accordingly lies in our faith in God's future, and not in our 'explanations' of the past and the present which do not do justice to the holiness of God, or the responsibility of man, nor as a result, to the structure of the covenant.

We find here a new perspective on the problems which gave rise to the so-called God-is-dead theology. On the one hand the questions were asked: Where was God in Hiroshima, in Auschwitz, Biafra? No actual answer has been given to these questions, probably because they were wrongly formulated. By virtue of the structure of the covenant, the questions should rather be: Where is *man*? It is us, the people, who have not discharged our responsibilities, who have not been fully human, i.e. not like Jesus, the real man! This is the 'explanation' of Hiroshima, Auschwitz, Biafra and Vietnam. Had the gospel been rightly proclaimed and believed in Germany there could have been no Auschwitz. If the rich western lands had rightly proclaimed and believed the gospel, there could have been no starvation in West Africa in 1974.

In the history of Israel too, not everything was ascribed to the will of God. Times without number the people were admonished, warned, called back from the wrong ways which they took contrary to the will of God (Isa. 53:6). And when the people in need were comforted, the comfort did not consist in the fact that the LORD had arranged everything and that nothing had happened against his will, but that he had intervened already in their history in decisive ways, such as in Egypt where he brought to an end the injustice that the Egyptians had inflicted on them against his will, and that he had promised to do it again. In the later exile, the consolation was based on the promise that he was preparing a new exodus, greater and more glorious than the former one. The Bible does not reduce everything to an ashen grey and call it the will of God. The Bible knows contrasts, distinctions in its interpretation of history. And for this reason, in times of need the people need not resort to a God-is-dead theology, but are reassured: 'Behold, the LORD's hand is not shortened that it cannot save, or his ear dull, that it cannot hear, but your iniquities have made a separation between you and your God, and your sins have hid his face from you...' (Isa. 59:1–2). As has already been shown, this is no final answer to all God's absences but it is a reminder that God cannot automatically be held responsible for everything that goes wrong. And the basis for his conclusion is the structure of the covenant, in which God gave to man his own realm of responsibilities.

All of this throws light on the second problem which gave rise to the God-is-dead theology – the question as to whether God is really needed in a world that is seemingly able to look after itself with all its scientific and technological advances. It was said: formerly we prayed, now we ring for the doctor. But this reflects a false view of the relationship between God and man. God actually gives to man certain responsibilities in the covenant. And he gives to man the 'living space' and the ability to meet these responsibilities. If man actually succeeds in realising certain aspects of his cultural task, in spite of the fact that for the greater part he has failed to do so and is accordingly responsible for the wretchedness and chaos on earth, and then proceeds to ask whether God is after all necessary, this is nothing less than blasphemy! The scientific and technological achievements of our times ought to bring us to God in gratitude for having favoured us with the opportunity to do so much – and the same achievements should bring us before him in sorrow because so little has been used to the benefit of mankind (e.g. atomic power), but on the contrary, so much has been developed as a threat to mankind. It is not 'they' or 'the 'people' that are guilty of this, but the church, because we have failed to proclaim the gospel in such a way that it was clearly heard in the world.[33]

THE COUNSEL OF GOD

In this connection it is necessary to look more closely at the concept of the counsel of God. It is obvious that the view of God as a detached being, unchangeable, self-sufficient, has definite implications for one's understanding of his decree (counsel) and providential purposes. According to this view his decree is eternal, in the sense of being before all time, and all-inclusive, so that history is nothing other than the working out of a detailed plan. It is true that various attempts were made to regain some sense of history, of human responsibility, of the covenant, and to accommodate sin in some way or another within this decree. It was claimed that sin was *contra* but not *praeter voluntatem Dei*, i.e. that sin was indeed against, but not outside of God's decree, and was therefore not beyond his control. This standpoint had praiseworthy motives, and was undoubtedly good in the context of a basically static concept of God. But in the final analysis, God and his divine counsel were implicitly or explicitly in competition with man and constituted a threat to him, the covenant and history. The dilemma, God or man, is to be rejected, but is understandable against the background of a static God and a minutely planned divine decree which had only to be unfolded in history.

In addition to the static concept of God in general, a mistaken view of the eternity of God is responsible for this unacceptable 'eternal' decree. It is striking that eternity in this context is seen exclusively in terms of the pre-temporal, so that an eternal decision was one that was made *before* creation.[34] And then, on the assumption that the eternity of God ended at the commencement of time, it was inevitably supposed that such a decision is unchangeable. In this way time and eternity are not only placed over against each other, which is dubious, but eternity seems to come to an end when God creates the heavens and the earth. According to this view, the eternal decree had been completed before time, and was executed only after creation. L. Boettner represents one of the most alarming examples of this line of thought.

Against this it must be asserted that the eternal God *was* the eternal God, *is* the eternal God and *shall be* the eternal God. Eternity does not cease with creation, but continues. Barth has spoken of God's eternity as pre-temporal, supra-temporal and post-temporal.[35] And while fundamental criticisms have been advanced against his views,[36] at least this is clear: God, as the eternal, continues to live, to work and decide in time, on the way to the final destination, the new earth. There is in fact no single reason, whether exegetical or theological, why we should assume that God made his decision once and for all before the world was created and is now merely executing it. Naturally this is not in itself a complete impossibility. God is free to choose to do things even in this way. But the

Scriptures do not allow us to accept such a view. In fact the concept of an 'eternal' decree of God supports a pre-temporal, supra-temporal and post-temporal decree. But before examining this, the idea of a 'decree' or 'counsel' needs further consideration.

First of all it must be pointed out that God's decree has been revealed. For too long there has been talk of the secret counsel of God, resting on Deuteronomy 29:29: 'The secret things belong to the LORD our God; but the things that are revealed belong to us and to our children for ever, that we may do all the words of this law.' The context in which this verse is found is not primarily concerned with the 'secret things', so that the emphasis in the verse does not fall on that aspect. In its structure, the verse shows that it is concerned primarily with the things that are revealed (the 'but' followed by a much longer section) and that were described in the preceding verse and chapters. This aspect is stressed even further by the fact that these 'revealed things' hold 'for ever' – to eternity. It is furthermore not suggested that the 'secret things' must and shall remain 'secret' for ever, nor that the 'secret things' represent the decree or counsel of God. There is no indication that the counsel of God (if that is what is being discussed here) is not found in the revealed things. Indeed the one-sided emphasis in the Reformed tradition on the 'secret things' is unacceptable, especially in the light of the fact that God's revealed will became 'only' (!) his 'precept'.[37] On the contrary, Scripture speaks of God's counsel as his *revealed* counsel (Acts 20:27), stressing that the *whole* counsel of God is proclaimed by Paul and thus revealed (see also Eph. 1:11; 3:3). In the Heidelberg Catechism we emphatically confess that Christ is 'our chief Prophet and Teacher, who *fully* reveals to us the secret counsel and will of God concerning our redemption' (answer 31). This shows how questionable is the viewpoint that in a one-sided way stresses the element of hiddenness in God's counsel, as though God did not live in Christ in all his fulness, as though Christ did not open up the 'full God' to us (Col. 1:19; 2:9; John 1:18). It is possible that the NAB gives the real intention of Deuteronomy 29:29, when it translates, 'What is *still* hidden...'. The utterance is intended to reassure the people that they do not need to be anxious about what they do not yet know, but they must take care to obey and do what the LORD has already revealed to them.

Acts 20:27 gives a somewhat clearer picture of what the counsel of God actually is. According to this verse, Paul had declared 'the whole counsel of God' to the community in Ephesus. We ought not to think in quantitative terms of a number of issues or truths, because it is clear that Paul did not preach everything that we have in the Bible today. Paul's letters make it clear that the gospel had a particular focal point, which enabled the Christian congregations to detect false doctrines even though they did not yet possess quantitatively all that would be taught in the various communities as different situations developed. Thus for example the Galatian community was to test what the false teachers were presenting against the gospel that they had received from Paul, namely the gospel of

Christ. Even though they had by no means received the entire Bible as we have it today, they were well able to apply the test because *Jesus Christ* had been preached to them. He is the focal point, the heart of the gospel; qualitatively he is the entire gospel, so that Paul was able to say: '*Him* we preach...' (Col. 1:28), and 'I decided to know nothing among you except Jesus Christ' (1 Cor. 2:2). This meant that even that which had been still concealed in the Old Testament was now revealed in Jesus Christ (e.g. that the heathen could be the people of God on an equal footing with the Jews – Eph. 3:2–7). When Paul said to the elders that he had preached to them the whole counsel of God, it is this point of concentration, Jesus Christ, that must be understood.

In and through Jesus Christ God has revealed his counsel. God's eternal plan of salvation is 'to unite all things in him, things in heaven and things on earth' (Eph. 1:10), which means that all things must first be reconciled by Christ (Col. 1:20). For this reason the counsel of God is repeatedly referred to in Acts in connection with the crucifixion of Christ. It was thus that the world would be reconciled to God. When the Jews rejected and crucified the Messiah, they did what God had decreed beforehand would take place (Acts 4:28; 2:23). We learn from this that God is able to bring forth good even from sin; in fact he is able to bring forth the best, namely, the reconciliation of the world. It is about this that the Christian community rejoiced; that God did not abandon the work of his hands, but that even when the Jews had murdered the Messiah, through that very murder he reconciled the world and them to himself. In the same way God accomplished the salvation of the heathen (which at the same time generated new hope for Israel itself because the Jews could now see what they had missed, Rom. 11:11 f) through the hardening of Israel, even though in Old Testament terms this would have meant that the heathen would no longer be able to see the light of the world. Naturally, this is not to say that the LORD predetermined Israel's hardening, or the fact that they rejected and crucified the Messiah. It was against his will that they rejected the Messiah, and hardened their hearts against him, but God is so wonderful that even then he accomplished his counsel (his will to save and deliver the world). In spite of their sin, and even through their sin, he still reconciled the world and brought salvation to the heathen.

When we understand the counsel of God in this way, certain utterances become clearer. For example, Luke 7:30: 'But the Pharisees and the lawyers rejected the purpose (counsel) of God for themselves, not having been baptized by him (John).' John baptized with the baptism of repentance. Through repentance the Lord wished the Pharisees and lawyers to share in his salvation. This purpose of salvation that God had for them, this counsel of God, they rejected, however, by turning their back on John and later on Jesus too.

In this connection Venema came to the conclusion that the counsel of God is God's plan of salvation to save a lost world and the active execution of this plan in and through Christ. Indeed the counsel of God does not mean that he first (beforehand) prepared a plan which he then afterwards only set out to fulfil. God's counsel includes both these aspects. It is his planned course of action in which he controls the run of events and in this way executes his will to save.[38] That Jesus was 'delivered up *according* to (instrumental dative) the definite plan and foreknowledge of God' (Acts 2:23) means that his counsel includes his activity in history, just as his eternity includes his involvement in time. For this reason his plan and his hand can be linked in Acts 4:28. The expression 'his hand' refers to his mighty deeds in history.

A few other verses where the concept of the counsel of God is found must be touched on briefly. Acts 15:18 has often in the past been made to say more than the best Greek texts will allow. The verse seems actually to say no more than that the LORD had made known long in advance that the heathen would come under his lordship (through Amos – cf. v. 15–17), something that was now happening through the mission to the heathen. Hebrews 6:17 is concerned with the promise of blessing to Abraham and his descendants. This is the counsel of God. And to convince them that his plan was unchangeable, that is, that he would fulfil his promise to Abraham and his descendants, God confirmed it with an oath. In the Old Testament too, such a specific decision in a concrete situation is called the counsel of God. According to Isaiah 46:10 ('My counsel shall stand'), God's counsel was to summon Cyrus (the bird of prey from the east) to allow his people to return to Palestine. The first part of verse 10 means no more than that God declared in advance of the actual event that it would happen, as distinct from the gods that had no power to influence the future (Isa. 42:23; 48:3 f). Because God proves himself to be God through his control of the future, the counsel of God will need to be understood in direct association with the so-called proofs of God in Israel's history.

THE PROOFS OF GOD

Much has been written in the history of the church and theology on the proofs of God. Almost automatically one thinks back to Thomas Aquinas and his five ways of arriving at the existence of God. Thomas was convinced that one could be sure of the existence of God without the use of Scripture, depending entirely on one's natural knowledge, i.e. by investigating reality and the concept of God and thinking logically about them. First of all we observe a great deal of movement, change, coming into being, and this suggests that there must be something or someone who is responsible for it. Secondly, everything that happens must have a cause, and therefore there must be a first cause. Thirdly, we are also aware that everything that exists is not necessary – which is to say that it could also not exist. There must therefore be one necessary being without whom nothing else would exist. Fourthly, there are good things, as well as better and worse things in the world. But these imply the absolutely good, that which is the best and without which it would make no sense to speak of better or worse. Fifth, there is a logical, intelligent order in the movement of the world, and this is only possible if there is an all-wise director of all things. These very brieflly, are the five ways by means of which Thomas tried to arrive at the existence of God.[39] These five ways played a tremendously important part in the theology of the Roman Catholic church, and some of these arguments are still used today in debating with unbelievers the question as to whether there is a God.

It will be helpful to gain a general impression of the nature of these five ways. For this purpose the first way will be discussed more fully. It is the most obvious way and it proceeds from the phenomenon of movement. It is a fixed fact, attested by our senses, that there is movement in the world. But everything that moves is moved by another. A thing can only be in motion to the degree that it is on its way to the goal of that movement. And something can only move to the degree that it has in a certain sense already attained its goal. Indeed, movement is nothing other than leading a thing from its potential to its realisation. But this can only be done by something that is already actual. But it is impossible that one and the same thing should simultaneously have attained its realisation (perfection of existence), and not have attained it. It is equally impossible that one and the same thing, in relation to the same being, in one and the same movement, at the same time moves something else and is moved itself, which means: It is impossible that something should move itself. Therefore, everything that is in movement must be moved by something else. When that through which something is moved is itself in motion, it in turn must be moved by something else, while this in turn must be moved by yet something else. But this cannot go on into infinity, for then we would have no first mover, and as a result no movement at all. For the later movers move only by virtue of the power of the first mover, just as a stick can only move in as much as it is moved by the hand. We must therefore assume a first mover that is not moved by anything else. The first mover is what all mean when they speak of God. Thus far, Thomas's first way. One may grasp it better by remembering that movement is not confined to physical motion, but relates rather to the realisation and the fulfilment of potentiality.[40]

It is clear that we have suddenly landed in a totally different and indeed, strange atmosphere. I have deliberately given this long account of Thomas's first way in order to bring out the radical difference between this and any other traditional proof of God and the way in which the Bible speaks about (or rather proclaims) God. The prophets and apostles speak differently about God. Never is his existence presented in such an abstract and neutral way as merely the realisation of potentiality. He is never called in afterwards to explain or clarify certain factual data. One sees this difference in the terms and descriptions which this proof of God led Thomas and his followers to develop: God is the *primun movens*, the *prima causa efficiens*, the *ens per se necessarium*, the *maxime ens*, the *summum intelligens*. (Translated, these mean more or less: God is the prime mover, the first effective and sufficient cause, the one existing being that is necessary in itself, the highest being, the highest intelligence.) Ebeling quite rightly asks: What has all this to do with God?[41] What affinity is there between such terms and the biblical message that God is the living God, the Father, the Deliverer, the One who is faithful and does not abandon the work of his hands? And where in the prophets and apostles is there anything that faintly resembles Thomas's Aristotelian proofs of God? The Bible declares what God has done and will do; in it men call on God and thank him; but there is no trace of any theoretical, formal proof that God exists! There are various reasons for this, such as the fact that it would actually be humiliating to God to attempt to prove his existence, especially since he proves himself on every hand.

Anyone who seriously tries to prove to an unbeliever today that God exists might mean well, but should consider what he is doing. He claims to be speaking about the almighty God that made heaven and earth, who has sustained them through the centuries, and who has reconciled all things to himself in Jesus Christ with a view to ultimately renewing them completely. The existence of this God he now wishes to prove! This is surely a colossal humiliation of God. If God is so great and has already done such breathtaking things, it is inconceivable that his supporters should still try to prove that he exists. Anyone who tries to do so cannot possibly expect the unbeliever to believe all the things which he claims for God, even if he is successful in convincing him intellectually. It boils down to something like a journalist who wishes to write about a marvellous boxer whom he is convinced will shortly take the heavyweight title of the world, but first of all he must prove by means of a lengthy newspaper argument that the boxer actually exists! If the boxer were indeed shortly to take the title, everyone would have known about him and discussed him, because he would have proved himself already. A journalist would therefore never attempt to prove the existence of a boxer. He merely writes reports on those boxers who have proved themselves. The others are not newsworthy, and it would not be worth the trouble to mention them in the newspaper.

Anyone who tries to prove the existence of God implies in fact that God is so unimportant and has done so little that he has not yet proved himself, and that there is not enough evidence of what he has already done. In which case the reaction of the unbeliever, consciously or unconsciously, is quite rightly: Is such a God worth believing in? Let him do something, and so prove himself, and then we will be able to speak of him.

Naturally, against this it could be observed that God does not function on the same level as a boxer. He asks us to have faith in him, to rely on him, and tells us that we cannot really know him without surrendering ourselves to him in dedication and trust. 'Without faith it is impossible to please him' (Heb. 11:6). But Thomas and his followers knew this, and for this reason they did not attempt to prove the fulness of God, or that which makes God God. It was only his existence that they wished to demonstrate. The result was that they became involved in abstract generalities. Even those who might accept the existence of a first cause or unmoved mover for purely logical, philosophical reasons, have not come to faith in the God of Israel, because his mere existence, even if it were demonstrable in this way, says nothing about his actual deity.

In this connection, Jüngel has said that a verification of God, outside of the realm of faith, was made impossible by God for man's sake. The reason for this is that if God could be proved, he would no longer be the true God. And if the true God does not exist, it leaves man without any meaningful and true existence. God and faith belong together inseparably.[42] Ott has investigated the same matter. That God is God means that his is Lord over man's total existence. This means that there is only one correct human attitude towards him and that is a life-long trust, and a surrender to him of the whole of one's life. Where this relationship of trust is missing man is no longer in a relationship with the living God, but with an idol.[43] Luther rightly defined faith as '*creatrix divinitatis non in persona, sed in nobis*' (faith is the creator of God – not in his person, i.e. not in his own independent existence, but in us). Because God is God, the God of Israel, Immanuel (God with us) and is not an object alongside other objects, we cannot distinguish between the knowledge of God and the attitude of trust in him. The Heidelberg Catechism also defines faith as knowledge *and* a hearty trust (answer 21).

We can now understand better what Jüngel meant when he said that the verification of God outside of faith is impossible for man's sake. God is not only, and does not wish to be only, God. He wishes to be *our* God, the One who makes our lives new. And for this reason he can only be truly known by those who give themselves to him. Jüngel had also said that we cannot speak correctly about God if we do not thank him. Consequently to be concerned logically, philosophically, with a first cause, is not to be concerned with the true God. So, from the perspective of the being of God (as Israel's God, as our God), the proofs of God are not necessary and of no use.[44] It may be the case that the recent reaction against the proofs of God stems from the realisation that they have little compelling power in the proclamation of the Christian message. Anyone who has tried earnestly to do 'missionary work' in this way would be able to confirm this. An unbeliever would but rarely find his way to faith in the true God along this route.

But not everything has been said yet. Two matters need further attention before we turn to the interpretation of history today. The one is God's proofs of himself, and the other the question of the signs of God.

In criticism of the proofs of God that have just been discussed, it is often asserted that there are no proofs of God in the Bible. If one means thereby that there is no attempt to prove God's existence in a philosophical way, but that the Bible simply presupposes from the existence and actions of the living God (Gen. 1:1), the assertion is correct. Such proofs are alien to the Bible, and to the times in which the Bible came into existence. During that period no one questioned the existence of gods, and erred rather in revering too many gods (Acts 17:22 f). A statement such as Psalm 14:1, 'The fool hath said in his heart, "There is no God"', must not be misunderstood (cf. also Ps. 53:1). The issue here is practical atheism, and not doctrinaire atheism. Here the existence of God is not denied. What is denied is that he is involved in our history and will punish injustice. Psalm 10 illustrates the point well. Verse 4 ('all the thoughts of the wicked are: "There is no God"') is in fact explained in verse 11 ('He thinks in his heart: "God has forgotten, he has hidden his face, he will never see it"'). In other words, 'God does not exist' means: 'God does not see what the godless do, and will therefore not punish them'. The deepest reason for this is expressed in Psalm 36:1: 'There is no fear of God before his eyes' and so in the realities of daily life no account is taken of God. The Living Bible gives a good translation of Jeremiah 5:12: 'They have lied and said: "He won't bother us! No evil will come upon us".' For the godless God has in practice no significance. The opposite of Psalm 14:1 ('There is no God') would be to enquire after God (14:2, The Living Bible, 'who want to please God'), but it is just this that the fool does not do – verse 4: 'They do not call upon the LORD'.

Theoretical atheism, as it occurs frequently today, is unknown in the Bible. If someone in the Bible denies the existence of God, it means that he does not take God into account in his life.

Now, in the Old Testament, such an attitude in life is folly, because there are more than sufficient evidences of God's 'existence'. He had proved himself in indisputable ways through his mighty interventions in Israel's history. This is what is meant by God's proofs of himself, and these proofs really do have persuasive power. Anyone who allows himself to be convinced by these, does not merely accept theoretically that 'there is a God' but gives his life to this God who by his control of history awakens the assurance that he will renew the earth. The biblical proofs of God are not attempts on the part of believers to prove to unbelievers by means of logical argument that there is a God, or a first cause of some description. They are God's actual interventions in history by means of which he proved himself against the gods and before the people in order to strengthen their faith in times of temptation. The prophets simply witness to these proofs, and the New Testament owes its origin to the greatest of these proofs of God, Jesus Christ.

Together with the countless greater and lesser interventions of God in Israel's history, through which only the lives of individuals or small groups may have been touched, and which served to prove God to them and sparked their faith in the LORD, there are in the Old Testament three decisive, major events: the exodus (including the journey through the wilderness and the entry into Canaan), the exile, and the return from captivity.

Rowley has indicated definite features in the story of the exodus that make it more satisfactory to accept the fact that God was active in it, rather than to suppose a series of 'coincidences'.[45] First of all there is the fact that the God who led the people out of Egypt had apparently not been served by them previously, except perhaps in a very sporadic way. (Cf. Exod. 3:6, 15, 16, where the LORD tells Moses repeatedly who he is, and Exod. 3:13 which assumes that Moses would have to explain to the people who had sent him to them.) The covenant that was entered into at Sinai, and the giving of the laws, and expressions such as Exodus 6:25–6 indicate that during the exodus a new relationship between the LORD and the people came into existence, and that before the exodus the people do not appear to have regarded themselves as the people of the LORD. Had Israel later on invented the story of the exodus, they would have made familiar gods, and not a new God, responsible for it. And if Moses had gone to them of his own accord (and had accordingly not met the LORD at the burning bush – Gen. 3), he would not have gone in the name of a relatively unknown God because of the possibility that they would not acknowledge that God.

Then there is the fact that they made no military contribution to their liberation from the powerful Egyptian Pharaoh. The LORD compelled Pharoah by means of plagues to let them go, and at the Red Sea it was only the LORD who delivered them. From their side, they contributed nothing. Were the story invented, the people would never have allowed such an opportunity to laud their military achievements to pass by. In such a case, Moses would have been portrayed as a military leader, who had whipped up the people's courage to great acts of heroism. But this element is entirely lacking in the story. Moses acts as a prophet and not as a military leader. He came only to announce to the people what the LORD would do to deliver them. Rowley mentions many other features in the story which indicate that it was truly the LORD's intervention in their history.

It is therefore not strange that this divine act should become the decisive event in Israel's history through which they were bound to the LORD, became totally dependent on him and were obliged and responsible to him alone. After the exodus their God became known as 'the LORD who led you out of Egypt (out of the house of bondage)', or 'the LORD, your God from the land of Egypt'. (See, for example, Exod. 20:2; Deut. 6:12; 8:14; 13:5, 10; 20:1; Judg. 6:8; 2 Kgs. 17:7, 36; Jer. 2:6; 16:14; 23:7; 32:20 f; Hos. 13:4; Ps. 81:10, to mention but a few of the countless utterances.)[46]

Just how extraordinary this intervention of God in Israel's history was, is evident from a passage such as Deuteronomy 4:34 f: 'Or has any god ever attempted to go and take a nation for himself from the midst of another nation, by trials, by signs, by wonders, and by war, by a mighty hand and by an outstretched arm, and by great terrors, according to all that the LORD your God did for you in Egypt before your eyes? To you it was shown, that you might know that the LORD is God; there is no other besides him.'

In this way the exodus was the supreme proof of God, a proof which had been enacted before the eyes of all Israel and the Egyptians.[47] Moses' fear that he would not be able to lead the people out of Egypt (note the repetition of 'I' in Exod. 3:11) was answered by the 'I' of the LORD ('*I* will be with you' – v. 12) and by his very real actions before the Egyptians. At first they attempted to refute the uniqueness of his acts, by producing magicians who could do similar things (Exod. 7:22; 8:7), but it soon became apparent that there was something happening here with which the local magicians and gods could not compete. After this had become clear (Exod. 8:8 f) the *motive* for the plagues is repeatedly mentioned: 'that you (Pharaoh) may know that there is no one like the LORD our God' (Exod. 8:10, 22; 9:14, 29). So Pharaoh and Israel were confronted with the reality of God who visibly, convincingly, and decisively intervened in history. Had Pharaoh come to faith in the LORD through this, as Israel did during the course of the exodus, it would have been very far from a leap in the dark. It would have been a responsible act motivated by overwhelming, ascertainable, historical evidence. For this reason it was sin when he failed to do so, and he bore the full responsibility and guilt for it.

It is important to observe that Moses did not attempt to prove to Pharaoh and the people, that there is a God, or that the LORD had really spoken to him. For the LORD himself did this in history. And this should not be regarded as an exception. Is it not possible for the One who created the earth to visibly act in it? It would be a betrayal of Genesis 1 (his work as Creator) had he not made himself known in history in demonstrable, convincing and verifiable ways. Israel did not believe in God in spite of the facts, or worse still, against the facts, but on the grounds of the facts, on the grounds of God's proof of himself in their concrete history, visibly before the eyes of the world (Ps. 77:14–16). For this reason it was sin (unnecessary, inexplicable deviations from the normal) when Israel or the surrounding nations did not place their trust wholly in the LORD.[48]

The second great intervention in Israel's history was the exile. At least two things are striking here when it is compared with the exodus: it is an intervention by God against Israel, and is announced in advance. (The carrying away of the northern kingdom comes into the same category – cf. the preaching of Amos – except that from it there was no return.) Westermann has shown that we have here a unique action on God's part. It was commonly accepted in Israel's environment that the gods did things for their people. But that God proved himself by doing something against his people, by letting his people be carried away into captivity, and that for this purpose he used great powers as 'flies' and 'razors', was unknown in the ancient east.[49]

While it is clear that the exile is a proof of God, like the exodus, it was not at that time experienced by Israel as a proof of God. Apparently, this

is because Israel, backed by the false prophets, was very confident in the
LORD and his support.

With the return from exile there is, however, a new situation. Here we
have a people who had been humbled, having spent decades under the
control of the nation that had carried it away. For Babylon, of course, it
was proof that their gods were superior to the LORD. That the persistence
of the exile was for Israel a terrible testing of their faith is clear from the
preaching of Deutero-Isaiah. (See 40:27 f; Ezek. 20:32; cf. Ps. 44:24.)
Although the prophets had told the people before the exile that they were
going to be taken away to Babylon as the LORD's punishment, the
progress of the exile and the oppression they suffered made them forget
this and prompted the burning question as to whether history was not
beginning to show that the gods of Babylon were greater than the LORD.

In this situation the LORD resolved to lead his people back. As with the
exile, and the carrying off of the northern kingdom in 720 BC, this too he
announced beforehand. But because Israel was now caught in the throes of
a trial of faith concerning whether the LORD was king or whether the gods
of Babylon were greater and stronger than him, his advance announcement becomes a central theme in Deutero-Isaiah's preaching and serves
as a proof that the LORD is the true God, the only true God, while the gods
of Babylon are not worthy of the name. This message occurs in several
pericopes, such as Isaiah 41:21–29. In a court scene the gods of Babylon,
and by implication their followers, are summoned to produce 'proofs'
(literally, strong things, strong words, and thus convincing arguments)
to show that they really are gods. (Verse 21. Cf. Psalm 82 which was
discussed in chapter 1.) These proofs could consist of two things: either
they were to tell in advance what was to happen (v. 22a), or that they were
to interpret the earlier things, that is, to explain the reason for the exile.
(This is the meaning of v. 22: 'Tell us the former things, what they are'.)

The gods were unable to respond to either of these demands. In doing
so they did not merely reveal their inability to offer proofs that they are
really gods; rather they provided positive proof that they are *not* gods[50]
(v. 24, 29). This shows the decisive importance of being able to act in
history as a proof of deity. Were the LORD also unable to act in history in
visible and convincing ways he would also be obliged to surrender his
claims to deity.

That the gods were required to tell in advance what was to happen
(v. 22) must not be formalised to such an extent that the weather forecasts
of the twentieth century could be divine proofs! The issues relate to a
particular matter in a particular situation. The situation was the relationship between the world powers in the latter half of the sixth century BC.
Would Babylon retain its command? This was the question that demanded
an answer. If Babylon were to fall, how would it happen, and through
whom? This the gods had to answer, but they could not. The LORD
answered, and made it happen accordingly. He announced that he would
raise up Cyrus, the Persian king, even before Cyrus had begun his

campaign against Babylon. In this way, Cyrus came to play an important role as a proof of God in Deutero-Isaiah. (See, for example: 41:2; 41:25; 44:28; 45:1 f; 46:11; 48:15 (in fact, the whole of chapter 48.)

It is striking that the return from Babylon is described in terms similar to those used of the exodus, although it is not seen as a mere repetition of the exodus but as a tremendously greater event. Anyone taking into account the eschatological meaning of Deutero-Isaiah's message,[51] will see in this similarity and superiority an analogy to what may be described as the restoration and surpassing of Genesis 2 in Revelation 21–22.[52]

The meaning of the fact that the return from exile was to surpass the exodus must now be considered. It has already been shown that the exodus was a convincing proof of God that formed the basis for the whole of the future life of the people, and that times without number the prophets appealed to this intervention of God for both encouragement and admonition. But Deutero-Isaiah goes to great lengths to convince the people that the return would be infinitely more glorious and wonderful than the exodus. While the exodus was the basis of their relationship to God, it was now referred to as 'the former things', which the people were 'to think of no more', and as 'things that happened before' to which they should no longer pay attention (Isa. 43:19). This was because God would do something new (v. 19). See also Isaiah 48:3–9; 49:8–13; 52:7–12. A study of the ways in which, and the degree to which, the return from exile surpasses the exodus reveals some interesting points. We will consider these more closely in chapter 4, in connection with God's relationship to the future.[53]

What is of importance here, however, is that God's earlier incomparable and unheard-of proof of himself will vanish as mist before the sun when he proves himself anew by raising up Cyrus, the Persian, to punish Babylon for its pride and to allow the people of Israel to return to Jerusalem. When it is remembered that the nations that were involved in the exodus, the exile and the return were Egypt, Babylon and Persia, the great powers of the world of their times, it is evident that God has repeatedly had the decisive word in the events of world history.

Shortly before 1945, which was a time of turmoil and confusion in world history, G. von Rad wrote a remarkable article under the title 'The way of God through history according to the witness of the prophets'.[54] He began the article by pointing out that the fourteen centuries of biblical history ran its course through five great world powers: Egypt, Babylon, Phoenicia, Persia and Greece. He continued by showing how striking is the ease with which the prophets, in the midst of these world powers, were able to distinguish and to proclaim God as the determining factor and as the LORD of history. How different things are with us! To us the super-powers dominate the scene. What will be the next move of America, or Russia or Red China? These are the decisive questions of the moment. Naturally God must come into the picture in some way or another. But how? And then we struggle to find a role for him somewhere on the periphery, or in some indirect way. Von Rad argued that for the prophets the position was exactly the reverse. To them God filled the whole horizon with his dispensations and the things in the foreground, the 'super-powers', which in our case almost totally obscure our vision of God, crumbled into nothing. According to Jeremiah 7:20 the mighty Assyria was but a razor in the hand of the LORD to shave Israel's harvests and people! Egypt was no more than flies, and Assyria no more than bees, on God's world-stage (Isa. 7:18). The decisive activity was God's.[55] History was contained completely within his hands. Von Rad concluded that faith therefore means to acknowledge God and his arrangements and not to allow him to be eclipsed by human manoeuvres.

It was through Deutero-Isaiah's expectation of an early end, and Trito-Isaiah's view of a delayed consummation, that the apocalyptic hope developed (cf. Daniel).[56] This hope, together with the whole promise-structure of the Old Testament, culminated in the coming of Jesus Christ in whom God himself appeared on earth in action. Martin Luther adopted the view that we see God in particular in the cross of Jesus Christ (but in the sense that the cross was the culmination of Jesus' *entire* life).[57] It might be regarded as a typically western imbalance that the cross of Christ is emphasised at the cost of his resurrection.[58] Opposed to this, the eastern biblical emphasis is on the resurrection. Indeed, in the early apostolic preaching the resurrection was linked with the cross by means of a 'but', in the sense of 'however': 'Jesus Christ of Nazareth, whom you crucified, (but) whom God raised from the dead' (Acts 4:10). While the word for 'but' is not found in the Greek, and does not occur in 2:23, 24; 3:15; 5:30; 10:39, 40 either, it seems that the 'but' is implicit in each case in that the Jews or Pharisees are said to have crucified him whereas *God* had raised him up. (In 13:30 'but' does occur in the Greek text.) From this we must conclude that the cross was not originally interpreted as a factor in salvation by the apostles, but as a gruesome murder perpetrated by the Jewish leaders, and that the true saving event was the resurrection, an event that cancelled the evil that the Jews had committed. Only later, possibly with Paul, was the saving significance of the cross seen and proclaimed, but always from the perspective of the resurrection.[59]

This meant, however, that in the resurrection of Christ, for the first time, God was proving himself in an apocalyptic, extra-historical and eschatological event. The resurrection of Christ has rightly been seen as an anticipation, a prolepsis, of the consummation. Something happened there that does not fit into ordinary history. Previously God had stirred up and called heathen kings to punish or deliver his people. But regardless of how clearly the prophets saw God's actions in the behaviour of such worldly princes, basically these actions were accessible for all the world to see. The surrounding nations could, for example, watch Cyrus move into action; they could fight against, or flee before, his armies. What mattered and made the difference were not the actions of *Cyrus*, for these were ordinary historical events, but the interpretation of the prophets: that God had called him and used him to punish Babylon and to release Israel from captivity. This interpretation was also accessible to the surrounding peoples, as has already been shown.

But the resurrection of Jesus Christ does not fit at all into the usual historical framework. Here is not something that everyone could observe, and that only needs to be interpreted correctly. The resurrection of Jesus falls outside of normal historical events. No one saw his resurrection. He appeared only to believers, and his resurrection body (or rather, life) clearly did not match the old reality in which he was present. So in his resurrection we are confronted with an apocalyptic or eschatological (supra-historical) event. God proves himself by giving now, in advance, a limited presentation of the consummation in Jesus. After his resurrection Jesus did not continue to live his old life as Lazarus had done, or the son of the widow of Nain. He lived a new life over which death had no further power. There is no analogy for this proof of God. It is a new turning in God's proofs of himself. When the invisible Holy Spirit is poured out, and Jesus Christ continues in a certain sense to live and work on earth through him in an invisible way, all kinds of problems arise which were unknown to the prophets in their preaching. Linked with this is the further problem that, while God undoubtedly continues to work and reveal himself, we no longer have prophets and apostles who can provide us with a reliable witness to, or interpretation of, his revelation and his work in history. This creates a new situation which was unknown before Christ, and which is responsible for many of the special problems with which theology grapples today. Problems such as: Where is God? What is he doing? What is there in history that we can ascribe to him directly? Is there anything in history now that is comparable to the exodus or the resurrection of Christ? Where do we find a reliable criterion for detecting his activity?

SIGNS OF GOD?

The first question is why the church finds itself in this dilemma. We have reliable prophetic and apostolic witness to the fact that God directed the course of history from the beginning until the resurrection of Christ and the pouring out of the Holy Spirit – or to express it more correctly in New Testament terms (but in a less accustomed manner) – until the apostles had reached 'the ends of the earth' with the gospel, which would be about the end of the first century after Christ. [60] What happened after this? Why do we have reliable witnesses through all the centuries before Christ and up to and including the activities of the apostles, but none for all the centuries after Christ. It is sometimes said rather bluntly that God completed his revelation in Jesus Christ, and that he reveals himself no further. Anyone thinking a little more deeply will quickly correct this and say that God has revealed himself in Christ but is not now revealing

himself, although he will reveal himself once more with the return of
Christ. But neither of these points of view can be acccepted. There is no
single reason why God should have revealed himself once but has ceased
to do so today. It is of course theologically sound that 'in times gone by'
he revealed himself 'in many ways and many places' through the prophets,
but 'in these last days...through his Son' (Heb. 1:2), and that the
revelation in Christ is final, and is infinitely greater and more glorious
than the revelation given in Old Testament times. God has indeed
nothing more to say beyond that which has been revealed in Christ. But
all this does not prove that God's revelation is closed, not even temporarily
until the return of Christ. Anyone who thinks along these lines has fallen
prey to the unbiblical idea that Christ has gone away and forsaken his
church on earth, and that we, either as individual believers or through
the Pope of Rome, represent Christ who during his absence has left his
affairs in our hands. This, however, is theologically unacceptable. No
one less than the exalted Christ is engaged *now* in the promotion of his
work in the world in and through the Holy Spirit. 'Lo, I am with you
always, to the close of the age' (Matt. 28:20). 'And the Lord (Jesus
Christ) added to their number day by day those who were being saved'
(Acts 2:47). Jesus Christ is the risen, living Lord. Through the Holy
Spirit he causes his kingdom to come *now*. If God has revealed himself
fully and finally in Jesus Christ in the past he is still revealing himself in
him *now*. Jesus Christ has not ceased being God's revelation in the meanwhile. There is indeed Christ's word to his disciples in John 6:12–13: 'I
have yet many things to say to you, but you cannot bear them now. When
the Spirit of truth comes he will guide you into all the truth.' We have
usually applied the last part of the verse to the apostles only, apparently
from the mistaken assumption that revelation has come to an end.
Anyone who believes in Jesus Christ as the Lord who is risen, living,
present and active, and also that God revealed himself through him, must
accept that God continues to reveal himself today.[61]

When this is our principal point of departure, the questions at the end
of our last section become even more urgent. Where is God? Where does
he reveal himself? What is he doing on earth now?

The real difference between the times of the prophets and the apostles
and our times is not that God revealed himself then but does not do so
now. The difference is that there were then reliable witnesses, prophets
summoned directly by God, appointed by him and addressed by him,
and apostles called by Jesus, equipped by him and enabled to be his
faithful witnesses,[62] whereas today there do not seem to be such witnesses.
In fact, the word witness ought not to be applied to us in its original
sense, since according to the New Testament only the apostles were
Christ's witnesses. We can at the most, simply confess his name. But
surely this is enough (cf. the Heidelberg Catechism, answer 32).

But the question 'Why?' has still not been answered. Why do we lack
an authoritative interpretation of his current revelation? It seems to me to

be related to the possibility that the times in which we live were unforeseen. I will give detailed attention elsewhere to the New Testament message concerning the near return of Christ, and show that all the New Testament traditions concerning his return proclaimed it as near.[63] Nevertheless, at this point it may be noted that the apostles did not anticipate the twenty centuries that have passed since then, and so did not have them explicitly in mind in their preaching. We are confronted with an unexpected duration of time which expresses something of the patience of God. In the preaching of the New Testament there is certainly room for these two thousand years (i.e. in the unique character of the concept 'near'), but no conscious expectation that the interval would be so long. In this sense we live in an unnatural period, and must therefore expect to encounter problems that did not arise in biblical times. For example, we live in a time when all the promises have been fulfilled, and we await the return of Christ which will bring about the resurrection, judgment and the renewal of the earth. Promises being fulfilled today are promises which have long since been fulfilled (e.g. the mission to the Gentiles – the heathen), but which are now being fulfilled again and again. This in itself is not strange. Think about the familiar idea of the repeated fulfilment of promises already referred to. But, and *this* is strange, in this unnatural and unforeseen time, we have no special seat of authority capable of giving an authoritative explanation of the revelation (work) of God. Rome has the Pope, but he makes no claim to receive new revelations. He claims only to give faithful interpretations of the revelation already given (testified to in the Scriptures and preserved – or, nowadays, clarified – in tradition). Protestants confess the testimony of the Holy Spirit, but he only leads them, and does not 'inspire' them as he inspired the apostles. There are claims here and there that the prophetic office persists in the church as a special gift of the Spirit,[64] but this claim raises the question in principle as to how one is to understand the nature of these times as unforeseen times.

The question, then, is whether during this unforeseen time, this long period in which the bridegroom delays his coming (Matt. 25:5; cf. the 'far land' of Luke 9:12) we can discern evidences of God. In the Old and New Testaments the people were wholly dependent on the prophets for their perception of the evidence of God in the exodus, exile and return, and on eye witnesses for the resurrection of Jesus. Can we see, and reliably distinguish, proofs of God without the aid of prophets? The answer is no. The meaning of the apostolic witness from which our New Testament comes was precisely that they gave a dependable interpretation of God's revelation in Jesus Christ. The church can of course *reflect* on whether significant contemporary events might be instances of God's personal intervention, and can test their reflections against his earlier revelations that have been reliably interpreted in the Scriptures, but the church cannot interpret any events in our times authoritatively and dependably as revelations or acts of God in history. For this purpose we lack the authoritative persons whom God provided in 'normal' times. This must be seen as one of the causes for the distressing questions concerning where God is and what he is doing, and whether it is reasonable to believe in him. We live in abnormal times, the first time in the known history between God and mankind during which he has not provided an authoritative body for the interpretation of his revelation. This fact alone explains why believers often resort to all kinds of devices to discern the presence and actions of God (Christ!) in history. While the traditional proofs of God have quite rightly fallen into disfavour, there are nevertheless other attempts to show that God is active in history, and to locate where he is and to explain what he is doing. Two main lines can be distinguished. First of all, the traditional belief in providence, and then the modern idea that there are signs of God in reality. The belief in providence must be seen as an attempt to promote the genuinely biblical proofs of God, namely, that God shows himself in history. The signs of God are an attempt to find an alternative to the unbiblical proofs of God's existence in which man aimed to prove God's existence by means of a rational interpretation of the structures of reality.

Let us first consider these so-called signs of God. Wolfhart Pannenberg is their best exponent today.[65] Anyone who perhaps is not a theologian, and who finds the discussion of the signs of God difficult, can go on to the next main paragraph. This material is certainly not vital to an understanding of the message of this book.

Pannenberg attempts to provide a radical correction to Barth's doctrine of God by using an apologetic natural theology. One could characterise Pannenberg as an apologetical theologian who considers it necessary and possible to show to an unbelieving world that it makes sense to believe in God, and that this does not clash with the basic structure of reality or with our modern view of life. He maintains that there are compelling signs, even though they may not be convincing proofs, of God's presence in reality. Here Pannenberg and Barth are sharply opposed, for Barth totally rejected any idea of a natural revelation. He saw the task of the church as the proclamation of the God of Israel revealed in Jesus Christ and the task of theology as the theoretical reflection on the revelation of this God; he rejected as idolatry all proofs or signs of God ouside this revelation and displayed an aversion to any and every general idea of God.[66]

Pannenberg is best understood against the background of Barth's thought. He argued that Barth, in effect, constructed a ghetto-theology, accessible only to the initiated. He rejected Barth's claim that it was only within the church and its proclamation to the world that it was possible to speak of God. In fact, Pannenberg regards this idea of Barth's as fatal to the life of the church, for two reasons. First, because Barth's acceptance of Feuerbach's criticism is so dangerous. Feuerbach, and after him, Marx and Freud – to mention only two – saw Christianity and the Christian idea of God as a human projection and as a product of man's alienation from himself. Barth saw this atheistic criticism as being valid for all other religions and views of God, but found an exception in Christianity.[67] Here we have a single, unique revelation. Pannenberg's argument is that Feuerbach's criticism left no room for this exception, and that Barth himself cannot make such a distinction between Christianity and the other religions, because there are in fact many points of similarity between Christianity and other religions.[68] Pannenberg shows that the biblical writers of both the Old and the New Testaments, as well as the theologians of the early church, all shared the conviction common to their environment that man must take cognisance of divine powers. This is part of their presupposition in what they said about the God of Israel, the Father of Jesus Christ. That which was special in their preaching only emerges when they claim that the God of Israel is the only true God. But his point of view assumes that it makes sense to enquire after a divine reality. For this reason the early church could link up with the philosophical questions concerning the true God and the pure form of the divine reality. In fact, this Greek philosophical reflection on the nature of the true divine reality was a partner to theology in the early church in its contest with popular polytheism, since the various streams of philosophy had already come to the conviction that god must be *one*. So then, by accepting the criteria that the philosophers had already formulated for the genuine divine reality, the Christian message could prove its truth to the mind of hellenistic man.

The second reason why Pannenberg rejects Barth's view that God can only be spoken of within the church, is that Pannenberg is convinced that the surrender of a general idea of God must result in the surrender of the God of Jesus, which in turn would mean the surrender of all that Jesus stood for, indeed the surrender of Jesus himself. He actually sees the God-is-dead theology and its related developments as a consistent development of Barth's (and Bultmann's) theology.[69] Pannenberg is of course right in his view that if you betray the God (Father) of Jesus Christ, you betray all Jesus' claims and all his significance. But Pannenberg is not convincing when he argues that the surrender of philosophical theology and a universal idea of God must necessarily lead to the surrender of the God of Jesus. Even if Pannenberg is right in his emphasis on the analogies between the belief in God in Israel and the ideas of God among Israel's neighbours, which is by no means indisputable, this does not alter the fact that Jesus was not dependent on the surrounding Gentile environment for his message, but preached the history of Yahweh with Israel, a history which the further it went, the wider it deviated from the histories of the heathen gods (Israel's environment).

These passing criticisms do not touch the real issue at stake in Pannenberg's thought, namely, that a universal philosophical God-concept is indispensable to the faith and proclamation of the church. He says briefly and pointedly that the surrender of the idea of God would bring the end of Christianity tangibly close.[70] The most important aspect of his doctrine of God is accordingly the endeavour to counter modern atheism by showing that there are reasonable grounds for believing in God.

Two matters must be kept distinct here. On the one hand there is Pannenberg's conviction that God reveals himself in the whole of history and will therefore only be fully revealed when history has run its course. As a result he rejects any division between salvation-history and world-history, which, so far as he is concerned, goes along with his rejection of the antithesis between faith and reason, and between revelation and natural science. On the other hand there is the basis on which Pannenberg defends the reasonableness of faith in God. For this he does not call on universal history or the whole of visible reality, but concentrates exclusively on man.[71]

Pannenberg is convinced that the traditional cosmological argument that God is the prime mover or cause of all things, or that God is the sustainer of all things, is no longer viable, because the principle of inertia has rendered the idea of God superfluous to physics. His ultimate hope in this direction is that a rediscovery of the fundamental importance of the contingency of everything might lead to a review of the way in which the principle of inertia is taken for granted. Until this happens it must be accepted as a fact that modern physics is methodologically atheistic.[72]

This means that from a traditional point of view, Pannenberg can find only one realm in which to rationally establish the idea of God, and that is in the doctrine of man (anthropology).[73] The decisive question then is whether the idea of God belongs to the humanity of man or whether, in contrast to this, it is possible to prove that the idea of God is a misunderstanding on man's part.[74] It all comes down to the question concerning the value of the religious dimension of the being of man. Stating the matter more broadly: If it cannot be shown that the 'issues with which religion is concerned, the elevation of man above the finite content of human experience to the idea of an infinite reality which sustains everything finite, including man himself, are an essential of man's being, so that one is not really considering man if one ignores this dimension – if this cannot be shown with sufficient certainty, then every other viewpoint with which one may concern oneself in this field is an empty intellectual game, and what is said about God loses every claim to intellectual veracity'.[75]

It is striking that Pannenberg bases the necessity for the idea of God on the freedom of man, which is precisely the point from which modern atheism launched its radical criticism of the idea of God. Pannenberg does this deliberately because he is an apologetical theologian; he is convinced that there need be no tension between faith and reason and therefore he wishes to convince modern man and the modern atheist that it is not unreasonable or senseless to believe in God. By basing the idea of God in the freedom of man Pannenberg radically differs from modern atheism (since Nietzsche), which has been convinced that the idea of God is an unessential product of man's spirit and is unnecessary to the full humanity of man in any form at all. Moreover it is convinced that every idea of God is an illusion and self-deception on man's part, which has hindered his full development by obstructing his access to an awareness of his own freedom.[76] This then is the question to which Pannenberg comes. Is freedom possible as something constituted by the subject as such, or can it be thought of as a freedom given to him, or even only as the experience of a liberation at some particular time?[77]

Of special importance in this connection is the way in which Pannenberg investigates the atheistic idea that God and human freedom are mutually exclusive. He concedes that certain 'Christian' propositions concerning God make human freedom impossible, such as the classical statements of Christian scholasticism. When God is seen as the one who is omniscient and almighty, the One who was already complete (German: *fertiges*) at the beginning of creation, then there can be no possibility of human freedom. His defence here is that this objection only affects certain invalid ideas about God, whereas the reality of God can be understood in such a way that he is conceivable as the basis for human freedom. This however means that theology will have to begin thinking differently about God. No longer can he be regarded as a thing (being) in the midst of, next to, and like other things (beings).

The basis of freedom cannot be an available (*vorhandenes*) being, but only a reality which opens up a future for freedom, i.e. the coming God.[78]

In passing it should be observed that Pannenberg finds himself here in a situation almost identical to that of Barth which he criticised so sharply, i.e. Barth accepted Feuerbach's criticism of god-concepts as human projections for all other religions, but claimed an exception for the God of Israel, whereas Feuerbach had precisely the God of the Bible in mind. The criticism of Nietzsche, Hartmann, and Sartre against which Pannenberg is addressing himself, was directed towards the Christian idea of God. While, like Barth, Pannenberg accepts the validity of these criticisms as applied to other religions and mistaken Christian concepts, he demands an exception for a correct Christian idea of God.[79] Furthermore, it is clear that the concept of God which Pannenberg is offering as legitimate is so decisively biblical that it is virtually impossible to believe that he could have arrived at it without the biblical message. And the question is whether he has not done exactly what Barth spoke of in relation to general revelation, that it is a reading into nature and history of the biblical message. In other words, is Pannenberg engaged here with a general philosophical idea of God, or with the living God of Israel? There is therefore the possibility that Pannenberg can only defend the absolute necessity, for the church and theology, of his general, philosophical idea of God, because unconsciously he has aready filled it with a biblical content, the coming God.[80]

For the sake of greater clarity it is still necessary to look more fully at the way in which Pannenberg bases the idea of God in the freedom of man. Pannenberg argues that man is the only self-transcending being. He is 'open to the world' (*Weltoffen*), i.e. 'man is "open" beyond every particular form which this world takes, capable of its alteration, but also dependent on a fulfilment which this present world cannot provide'. This means that man stands over against himself in a theoretically-critical and practically-changing relationship. But this also means that man is open to the future and that he still awaits fulfilment. His openness to the world[81] makes him aware of his limitations and his bondage to his environment and constantly stimulates an enquiring disposition in him, to such an extent that Pannenberg also speaks of the *Fraglichkeit* of man, i.e. 'the evidently problematic nature of man's being'. Man's quest is essentially for a supporting power over reality, which will carry him over the bounds of his limitations.[82] Pannenberg sees *Fraglichkeit* and *Weltoffenheit* as the most characteristic aspects of man's being. Of course, the fact that man is a questioning being is no proof of God (something which Pannenberg never claims). Rather, it is a sign of God,[83] and that in a double sense. First of all, it means that the idea of God is not senseless and unreasonable. On the basis of the structure of the being of man Pannenberg has shown that it is reasonable and meaningful to enquire after a power that transcends what is all around us. Here we have at least a basis on which it is possible to discuss the acceptability of a divine reality.[84] But of course a question presumes an answer. Anyone who knows absolutely nothing about a matter cannot even ask a question about it. But where does he then get the draft-answer that he has in mind when he asks the question, in this case, concerning the 'supporting power'? It would be an abstraction to imagine the questioner as having no relation to the reality about which he is enquiring. Rather, the question is always framed only in association with the reality in question. This is particularly true of the question which man not only asks, but actually *is*. In that man's existence is animated by the question about his destination and fulfilment, he is already borne by the reality to which such inquiry is directed, i.e. God. Man always already stands in the experience of the reality about which he is asking.[85]

This is also naturally not intended to be a proof of God. Pannenberg points out repeatedly that it is always possible for man to deceive himself in this respect.[86] This, however, is merely a bloodless concession to atheism since this possible self-deception does not feature in his thinking. The reason for this must probably be sought in the question which has already been addressed to Pannenberg in passing namely, whether, in Barthian fashion, he has not begun by reading into man's question his own biblical faith in God, and thereafter does not take with complete seriousness the possibility that man might be deceived about the existence of God. Pannenberg cannot be blamed for this since it really is doubtful whether a person can in practice know the living God and then suspend this knowledge and argue theoretically about a concept of God. But if this is not possible, and I am of the opinion that the evidence of Pannenberg's thought shows that it is not, then his critique of Barth must be revised.

This criticism of Pannenberg should not blind one to the positive value of his thought. It is true that the earlier dialectical theology and its later developments in various directions (e.g. Barth, Bultmann, Tillich) did not solve the problems raised by 19th century theology – either those of liberalism or those of modernism. Walter Kasper (Roman Catholic), who shows remarkable similarities to Pannenberg,[87] has written in this connection: 'A genuinely biblical theology and proclamation, based only on the Word, reflects neither the Catholic tradition nor a theological perception of what the faith is all about...As a human act, faith cannot be an arbitrary decision. It must be humanly meaningful and intellectually reasonable and responsible...It is therefore not satisfactory to dish up dogmatic formulae to the congregation in our preaching, and say to them: "Eat up birdies – or die".'[88]

In passing it may be mentioned that while Kasper does not go into the problem as deeply as Pannenberg, he does display a broader approach. The exclusively anthropological foundation for the signs of God that Pannenberg proposes, with the deliberate exclusion of the cosmological proof of God, can also create the impression eventually of a 'God of the gaps'. According to Pannenberg, physics no longer needs a first cause or a continuing mover. From this he concludes: The methodological atheism of modern natural science shifted the whole burden of the question of God onto man.[89] But the next question is what will happen when anthropology no longer regards the *Fraglichkeit* and the *Weltoffenheit* of man as essential to his humanity but as passing phases arising from certain deficiencies in man's control of nature?

In the light of this a fuller consideration of Kasper warrants our attention. He, too, rejects the cosmological approach, but he also rejects an exclusively anthropological approach, and does so for two reasons: because it aways remains possible that Feuerbach was right, and that in his thought of God man actually does project his own finitude into an absolute subject; and also because Marx has rightly asked where we are to find 'the man'. The only people there are, are the people we actually encounter in history. Even the question concerning meaning is therefore a question concerning the meaning of man's history. Kasper concludes: 'We can proceed neither from reality alone nor from the being of man alone...As a result we can only pose the question about meaning in a historical perspective.'[90]

This question concerning meaning encloses all other lesser questions because it relates to the purpose of the whole of reality – a question which science and technology do not in any sense answer. Kasper uses two approaches in trying to show that the biblical message about God is a meaningful contribution to a meaningful humanity. First, by way of injustice and suffering; and second, by way of man's finitude (death). Injustice and suffering call for absolute justice because man cannot accept that the injustice and suffering that he experiences should be the last word. If this hope is not futile and we do not radically doubt the meaning of history, a qualitative leap and a qualitatively new beginning are necessary, something totally new which cannot be derived from our present history or from what we can plan and effect as human beings. This absolute future we 'have', but only in the form of hope. It would seem, therefore, that the question concerning the meaning of our existence and our involvement in history provide a possible perspective on the God who in the Scriptures is called 'the God of hope' (Rom. 15:3). Not that we could prove God in this way. But the message about God would seem to be a meaningful contribution to a meaningful life and at the same time an encouragement to become involved in the movement of history.[91]

His second way considers the problem of death, and exhibits the same type of structure.

Therefore Kasper's procedure reveals a somewhat broader approach than Pannenberg's, although Pannenberg's view is dependent upon a more comprehensive anthropology. At the same time, the critical questions posed in relation to Pannenberg hold for Kasper as well. It seems that a problem remains which has not yet been resolved. On the one hand, there is no escape from the demand of Pannenberg, Kasper and others, that the preaching of the church should make sense and should at least not be irrational. To be a Christian does not demand a sacrifice of the intellect. On the other hand, it repeatedly seems that the believing partner in the dialogue is influenced in advance by his trust in the God of the Bible and is therefore not in a position to engage in an open dialogue, the outcome of which is not settled in advance. Such a dialogue would not be a genuine dialogue, and would as a result make an untruthful impression on the other partner in the conversation. For this reason, such a rational approach can never displace Barth's legitimate point of departure: that is, that the church must, in the first instance, proclaim God. It is possible that the ability of the church to do this relevantly ought not to be sought in an endeavour on the part of the Christian to convince the unbeliever of the basic reasonableness of his faith in God, but in the Christian's knowledge that he has something in common with the unbeliever and with the atheist, and that is his own ultimate possibility of being an atheist.[92]

Let us then evaluate the attempts of Pannenberg and Kasper to discover signs of God in reality. Four points can be made.

Firstly the motive behind the endeavour is important. They work in an atmosphere in which most find it absurd and something of a joke to believe in God (in fact any god). Such people find it beneath their human dignity to take the trouble to find out more about the Christian message. Whether the reason for this must be ascribed to Barth's so-called ghetto-theology is, as far as I am concerned, at least an open question. But whatever the reason, we have here a necessary and praiseworthy attempt to show once more that it is neither senseless nor childish to believe in God. Pannenberg turns to specific signs in reality to show the meaningfulness of believing in God – or at least that it is more meaningful to believe in him than not to. Pannenberg chooses man and his freedom because it is in this realm that the most powerful arguments against the existence of God are being advanced today in Western Europe. By pointing out the structure of man's being as open, incomplete and directed towards the future, he sets out to show that man cannot be fully man if there is no answer to his question concerning the basis of his existence and his openness to the future. When this basis that carries him along is God, it is essential to man's full humanity, or full self-realisation, to believe in God. This attempt, and the success that it might achieve in preparing people to listen once more to the message about God, must be welcomed. There were times when God was a presupposition in every westerner's view of life. In such times Pannenberg's attempt would have been unnecessary. Today, for thousands of people, God is dead, unimportant, irrelevant. In such a situation, Pannenberg and his kindred spirits are to be welcomed.

Secondly, the limitations of this attempt must be noticed. It is not concerned with *proofs* of God, but with *signs* of God. Pannenberg is fully aware of this. Even if his arguments were to persuade the atheist that it makes more sense to believe in God than to deny his existence, this would still be no proof of God, because as long as we remain in this world of pain and misery and oppression we can never provide a proof of a God of love. If the existence of a supernatural power in this situation could be proved it would be more reminiscent of the devil than of a God of love. God's existence will only be proved in the future. For this reason Jesus also preached the *coming* kingdom (lordship) of God. The reality of God will accordingly be debatable (*strittig*) until the full revelation of God's sovereignty. But, in a situation where people do not even consider the possibility of the existence of God, Pannenberg nevertheless attempts to show that this possibility does exist and that it is meaningful to believe in God. So by means of the discussion of the signs of God, he simply wishes to keep open the debatability of God.[93]

Thirdly, this limited objective creates definite problems. The first of these is that Pannenberg speaks too generally and vaguely about God. Concepts such as the 'idea of God' (*Gottesgedanke* – usually in the sense of a general philosophical concept of God), and God as the power of the future, are altogether too empty and indefinite. Berkouwer is of the opinion that it is precisely here that the difference between Barth and Pannenberg lies.[94] The word 'God' and (especially) generalised signs of God become meaningless when they are no longer used in the biblical sense. There no attempt is made to speak in a generalised way about 'a God', but from the very beginning a distinction is drawn between the true God and the gods of the nations. For example, 'I am the LORD your God. You shall have no *other* gods before me.' Jüngel especially has pointed this out over against Van Buren.[95] So long as Pannenberg does not do justice to a way of speaking about God that points to his distinctiveness, but rather allows the analogies between the God of Israel and the heathen deities to dominate his thinking, the actual gain in his signs of God becomes smaller. There is no guarantee that a person convinced by this line of argument will necessarily come to believe in the true God. This is especially true of Kuitert's popularisation of Pannenberg in a recent book, in which he claims that the general norm to which all religions, Christianity included, must be subjected, is whether they offer an orientation-scheme for the whole of reality, which man himself cannot grasp, but which gives him the courage to intervene creatively in this whole.[96] Pannenberg will have to search for signs of the true God, the unique God, in order to make sure that his service is in the interests of the gospel. In other words, it will be necessary to show that the uniqueness of God dominates the analogies with other gods, and that there are more convincing signs of this particular God than there are of a general philosophical idea of God – exactly on the basis of his own concept of God as a person.

Fourthly, the real value of Pannenberg's apologetic work cannot be denied. Precisely because he works in an environment where the word 'God' is for the greater part synonymous with the God of Israel, and because Pannenberg himself is a Christian whose ideas of God are decisively biblical, regardless of how philosophically he reasons, his work is aimed at creating an atmosphere in which there is a greater openness to the preaching of the gospel. In this sense, it is my conviction that Pannenberg does not displace Barth, nor does he wish to do so,[97] but is engaged in very important preparatory work which creates greater scope for the preaching of the gospel (Barth). Rather than one-sidedly stressing Pannenberg's opposition to Barth, it will be more useful to see him as critically preparing the way for Barth. Barth certainly did not face up to the natural sciences. If Pannenberg rectifies this omission we can be grateful.

This much, at least, must be said for Pannenberg: If in the whole of creation and history there are no signs or traces of God, a God-is-dead theology and even atheism might indeed seem justified. We must guard against speaking of God in such a way that his acts relate only to undemonstrable, spiritual aspects of our lives (repentance, rebirth, peace of heart) – things which unbelievers could always attribute to other psychological factors. We confess God to be Creator of heaven and *earth*. If there are no traces of his footsteps in his creation, in spite of man's sin, grave doubt may well be cast on our belief in his act of creation and thus on our faith in him. For this reason we must give attention to his acts in history since the time of the apostles as well.

THE INTERPRETATION OF HISTORY

The biblical witness makes it quite clear that God works in history – in profane, world history. It has become progressively more obvious that he did not deal with Israel in a separate, isolated history, independently of the nations surrounding them. The decisive event in Israel's history, the exodus, was an act of God in world history, a history which involved not only Egypt but all the nations along the route which Israel took, and those that were in Canaan when Israel entered the land. The whole of Israel's later history took place in the midst of a world of nations involving both the small and the great – from the Ammonites and the Philistines to the Aramaeans, Babylonians, Persians and Greeks. Later in the Old Testament it became clear that God was not only making history with Israel in the midst of the surrounding peoples, but that he was directing world history itself towards its consummation. (Especially in the apocalyptic literature of the Old Testament, and afterwards that of the New Testament.) Through the missionary commission of the church in particular all nations came explicitly within the sovereignty of the Holy Spirit because the whole world was reconciled through Christ.

Several things are important in this connection. The first is that God's actions in history were never recognisable as his acts without faith and trust in him. In spite of the reasonableness of faith in the God of Israel, to which reference has repeatedly been made,[98] the exodus could still be described by an unbeliever as the surprising success of a slave people who, aided by a few co-incidental freaks of nature, managed to escape from their masters. Indeed, the possibility remains that Egyptian historians might have interpreted it as a punishment by the Egyptian gods on the Egyptians on account of transgressions against these gods. Similarly, any of the later spectacular events of world history which were performed by God (the carrying away of the northern kingdom in 722, the exile, the liberation through Cyrus the Persian) could be interpreted in other ways by those unwilling to believe in the God of Israel. Even the appearance of God's ambassador Jesus Christ was interpreted as the work of the devil, and Gamaliel very calmly suggested later that they should wait and see whether Jesus had been sent by God or not. John 7:17, 'If any man's will is to do his (God's) will, he shall know whether the teaching (of Jesus) is from God or whether I am speaking on my own authority', does not hold only for Jesus, but for all God's actions in world history. The entire struggle between the false prophets and the true prophets in the times of Amos and Jeremiah, to mention but two examples, and the uncertainty in which the people sometimes found themselves, at least for short periods, as to who were the true prophets, are evidence that God's actions in history were not obvious. For this reason God did not merely act, but from earliest times appointed prophets to interpret the things that he had done and was about to do. For example, they told the people that Nebuchadnezzar was not too strong for God, but that God was using him to punish the disobedience of the people; and that the marching armies of Cyrus were not merely an unexpected threat to Babylon, but the means by which the LORD would deliver his people. So even in the times of the prophets there was no question of a simplistic and straightforward interpretation of history. Men endowed with God's gifts were needed to interpret history as the actions of God, often against the wishes of the people, as in the case of Amos and Jeremiah. In this sense it is correct to say that an interpretation of history was needed from the beginning, although this should not imply that salvation-history and world history can be separated, as though God's salvation for his people and for his world was something he was working out in a little corner, while the great world decisions were taken independently of him. This necessity for the interpretation of history is evident from another aspect of the prophetic preaching. The prophets never ascribed everything that happened to God. The simple fact that they emphasised certain events (exodus, exile, return, Messiah) so strongly as God's acts in world history, implies that they did not ascribe everything that happened everywhere in an un-differentiated way to God. In fact not even all the elements in a particular event are ascribed to God. For this reason Babylon was later punished, though God had previously used Nebuchadnezzar, because they had been too severe on Israel (Isa. 47:6 f). So long as Israel interpreted the exodus from Egypt by faith and accepted obediently the responsibilities which flowed from it, this event was incomparable; however if they became unfaithful, the exodus would, in effect, have no more significance than the mundane population movements of the Aramaeans and Philistines, of which Amos speaks (Amos 9:7 f).

When one separates salvation-history from world history on these grounds, it means that God has realised his salvation in particular, decisive events in world history but that we cannot ascribe to God everything that happened then or now. In fact, anyone wanting to ascribe the whole of the last 1900 years of history to God, will arrive at a 'God' with horrifying demonic features. The mere fact that history needs to be interpreted presupposes that there must be a differentiation between salvation-history and world history.

On the other hand it is striking how the prophets saw the hand of God almost as self-evident in certain decisive events in world history. Whereas, to the eyes of the unbelievers, it seemed as though everything depended on the power and strategy of the great powers, the prophets could describe them without any difficulty as trivial instruments in the hands of God, by means of which he would achieve his objectives. (Von Rad has written compellingly about this in at least two articles, both of which were referred to earlier in this chapter.)

The decisive question, however, is how we in the post apostolic age are to interpret history. The greatest problem in this connection is the fact that in the time of Israel and the apostles, God himself interpreted history through his servants, with the result that in the Bible we have a reliable interpretation of history. While the same God is still working in history to achieve his objectives, he does so more secretly. In contrast to the 'revealed' actions witnessed to in the Bible (disclosure-situations)[99] we today face unclear situations in which good and evil intermingle and for which we possess no reliable and authoritative interpretation. There is then, on the one hand, the view that we cannot interpret history today because God is working secretly. According to this view we can believe and confess that he is at work, but we are unable to point out his actions. This point of view is strengthened by the lamentable failures of most attempts in the past to interpret history, such as for example the many attempts to calculate the date of the end of the world; or the interpretation of the rise of the Third Reich in Germany by some as the hand of God, and even as a new outpouring of the Holy Spirit. These things should serve, according to this point of view, to caution us against interpreting certain unusual things as either the work of God or the work of the devil. Christians are not called to *interpret* history, but to dedicate themselves to *do* the will of God in history.

While there is an element of truth in this point of view, it also presents a serious problem. This contra-distinction between interpretation and dedication is impossible. Every act of dedication to do the will of God presupposes some measure of interpretation. It assumes a choice for or a choice against. If for example a church becomes a member of the World Council of Churches, it presupposes an interpretation that God is working in it, regardless of how imperfectly the World Council actually reflects this. A decision not to join, or to terminate membership, presupposes the interpretation that God is not working through it. Thus, the church is certainly called to undertake the risk of interpreting history, at least to the extent and degree that it is necessary to make tangible our dedication to the work of God. The same holds true for the personal life of the Christian. He believes that all things work together for the good of those who love God. And yet he has to enquire repeatedly after the will of God in his life and take corresponding decisions. Then only later on does it become clear whether or not the decision was indeed in accordance with the will of God. Whatever the outcome, however, our belief that God wishes to guide us in our personal lives is not threatened. In the same way, it might become apparent later that a particular church or Christian made a wrong judgment in a particular situation, but this does not deprive us of the right or the duty to repeatedly risk an attempt at interpretation. In the final analysis the church lives in the belief that God will lead it through his word and Spirit and that sooner or later the church will receive clarity on things that for the time being are obscure. And in this situation the community of the faithful, and therefore the continuing contact between the churches, is indispensable.

A further question is whether we have any guidelines today that will help us in our interpretation of history. The answer would seem to lie in the simple fact that we are Christians, that is, people that have come to believe in Jesus Christ through the apostolic witness and in the God whom he called Father – the God of Israel. Jesus and the apostles recognised the Old Testament as their 'Bible' and used it freely. This means that they accepted as dependable the prophetic view of history.

For our part we follow the apostles because we believe that they preached and recorded a dependable message concerning the decisive historical acts of God in Jesus Christ.

This means that we do at least have examples that we can follow in our endeavours to interpret the history in which we live. In making this attempt it is of decisive importance to remember that the apostles did not see all the acts of God as being on the same level, but, as Deutero-Isaiah once saw the return as infinitely greater than the exodus, they proclaimed the action of God in Jesus Christ as having infinitely greater significance, and even absolute importance, for world history. No one has dealt with this more arrestingly than Karl Barth.[100] The whole of world history is played out in Jesus Christ. In the incarnation, humiliation, judgment and crucifixion of Jesus Christ God brings to an end the old disastrous history of the world, demonstrating irrevocably that the disobedient, apostate, hostile world has no future and that God has no interest in its continuation. Jesus is crucified and dies, as *the* man, as the representative of mankind, as the last Adam. So God is not simply intervening once more through him at a decisive moment in world history as he did in the exodus, exile and return, but in Jesus Christ God *ends* world history. Jesus *dies*! And when God raises him, he does not restore to him his old life, as happened in the case of Lazarus and the son of the widow of Nain, but gives him a *new* life, the so-called resurrection body, over which death no longer reigns (Rom. 6:9 f). This means that in Jesus God created a new humanity, a humanity which has behind it its history of a broken covenant and unfaithfulness, and ahead of it only obedience, love and faithfulness. So when a man, or mankind, or a part of it, or even the major part, continues to be unfaithful to God, and is estranged from other men, that which is really past and gone lives on. In the history which he is now making, God is bringing about existentially, i.e. in our life and in this world, his purpose which has already been realised in Christ.

In general, we have then two criteria for evaluating our history. The first (more formal) is the fact *that* God does intervene in history and at particular points does direct it in certain ways (as in the Old Testament examples). The second (more material) criterion is the fact that God has given to this history a specific content and goal in Jesus Christ, a content of reconciliation, peace, righteousness, and the new earth.

The task of the church, among other things, is to use these fixed criteria as a means of discerning something of the revelation and acts of God in our own world history.

One further remark is necessary. As in the case of the prophets, there can be great differences today as well, even within the church, concerning what God is doing in our times. It is important to remember that false prophets were not necessarily always subjectively false, nor necessarily did they deliberately want to make the people untrue to God. A. S. van der Woude[101] has pointed out that their subjective intentions were probably often completely innocent, and it is clear from the confrontations that Amos had with them that they appealed to old and acknowledged elements in the faith, or rather to the form and letter of these elements. Rather the falseness of the false prophets usually lay in the fact that they did not have a grasp of the 'hour of truth' and that they did not understand the unchangeableness of God, believing that he always, regardless of the reaction of the people, would do what he had once promised in a particular situation. For example, 'I am with you', to which there is a passing reference in Amos 5:14. This means that the church must live constantly in a vital obedience of faith in which it carries out here and now the task given to it by God.

In the previous sentence I deliberately spoke of *the church*, because it creates almost insurmountable difficulties when specific parts of the church (the so-called 'churches'), which often represent only a single country, language or culture, give a certain interpretation to an event involving other people belonging to a different church. The Second World War provides a forceful illustration of this. In Germany, a certain part, indeed the greater part, of the church supported the German leaders, while the churches in those countries which were Germany's enemies aligned themselves with the allied powers.

Let us consider this a little more fully. In what follows we give two declarations made by groups of German theologians in the year 1933: 'We are full of thanks to God that He, as Lord of history, has given us Adolf Hitler, our leader and saviour from our difficult lot. We acknowledge that we, with body and soul, are bound and dedicated to the German state and its Führer. This bondage and duty contains for us, as evangelical Christians, its deepest and most holy significance in its obedience to the command of God.' 'To this turn in history (i.e., Hitler's taking power) we say a thankful *yes*. God has given him to us. To him be the glory. As bound to God's Word, we recognise in the great events of our day a new commission of God to his Church.'[102]

Against this 'German' interpretation, a 'Russian' interpretation of the same history may be mentioned, for example, the one by the patriarch Sergius who called Stalin 'the *divinely* appointed leader of our armed and cultural forces, leading us to victory'.[103] And which South African will forget – without mentioning any more! – the blessing on the Russian weapons, spoken by our own prime minister of the time?

History can provide countless examples of such contradictory interpretations of particular events. One of the most striking is certainly the one related to the fall of Rome in 410. Augustine denied that the Christians were responsible for this because of their failure to honour the old heathen deities, as was alleged by the heathen side, but squarely opposed to Augustine was Salvianus, also a Christian, whose interpretation was that it was precisely the moral decline of the Christians that was the principle reason for the fall of Rome.

The South African situation also affords some interesting examples.

On the one hand there is the generally accepted interpretation among the Afrikaans people and churches that at Blood River (where in 1838 a handful of trekkers defeated thousands of Zulu warriors) God clearly intervened in the history of the Afrikaner people. But there is also an earlier interpretation, less familiar and not yet fully researched. In the Cape Province the Afrikaner Christians of the time saw the murders of the Voortrekkers in Blaauwkrans, Weenen and other places, as the clear judgment of God on the Great Trek, because the trekkers had rejected the legitimate ('God-given') authority of the (English) government in the Cape (Rom. 13). See in this connection, the so-called 'Third letter of a minister in South Africa to his congregation'.[104] South African history, in fact, presents plenty of similar problematic instances. The Rebellion of 1914 was an armed, violent uprising of Afrikaners against a government that had been democratically elected, an election in which even the rebels had had the right to vote. The Afrikaans churches never condemned this rebellion nor did they discipline any of the rebels, and at least one of them lies buried in the 'Heroes Acre'. I must honestly admit that as an Afrikaner I have readily accepted the traditional interpretation of Blood River and the Rebellion, but I am very much aware that these events have not been explored in a responsible way, biblically and theologically, in our view of history. Nor have Afrikaners given enough thought to the problem that the violence of 1914 (against a democratically elected government) is accepted without criticism into their view of history, while the violence of others today is condemned on the basis of Romans 13 (even though they have no vote). Afrikaners will have to look very hard at this problem in spite of the great differences there indeed are between the limited and almost incidental violence of 1914, and the comprehensive and well-planned violence of today. Someone has observed that the present attitude of the World Council of Churches towards violence is uncomfortably close to that of the Afrikaans churches in 1914. Fortunately, in spite of this measure of agreement, a major difference can be pointed out: the Afrikaans churches did not approve or support the violence – they simply kept quiet about it.[105]

The foregoing discussion has indicated clearly enough that the lack of unity and catholicity among the churches constitutes one of the greatest problems in trying to identify positively the work of God. And yet the situation is not without hope, so long as the following three conditions are kept in mind: That God does intervene decisively in history; that history has already been realised and filled with content in Jesus Christ; and that God's historical acts can only be interpreted by faith, that is, as the church discharges its task in the obedience of faith. Using these three criteria, an interpretation of history is possible even if it is only provisional and hesitant. I have often expressed the conviction that Blood River really was an intervention of God in the history of South Africa.[106] But using the criteria mentioned above this would then mean that we could only claim God's intervention there if we accept the purpose of that intervention as the reconciliation, righteousness and peace between God and man and between man and man that he had already embodied in Christ and which through his intervention he wishes to carry into the world. This means that only those who preach and actualise the gospel of reconciliation, through the power of the Holy Spirit, with all the means at their disposal, (which in South Africa includes affirming the possibility that all should share in the prosperity that at present belongs to only a part of the population) can interpret Blood River as God's work. Even more specifically: Only those who are really working to ensure that black and brown participate in the same privileges that whites enjoy can celebrate the Day of the Covenant (the celebration of the victory at Blood River) in a way well-pleasing to God. Let us follow this through: The land that is allocated today to the black population, and the room that is provided for the brown people are not adequate. At Blood River, God was not concerned with the establishment of an everlastingly privileged white group and an underprivileged black group. This serves to demonstrate that the final question is not whether God's hand can be detected in a given historical situation, but what his intention may be. This can only be discovered in the obedience of faith towards him who called us, and enabled us, to love our neighbours as ourselves, and to do to others what we would want them to do to us.

Many other points are also raised by this question of the interpretation of faith. In recent years there have been repeated attempts to draw up 'lists' of particular developments in the modern world which might be interpreted as the acts of God. In 'God in Nature and History', for example, it is said that God calls us to act against hunger, suffering, poverty, discrimination and oppression, and thus to throw ourselves into the struggle for welfare, freedom, equality and brotherhood.[107] This choice for and against presupposes of course an interpretation of what is God's work today, and what is not. Vatican II's comprehensive 'Pastoral Constitution on the Church in the Modern World' deals repeatedly with modern world developments and interprets particular trends as the work of God.[108] On the one hand the church is referred to as the place where the universal brotherhood of man has already taken shape. In this sense the church then has the task of exhibiting itself to the world as an example of what God's ultimate goal for all mankind is, and to call the world and inspire it to work towards this goal. On the other hand reference is made to the tremendous efforts of humanity, individually and collectively, through the centuries to improve their circumstances in life. This, too, is positively appreciated as in accord with God's purposes. It is in fact seen as a further development of the uncompleted work of the Creator, by means of which man in his ordinary, everyday life makes his contribution to the historical fulfilment of the divine plan. In this light it is not surprising that a very close link has been seen between man's cultural task and the coming of the kingdom of God. While the development of the world must be clearly distinguished from the growth of the kingdom of God and must therefore not simply be equated with the coming of the kingdom, it nevertheless has great significance for the coming of the kingdom in so far as it can contribute to a better organisation of human society. The one development that features frequently in this document is the contemporary unification of mankind, the process in which all men are becoming increasingly dependent on one another. This is spoken of as 'socialisation'. The development is welcomed as in accord with the plan of God that all men should be one family. It is both an anticipation of the eschaton (God's final goal) and a development towards the eschaton. This socialisation and everything that goes with it and promotes it, is then specifically interpreted as in harmony with God's purpose for creation.[108]

Rather than evaluating this 'list' of God's works in the modern world, I want to look a little more closely at why the *church* is so often totally uninvolved, and at best only indirectly involved, in such developments. Two examples, one from the last century and one contemporary, may illustrate the problem clearly: the first, the abolition of slavery, and the other, decolonisation.[109] In both cases, certain churches gave their support only after the actual event. This means that we will have to accept that the works of God in history are not limited to what he might do through the church, but that he uses all kinds of secular bodies (Cyrus) in his service. Thus, even much of the modern methodology of world politics – negotiations, dialogue, compromise – is certainly a process of God-willed humanisation, even though it is outside the direct influence of the church, when seen in contrast to the cold-blooded methods of earlier centuries when thousands of people might have been cut down by the sweep of a tyrant's hand.

A further point that needs to be mentioned is that much of what God gives to humanity in these things is lost because it is not interpreted in faith and is therefore not accepted from his hand in obedience to him. Many former colonies gained little or nothing in their actual living conditions through their independence. It is not inconceivable that some now suffer greater tyranny and exploitation than in the colonial days. Thus, anyone who does not receive God's gifts from his hands in faith may find, like Israel, that God later judges those whom he had previously privileged (elected) (Amos 3:2). On the other hand this possibility underlines the tremendous responsibility of the church to convert (= to make Christian, in the widest and deepest sense of the word) the inhabitants of those states that have become independent in the last few decades. Freedom from a colonial overlord is still not freedom from all the powers of evil. We will touch later on the responsibility of the rich lands towards the poor.

THE PROVIDENCE OF GOD

While we cannot go into detail here about the church's confession that nothing happens outside of the will of God, a confession that affects very deeply our view of history, a few comments are necessary. First of all, there is the equally important confession that much does happen that is against his will. In practice in our life of faith, the first utterance tends to dominate the second almost completely. This results in an attitude of dull resignation, which often appears more like an acceptance of fate, as though God could do nothing about one's circumstances – a kind of God-is-dead theology in practice. In contrast to this we must affirm that much happens against the will of the Lord. It would be a terrible God who could accept responsibility for the present condition of the world. Who would be able to worship and respect such a God? How many murders and outrages do not take place every day! How much deceit! And Vietnam and Biafra! And children abused by their parents! These things are against the will of God. He hates sin (Ps. 5:4–6). He judges every form of injustice. Berkouwer has rightly reminded us that there is only one 'relationship' between God and sin. He is against it, he judges it. But thank God, he also reconciles the sinner, and eliminates his sin,[110] so that righteousness (all that is right) may dwell on the new earth (2 Pet. 3:13; cf. also Rev. 21:4). There God will bear responsibility for everything.

But what does the church mean by the equally important confession that nothing happens outside of the will of God?[112] A few things must be remembered if we are to understand this. This confession is surrounded with qualifications and explanations. The Belgic Confession, art. 13, reads: '...that nothing happens in this world without (God's) appointment', but this is immediately followed with the explanation: 'Nevertheless, God neither is the author of, nor can be charged with, the sins which are committed'. Thereafter it is said that this message is intended to *comfort* the *believers* (both these words are very important as is clear from the rest of the article); that is, it is designed to assure those who trust in him, but are in trouble, that it is worth continuing to trust him, and to persuade them especially that there is no such thing as 'blind fate', and that things do not simply come upon them 'out of the blue'. The objective of this confession becomes clearer if we read the last sentence and realise what it is aimed against: 'And therefore we reject that damnable error of the Epicureans who say that God regards nothing, but leaves all things to chance.' In this article it is thus actually confessed that God is involved in history. Quite correctly, reference is made to Matthew 10:29–30 in this connection, where Jesus wishes to comfort his followers in three extreme needs (v. 28). And the conclusion to his message is not that we can explain everything that happens in the world, or must submissively accept all that happens, but: 'Fear not therefore' (v. 31). Indeed, when we confess that 'food and drink, health and sickness, wealth and poverty and all things do not come to us by chance but from his fatherly hand' (answer 27, Heidelberg Catechism) it is clear that not *all* sickness or poverty (or even wealth) come from his fatherly hand. There is wealth that has been acquired through injustice, and against which God's wrath flames (Amos). There is poverty that comes from laziness, and there is sickness that is our fault. But the contrast in the confession is not between God's reponsibility and ours, but between God and chance ('that nothing can befall us by chance, but...'). Faced with this choice we confess: not by chance, but from his fatherly hand. This does not relieve us of our responsibilities; it does not deprive the history which God is making with us of its covenantal character (in all covenants there are two sides). It means that God can be against our unjust profits and unnecessary poverty and sickness without thereby opposing himself and *his* work, but opposing *us* and *our* works.

During recent years there has been a definite development in our view of reponsibility. In earlier times man was regarded far more as being set in unchangeable structures and left in the hands of supernatural powers. Examples of such structures would be the master-slave relationship, the rich-poor relationship, rain-drought. These were usually regarded as unchangeable conditions, in which people simply found themselves, and about which they were not supposed to try to do anything. Nowadays it is being increasingly realised that a far greater part of our life is genuine history and not merely a tiny enclosure with given, unalterable structures, within which we endure. Our responsibilities become correspondingly greater, covering ever wider areas. This does not mean that God is being eliminated from our lives, but that we are understanding more fully what his cultural mandate to us involves, and how dependent on him we really are for strength and guidance to cope with the tremendous issues with which we are wrestling in these days (over-population, the environment, hunger, energy crises – not to mention the growing unbelief in the world). Truly did Jesus say, 'Without me you can do nothing' (John 15:5).

In our confession that everything comes to us from God's hand and not by chance, we derive the comfort that we are able to discharge our task, because it is not fate that causes things to happen, but the living God who is accompanying us on our way through a genuine history to his ultimate goal, the new earth.

While the confession concerning the providence of God is a comfort in times of need, it does not solve all problems. The problems of suffering, pain, disasters, for which people are not responsible have always posed questions to believers concerning the love and even the justice of God. 'Can a God of love permit that?' is a familiar question. In this connection one ought not to think too theoretically about 'suffering' or 'misery' as abstract phenomena, but should visit a few institutions where the blind and crippled and spastic are cared for.

In this connection Pannenberg pleads that we should think of the omnipotence of God as an eschatological concept[112] that will only take form in the future. While there are many difficulties in this idea, it does remind us of the biblical view that God has still not reached his goal, that he is still on his way with his creation, and that we must pray daily: '(Let) thy kingdom (thy dominion, thy reign) come.' God's dominion has certainly not taken its full form on earth yet. While Jesus drove out evil powers and showed himself entirely their superior, the annihilation of their power on earth is a task which he (fortunately, *he*) continues to pursue. For this reason the Christian faith is always strongly orientated towards the future. Without the faith in a God who will awaken the dead and liberate the earth from all evil powers, the Christian faith cannot be authentic. For this reason it is far better to shelve the problem of suffering as insoluble in terms of our present knowledge and to pray for the coming of the Lord Jesus when the fullness of God's kingdom will also come and he will be all in all. The solution that the apostle Paul gives (Rom. 8:18 f) to the misery and sorrow of mankind is the return of Christ and the glory that will be revealed at his coming, a glory that will infinitely transcend all the present sufferings of creation. In chapter 2 we showed that God is not cold and indifferent to our suffering. Nowhere can we see more clearly the seriousness with which God concerns himself with our suffering than in Jesus Christ, who from the beginning of his incarnation to the end of his life on earth suffered, to such an extent that in the Apostles' Creed his entire earthly life is summed up in that one word, 'he suffered'. So anyone who believes in God need not doubt his concern for our suffering for a single moment. He once led his people out of poverty and injustice as a prophecy that he would tolerate no form of suffering on his new earth, not even tears (Rev. 20:4). But while we proclaim his glorious future, we must never forget that he himself was not content with only preaching about future bliss – about 'a pie in the sky, by and by, when you die'; he did something for the needs of people. He continues to do this, working through the Holy Spirit in the church and outside the church, so that his people may proclaim by word and deed his salvation – in the comprehensive sense of the word *shalom*, peace – and erect signs now of the perfect righteousness that he has promised us. In this sense the church is an eschatological sign of the new earth, because here in this community of redeemed people, it is God's will to give the world a glimpse into his thoughts for the future.

4

God and the future

There is an old and widespread conviction that eschatology, with its future orientation, made a very late appearance in the Old Testament and does not altogether fit in with its message.[1] This belief derives from the fact that the concepts commonly associated with eschatology – for example, the resurrection – are only clearly represented in the very late passage, Daniel 12:2. Other utterances cited in support of the concept, such as Isaiah 26:19, are also late, and do not indisputably imply an individual resurrection from the dead.[2] Similarly, the development of apocalyptic ideas (i.e. ideas relating to a supernatural end to world history) are a late phenomenon and occur also especially in Daniel. In themselves these affirmations are correct. And yet it is clear that such beliefs were in part responsible for the fact that for several centuries eschatology was a step-child in the preaching and the theology of the church.

However, one ought to query the assumption that eschatology should be confined to certain things such as the end of the world and the resurrection of the dead. In the forthcoming Part 2, *Jesus the End*, I shall attempt to show that eschatology should be viewed much more broadly, for the principal reason that it is not primarily concerned with the last *things*, but with the Last One: Jesus Christ himself. Since he is called the Eschatos, since he represents the goal of God's creation, since the future is linked with the achievement of this goal, and is not a mere end which might just as easily be an end brought about by failure and disaster, I have endeavoured to construct an eschatology from Christology. My basic position is that Jesus Christ realises God's goal in creation, and that this is the reason why the New Testament describes the whole history of Jesus Christ from the crib to his return in splendour, in eschatological terms.

This point of view means that there can be no talk of eschatology in the Old Testament because God did not achieve his goal in the history of Israel. Israel failed repeatedly and persistently to be the faithful covenant partner of the LORD. So, in spite of the enduring faithfulness of the LORD, the covenant did not take form and develop. Jesus Christ came to take up the functions of the 'remnant' and the 'servant of the LORD', which were titles originally applied to Israel. God's goal was thus achieved in Jesus Christ, and not in Israel's history. He did what Israel was called to do but failed to do. He is the LORD's true covenant partner. His 'meat' is to do the Father's will, and always to please him. He discharges the duties placed on him (John 4:34; 8:29; 19:30). Thus, if eschatology is concerned with the reaching of a goal, then there can in principle be no eschatology in the Old Testament. It is only possible in and through the history of Jesus Christ. This was the main theme of my thesis.

When I now argue that the future is central to the preaching of the Old Testament because from the beginning God was aiming at the future, this in no way conflicts with this definition of eschatology. The point at issue is that eschatology is not simply to be equated with a future expectation.[3] In terms of the foregoing concept, not all future expectation is eschatology, because eschatology is concerned with the LORD's goal, and with its achievement and fulfilment. When one sees Jesus Christ as the achievement and fulfilment of God's purposes, and when his history is identical with eschatology, it follows as a matter of course that since the coming of Christ, eschatology relates not only to the future, but also to the present, and even to the past. Things that were still a future expectation in the Old Testament, such as the last days, were present and even past for the apostles. 'In these last days God *has spoken* to us in his Son' (Heb. 1:2, indicating the incarnation and earthly life of Jesus Christ); the Holy Spirit *was poured out* in the last days (Acts 2:17) and according to John the Christian community was living in 'the last hour' (1 John 2:18).[4] In contrast to this, the Old Testament still spoke of 'the last things' as an expectation in the distant future. Thus, what was a future expectation in the Old Testament was in the New Testament regarded as fulfilled, and could be spoken of in the past and present tenses. Indeed the concept of 'the last days' is not used for the future at all in the New Testament. That which the prophets had anticipated in the last days was fulfilled in the coming of Jesus Christ and the Holy Spirit: e.g. that the people would stream to Jerusalem (Isa. 2:1–4 and Acts 2:5 f).

If by definition eschatology is concerned only with the history of Jesus Christ because it is he who actualises God's purpose, and there can thus in principle be no talk of eschatology in the Old Testament, this does not mean that there is no future expectation or future orientation in the Old Testament. It would in fact be strange if the God who achieved his goal in Jesus Christ had not been aiming at this goal from the very beginning and had not revealed something of his purposes to his people. So then, when eschatology is defined as future expectation, as it still is by most Old Testament scholars, this implies that the Old Testament is eschatological from the very beginning and not only in its later parts in which certain new elements come to the fore – such as the end of the world and the resurrection of the dead. This idea has been corroborated in recent times by Old Testament scholars who have shown that 'eschatology' (defined as future expectation) was part of Israel's faith from the start; indeed, that faith in the LORD *is* future expectation.[5] But since I have not defined eschatology as future expectation, I will, in what follows, not speak of the 'eschatology' of the Old Testament, but in preference use such concepts as future expectation and future orientation.

This is a matter which affects the doctrine of God very closely, but before considering it in greater detail it will be helpful first to think about the concept of the future.

In theology the concept of the future is closely linked with the idea of history (cf. chap. 3). In the biblical message, history, as God's acts with his people Israel leading to his actions with all mankind, is directed towards a particular goal, a goal to be reached in the future. This means that one can therefore expect the Bible to have its own view of the future. In Israel's environment there was as little understanding of 'history' as there was of the 'future'.[6] Cullmann's attempt to show that the Bible presents a linear view of history, in contrast to the cyclical view of the Greeks, is familiar.[7] In recent times Preuss has confirmed that Israel experienced time and history in a linear way.[8] In chapter 3 reference was made to another feature that confirms this finding, namely the way in which Israel transformed the nature festivals into historical celebrations commemorating historical events.

While this biblical message with its future orientation has to a large extent moulded and dominated our western thinking, and while we have accepted the future as a self-evident element in our cultural heritage, some radical questions have been posed in recent times concerning our future expectation. They do not so much query our biblical future expectation (the return of Christ, the new earth), but our 'direct', or secular future expectation. If 'vertical' and 'horizontal' were not such utterly undesirable contrasts, one might suggest that it is our 'horizontal' future that is being queried here. From various sides the future continuation of life on earth has been seriously called into question. The publication which in the early seventies achieved fame in a few months, *The Limits to Growth*, calculated that existing resources, regardless of how they might be utilised, could not last for more than a century. Pollution was shown to be something that could bring all life to an end. And if pollution were to be radically curtailed, the consumption of energy would be so greatly increased that its supplies would be exhausted within a foreseeable period. It asserted that even given a drastic reduction in population growth, people have become so obsessed with an increase in their living standards that energy reserves would in any case not be able to cope with their growing demands. Elsewhere another example was given of how real the danger is that energy reserves will be exhausted. The Americans (representing six per cent of the world's population) used, during the decade of the sixties more of the world's natural resources than the entire population of the world in its entire history up to the nineteen-fifties. It has also been calculated that one American uses as much of the world's natural resources as fifty Asians.[9]

Anyone surveying the past three decades must sense something of the expansion of the scale of life that we are experiencing in every realm –

even in the hope and despair of mankind. After the ruinous Second World War, Europe experienced despair and soberness. Existentialism flourished in the fifties and the cynical question was asked: What is the meaning of life? And yet there followed the sudden reversal in the sixties in which optimism banished this despair. The tremendous developments in technology and the natural sciences pointed to the year 2000 as an idyllic dream ahead of mankind. What a wonderful community could be built up during the following thirty years, so that by the end of the century a carefree world would be able to eat the fruit of its labours. Consequently it was symptomatic that during these years of hope Moltmann wrote his *Theology of Hope*. On the other hand, it is also indicative of the reversal in the mood of mankind in Western Europe, that in 1972 Moltmann published *The Crucified God*. While Moltmann himself sees the crucified God (the theme of suffering) as the reverse side of the theology of hope, it is striking that he inverts the sequence of the New Testament in the order in which these two books appeared. According to the New Testament the crucifixion (suffering) comes first, and then resurrection (hope). But Moltmann begins with hope, and follows this with cross and suffering. It would seem that this is related to his delicate sensitivity to the mood of the times, which explains why he wrote about hope in the sixties and suffering in the seventies. After the optimism of the sixties, the world has entered an era in which the year 2000 appears to be anything but inviting and the future appears foreboding. The question: is there a future? once more intrudes upon us. although with an entirely different significance than it had for the Greeks with their *cyclical* view of time. This question is far more radical than the mere lack of insight into the future, that was characteristic of the people surrounding Israel. Now the continuing existence of mankind is threatened. Now we are confronted with the shocking discovery that it is our own scientific and technological achievements that are in the process of strangling us. The dream society (comfort, abundance, progress) is so costly that the earth cannot afford it. Ominously suspended over our own 'creation' is the literal possibility that all mankind can go bankrupt and perish.

And what does all this have to do with God? It was very sobering to me when this question was asked in a Christian discussion group and there seemed to be no grasp of the problem. That God might have something to do with the 'limits-to-growth debate', and that the gospel ought to have something to say about it had apparently not occurred to the participants in this discussion.

But the question is being addressed to Christianity from another quarter. One of the members of the 'Club of Rome', and one of the compilers of *The Limits of Growth*, D. L. Meadows, ascribed responsibility for the crisis indirectly to the biblical message and Christianity. In an address given at the end of 1973 he said that there are two main views of man that dominate the thought of mankind. The first is that of the *homo sapiens*, man as the unique creature which has not only the ability but the right to exploit all other creatures and everything in the world for his own technology. He is able to remove any obstacles in his way by means of his technology. According to Meadows, this view of man is anchored in the Judeao-Christian tradition, and it is this view of man that has led to the achievements of the past decades but that has now poised man on the brink of destruction.

The other view of man, which he finds mainly in the eastern religions, proceeds from the idea that man is but one creature in the midst of many others, and is intimately interwoven with the context of natural processes. This inter-relationship may not be disturbed, and it is precisely the short-sightedness and greed of modern man that have provoked him into disturbing this inter-dependence, even to the extent of threatening his own existence. According to this view of man it is seriously doubtful whether the technology and material growth which have contributed so much to the crisis can make any further contribution to the solution of the problem.[10]

Christianity, with its view of man and uncontrolled growth, of progress and development, is here accused of being the greatest single factor in precipitating the present crisis threatening man's continued existence. When theologians consider this charge more carefully, as Lohfink has done in the article referred to earlier, it is not merely to ask whether or not Christianity really is guilty, and perhaps to try at all costs to prove that it is not, but rather to consider again what the biblical view of man is, that the church must proclaim, and what meaning this view of man might have in the present crisis.

One might well ask what all this has to do with the doctrine of God. But it must be remembered that man is created in God's image, which means that there is a certain 'agreement' between God and man, a matter that was dealt with in chapter 2. It must also be remembered that the picture of man, of growth and progress, rests heavily on Genesis 1:28, and that the context of this verse is concerned precisely with man as the image of God. So the question resounds whether God, of whom man is the image, who is related so strongly to the future, and in fact created the future by means of his promises, and directed man towards the future (a point to be dealt with shortly), actually willed the unbroken growth and progress of man, and commanded it, and accompanies man in it – or rather, carries mankind along with himself in it? And the answer seems to lie in the biblical view of the new earth with its abundance (Rev. 21–22).

But this interpretation of the biblical view of God and man has been rightly disputed. Lohfink, among others, reacted against this view and has taken a closer look at the meaning of Genesis 1:28. This verse is usually regarded as the basic command regarding the Christian, biblical cultural mandate. It is striking to consider what a tremendous influence this verse has had on the interpretation of our cultural responsibility, and how unreflectingly and uncritically it has been used in this connection.[11]

Genesis 1:28 states: 'And God said, "Be fruitful and multiply, and fill the earth and subdue it; and have dominion over the fish of the sea and over the birds of the air and over every living thing that moves upon the earth."' Anyone taking a closer look at the meaning of this will discover the important role it plays in Genesis as a whole in the form of a command or a promise (Gen. 9:1–7; 17:6 f; 17:5 f; 35:11), but in Exodus 1:7 where the focus is on Israel, it seems to find a particular fulfilment: 'But the descendants of Israel were fruitful and increased greatly, they multiplied and grew exceedingly strong; so that the land was filled with them.' After this it seems to vanish, playing no significant role in the rest of the Old Testament or in the New Testament.

Linked with this is the fact that the Exodus from Egypt and the entry into Canaan create the impression of a rounded-off entity. For example, read Exodus 29:45–46: 'And I will dwell among the people of Israel and will be their God. And they shall know that I am the LORD their God, who brought them forth out of the land of Egypt that I might dwell among them. I am the LORD their God.' One could say that Israel, representing mankind as a whole, multiplied in Egypt and expanded and filled the land, and that the LORD then led them out to enjoy his fellowship as a fully-fledged nation in their own land.

I think Lohfink is correct when he confines the primary meaning of Genesis 1:28 to this original context in which it occurs. The fact that the utterance occurs repeatedly and plays a definite role in *this* part of the Bible, and thereafter is not consciously used again, also confirms Lohfink's right to investigate further the actual meaning of Genesis 1:28,[12] and especially the connection that it might have with the present exploitation of the natural resources of the earth in and by the Western world. Several of Lohfink's conclusions are important. First of all, he shows that the idea of 'having dominion over', in Genesis 1:26 and 28, has had an unjustifiably important role in our idea of controlling nature. In the Bible this concept has only living creatures in mind, so that this command means that man should 'rule over' living creatures, and not nature. Furthermore, in the remainder of the Old Testament, the idea has a 'soft' meaning. So far as the animals are concerned (as it is used in Genesis 1:26, 28) it apparently means to 'tame', or 'domesticate' or to take into service in some way. Concretely it means that man has 'dominion' over the animals when he watches over them while they are grazing, when he harnesses them as draught animals, when he gives them commands to obey. The 'dominion' of Genesis 1:26, 28 says nothing more than this. In passing it should be observed that the words 'over all the earth' in verse 26 must be interpreted in the context too and in the light of the fact that 'having dominion over' elsewhere refers only to living creatures; the idea would then originally have been, 'over all the wild animals of the earth'. How 'gentle' this dominion was to be is also clear from verse 29 where there is no suggestion that the animals should be slaughtered for food. When animals were later given to man for food (Gen. 9:2 f) the words

used are much more severe ('fear', 'dread', 'delivered'). A further indication of the 'soft' meaning intended is the fact that where more severe
treatment is meant, extra words are used. (Examples can be found in
Leviticus 25:43, 46, 53; Isaiah 14:6 and Ezekiel 34:4).

The second important conclusion drawn by Lohfink relates to the
words 'fill the earth and subdue it', in verse 28. He compares Numbers
32:22, 29 with Deuteronomy 3:20 and Joshua 1:15, and comes to the
conclusion that the Hebrew word for 'subdue' in the first two texts is
explained by the Hebrew word for 'take possession of' in the second pair,
which he sees as parallels to the first. On this basis he interprets 'subdue'
in Genesis 1:28 with 'take possession of', so that the command then
reads: 'fill the earth and take possession of it'. There is room in the
Hebrew for this meaning because it is related to an original Hebrew
expression which means literally, 'to place your foot on something', but
actually, 'to place your hand on something'. This meaning fits the
context well because it is followed immediately by the command to have
dominion over the animals. This would then mean that as mankind
increased and various peoples began to occupy the earth (cf. Gen. 10)
they would have to take possession of those areas where wild animals still
had free run, would have to tame them and take them into service. So, in
brief, Genesis 1:26, 28 means that man was to increase, spread over the
earth, each nation living in its own land, until the earth (or various lands)
was filled, and that they should domesticate the animals and put them to
work.

It is immediately apparent that this does indeed say something about
our cultural mandate and view of man. But it is equally clear, and in this
context very important, that it does not provide a basis for the so-called
Judeao-Christian view of man against which Meadows was campaigning,
a view of man which was summarised by Benno Jacob in his commentary
on Genesis as follows: 'These words [subdue the earth] gave to man an
unlimited sovereignty over the planet "earth", so that nothing that man
does with the earth such as, for example, tunnelling through mountains,
or levelling them, or drying up the rivers, or changing their courses, can
be regarded as violations of the will of God.' It is immediately clear that
this view of the unbridled sovereignty of man over the earth lays the
foundations for the contemporary view of man that is so rapidly leading
to the exhaustion of the natural resources of the world. It is totally
unjustified to regard the growth mania of the economies of the Western
world as the execution of our Christian cultural mandate, as this is
derived from Genesis 1:26, 28. To take the American situation again as
an example, it is clearly sin to sustain, and even to seek to raise a standard
of living that is already higher than what the rest of mankind, or even a
significant portion of mankind, can ever hope to achieve; a standard of
living that will exhaust the energy resources of the world within a
foreseeable period, and which will therefore be responsible ultimately for
a situation on earth which God would certainly *not* will: namely, that the

earth will be desolate, and empty, and uninhabitable (Gen. 1:2; Isa.
45:18). The goal of man's cultural mandate is not to live in increasing
luxury and damaging affluence at the expense of the majority of mankind.
Nowhere more clearly than in Amos do we hear the wrath of God
proclaimed against those who live in abundance at the expense of others.
Theologically expressed: the covenant is God's goal for creation. The
meaning of life is not to be found in economic growth leading to ever
greater luxury, but in fellowship with God. God created man so that he
might be his God, and so that through his care and love for him man
might live happily in fellowship with God, and so that man might be his
man, and would therefore find the meaning of his life in enjoying the
loving care of God, and so serve and glorify him in gratitude. Cultural
elements are included in this, but in the present crisis-situation the task
of the church is to proclaim that it is not economic growth, but fellowship
with God and the loving service of our fellowmen, that must now assume
global proportions, that represent the meaning of life. This might mean
that the church, especially in the west, will have to begin to preach
against economic growth, or rather in favour of the application of our
economic progress to the advantage of the greater part of mankind which
cannot find a truly human existence within our present economic
structures.

Yet it is clear even from this brief discussion that we are now moving
more in the realm of the present or the 'little' future, a realm in which the
ethical teaching of the Bible provides a great deal of guidance, rather than
in the 'absolute' future (Rahner), or the 'great' future. That God is
concerned with our 'little' future, our future as the continuation of our
present life on earth, is already apparent. Theology will have to give
urgent attention to this aspect. But the interest in this chapter is not
primarily in that future, but in the 'absolute' future, the eschatological
future, the future in which God is coming to us in order to achieve his
ultimate and final purpose for creation. We must now give attention to
this future and the relationship in which God stands to it.

GOD'S FUTURE ORIENTATION – IN THE OLD TESTAMENT

In recent decades a great deal of attention has been given to the theme of
the future in theological literature. W. D. Marschs gives a good survey of
the contemporary debate.[13] What is important in this connection is that
one should not approach the issue with an empty, unfilled concept of the
'future'. Ott suggests that neither a stone nor a dog have a future because
their 'future' does not influence their present. He proposes that personal
being is a condition for a genuine future.[14] Criticism of an empty concept
of the future is offered from another angle as well. With reference to the
Exodus Zimmerli says that its meaning as a 'future-opening' event
cannot be used to establish the Exodus as a principle ('*Prinzip Exodus*')
from which in turn hope as a basic principle ('*Prinzip Hoffnung*') might

be derived. In this connection he refers to Bloch, and adds: it is not the mere fact of an exodus which can lead to a variety of other exoduses into the future that offers a true interpretation of the actual content of the exodus, but the fact that in its exodus Israel met that God who had compassion on the captives.[15] Out of this emerges the fact that the decisive character and content of the biblical future is that God, Israel's God, promises and brings this future to pass. It will also be seen, and this aspect is crucially important for this chapter, that the God of Israel promises this future and brings it to pass because he himself is orientated towards the future, and that it is precisely his activity that gives to Scripture its message which directs the believer radically towards the future.

In the next few pages we shall consider the future orientation of the LORD, and shall do so on the basis of the revelation of his Name. Thereafter we shall consider other matters that flow from this revelation: creation, the call of Abraham, the exodus, a number of 'new' things as the repetition of the fulfilment of certain promises, such as a new exodus and a new creation. The LORD's future orientation may also be demonstrated from the new possession of the land, the new covenant, the new David, the new Jerusalem, and from the day of the LORD, conversion, and a variety of concepts such as kingship, peace, history and faith.[16] It will be seen that all these facets of the message are future related and awaken hope precisely because they point to the LORD's actions, or are reactions to what he has done or has promised. It should be clear by this time why this method is being followed (that is, the method of deriving the being and thus also the future orientation of the LORD from his revelation in words and deeds) rather than proceeding from an abstract concept of a *Gott-an-sich* (God in himself). First of all, we only know God through his revelation, and in his revelation he always makes himself known in certain relationships. For this reason we always reflect on God through the medium of these relationships (God and the gods, God and man, God and history, God and the future). But as a result we know the true God, God as he really is, in this revelation. For this reason we do not need to look for the actual God behind his revelation, any more than we need to search for his actual will, sometimes called his hidden will, behind his revealed will.

R. Rendtorff[17] has shown that the revelation of God took the form in the beginning of appearances in certain places (such as Gen. 12:6; 26:24 f; Exod. 3). This was not in itself unique in comparison with Israel's neighbours. But what is noticeable from a very early stage is that in his appearances, and in other forms of revelation, the LORD gave specific promises. Thus, the actual content of Genesis 12, 18 and 26 (12:7; 18:10, 14; 26:24) and Exodus 3:7 f is expressed in certain promises. And these promises (as did all his promises) directed his followers to the future with eager anticipation. The glory of the LORD plays a special part in his revelation (e.g. Ps. 97:6; Isa. 6:3), and as time passed the revelation of his glory was also expected increasingly in the future. Thus Isaiah 40:5 proclaims: 'And the glory of the LORD *shall* be revealed, and all flesh *shall* see it together.' Compare also Numbers 14:21; Psalms 56:6, 12; 72:19; 102:16 f; 108:6. When we remember that the revelation of the LORD's glory has as its deepest meaning the revelation of his power, it becomes clear why the people in exile waited so fervently for the revelation of his glory, and why it was that at that particular time they heard the message that his glory would be revealed. His people were then indeed in the depths!

The revelation of the LORD that was given in order that the nations (the heathen) might learn to know him was also directed towards the future. The hope is repeatedly expressed that the nation might come to know him in order that they might in the future remember him and enjoy his blessing by living in fellowship with him. Even the plagues in Egypt had the effect of revealing the LORD so that he might be known (Exod. 6:6–7; 7:17; 8:10, 22; 14:4, 18). Both here and in 1 Kings 20:13, 28 the reason why the LORD should be known was, of course, that Israel might trust the LORD *in the future*. As with the glory of the LORD, it was during the exile that these 'self-proofs'[18] of the LORD were increasingly promised and expected. Deutero-Isaiah especially gives as the LORD's great proof of himself, his pending arousal of Cyrus, the Persian, who would send the people of Israel home (Isa. 45:1–6; 49:3, 23–26). While the coming revelation of the LORD appears in a different context in Ezekiel, it occurs so often that it could almost be called the theme of this prophet's preaching: 'and you shall know that I am the LORD' and similar expressions. (Cf. Ezek. 6:7, 13, 14; 7:4, 9, 27; 11:10, 12; 12:15, 16, 20 etc.)

From the facts presented so far two sides of the same matter have become clear. On the one hand, the LORD's revelations repeatedly directed Israel to the future, by way of prophecies and promises; and on the other hand, certain decisive revelations were expected with increasing intensity in the future. The conclusion to which Rendtorff comes, and which is expressed in the last sentence of his article, is very important: at the time when the canon of the Old Testament was closed there was no thought that the history of the LORD with Israel and with the world had come to an end, but that on the contrary, the last writings in the Old Testament still awaited the final revelation of the LORD.

Indeed the Name by which God revealed himself in the Old Testament, the LORD, Yahweh, reflects an openness to the future. Preuss has rightly affirmed that the meaning of the name cannot be derived from a mere analysis of the concepts implicit in the word Yahweh. As in the case of the 'image' and 'likeness' in Genesis 1:26, it is the context that gives the clue to the meaning. Consequently it is not all that important to decide from which Hebrew root the word Yahweh is derived.[19] Actually, the normally sound practice of analysing basic concepts in order to arrive at their original meanings can sometimes obscure the real meaning of a word. The meaning of a word cannot be determined by its 'original' meaning, nor from the parts which comprise it. To attempt to arrive at 'butterfly' from 'butter' and 'fly' would be to miss the reality entirely! Similarly, it would be insufficient, when preaching from 2 Corinthians 5:20 merely to elaborate on the meaning that 'ambassador' had in Greek or Roman culture, because that is not necessarily the meaning that Paul had in mind. Only when such a meaning serves to illuminate what the apostle had in mind should it be used as illustration. What Paul meant by the word can only be discovered from Paul himself, by considering the context in which he uses it, and other portions in which it might appear.

In the same way it is the context of Exodus 3 that must be used to arrive at the meaning of the name of the LORD. And the direct context makes it clear that Israel heard a distinct connection between Yahweh and *hyh* (to be). This 'to be' is in the fullest sense a verb, a verb that above all indicates an event, and that is used in expressions such as: 'And the word of the LORD *came* to...' In 'I am that I am' there is accordingly a dynamic, an event, a history enclosed. The broader context shows that these events lie in the *future*, and first of all in the liberation from Egypt that the LORD promised to his people at that time. So Preuss translates 'I am that I am' with the words, 'I am what I will demonstrate', and paraphrases as follows: He will be there as the working God; he will lead them in actual deeds (*tätig*); he will accompany them until his purposes are achieved. Thus the LORD's future orientation was enclosed within the Name through which God revealed himself – as A. Deissler has rightly deduced from the form of the verb (the imperfect in Hebrew is also used for the future).[20]

One can come to the same conclusions from an observation of God's works and the reactions of Israel and of individuals to them. Creation itself is in a certain sense an incomplete work of God, through which he has created the realm within which his covenant with man can be actualised. And because the covenant is the goal of creation (cf. the covenant in chap. 3), and the covenant has 'two parts', history, which is made by way of the covenant relationship between God and man, only *begins* with creation. The first words which God speaks to man constitute a command that directly affects creation no matter how it may be interpreted (a problem discussed earlier in this chapter). If man is made in the image of God, this means at least that God himself is a working God who is accompanying creation into its future.

The way in which God called Abraham says a great deal in this connection. Like Israel later on, Abraham's history began with an exodus which set him on a road which he travelled together with God towards an open future (Gen. 12:1). Preuss rightly introduces election here as an act of God which directs both himself and his elect towards the future. When God chose and called Abraham he promised him certain things. Four basic things can be distinguished: the land of Canaan (Gen. 12:1, 7, 14 f; 15:7, 18 f; 17:8; 24:7); a son and a great number of descendants (Gen. 12:2; 13:16; 15:2 f; 17:2 f, 19; 22:17; 26:4, 24 etc.); that he would be a blessing to others (which was a promise to Abraham, Genesis 12:2–3; 18:18; 22:18; and to Isaac, 26:4; and Jacob, 28:14); and finally, that the LORD would be with him (them), by implication at first, but later more explicitly (Gen. 26:3, 24; 28:15, 20; 31:3). These promises, as election promises, i.e. promises giving substance and meaning to election, directed Abraham and his descendants decisively towards the future; and because they were promises given by God who accompanied Abraham into his future, they bear witness to God's future orientation. In Hebrews 11 many significant conclusions were drawn from this 'being-on-the-way' towards the future. Abraham went out (v. 8); he lived as a stranger in the land promised to him (v. 9), but he was prepared to do this '*because* he looked toward the city which has foundations…' (v. 10) which, without doubt (in the light of v. 13–16), refers to the new earth and the new Jerusalem! This is how radically the writer to the Hebrews interpreted the orientation towards the future in God's call and the journey of Abraham.

The exodus itself, the decisive act of God in which he established the people of Israel as a nation and began a journey with them into the future, was the fulfilment of a promise (Exod. 3:8, 10, 17). Eventually this turned out to be the message around which a great deal of prophetic preaching revolved, both as warning and admonition, as encouragement and as a message for the future (the 'new exodus'). One might describe the entry into Canaan as but the first station on the way into the future. And yet the exodus may not be made into a principle from which we might conclude that everything must always change in a similar revolutionary fashion. The meaning of the exodus does not lie in the exodus as a phenomenon, that is in change, in being on the way, in openness as such. The meaning lies in the fact that the LORD chose these oppressed people, liberated them and took them into the future under his care, until the complete and perfect fulfilment of the covenant would be achieved: 'I shall be your God and you shall be my people'. This is the criterion by which all new departures, all renewal and all openness to the future must be measured. The issue is: How does God come into his own as our God, the God who has promised us freedom and righteousness? And how do we come into our own as God's people, who may enjoy his love and offer him our praise for it?

On the other hand it must be emphasised that by means of the exodus God did lead Israel into the future, and from time to time thereafter, into new futures, because his covenant cannot be completely fulfilled in any 'here and now'. His promises are too rich, and the sin and structures that have been deformed by sin provide too little scope for a final fulfilment. Because God will only come fully into his own on the new earth, his people, his church can never sanction any status quo. This would be a denial of the greatness of God and a betrayal of the promises concerning the return of Christ. Equally, it is necessary to ask what the alternatives are, and whether the proposed change might not represent a worsening of the present conditions (status quo). On the way to the promised land Israel quite frequently wished to bring about 'changes' – back to the flesh-pots of Egypt! Journeying, being on the way, as such is not enough!

A singular characteristic of God's future orientation relates to the 'new' things which are always a re-fulfilment of promises that have already been partially fulfilled. Among these are the new exodus, the new Jerusalem (Zion), the new covenant, the new David, the new creation. We shall briefly give attention to the new exodus and the new creation.

Of the various new things, the new exodus (the return from Babylon) was by far the most important. It is mentioned indirectly in Jeremiah, but plays a more central role in Hosea, Ezekiel and Deutero-Isaiah. Once more God would bring his people out of a strange and hostile land, back to the land that he had promised to their fathers (Hos. 2:13 f; 12:10; Exek. 20:33–44). The new exodus appears vividly in the foreground in Deutero–Isaiah. What is unique to this prophet is that there is no longer any mention of judgment at the time of the new exodus as there is in Hosea and Ezekiel. (Cf. e.g. Isa. 41:17–20; 43:16–21; 48:20–21; 51:9 f; 52:11–12; 55:12–13.) The most significant characteristic of this new exodus (the return from captivity in Babylon) was that it would far excel the first exodus. When one remembers what a dominant role the first exodus had had in the history of Israel, one realises just how glorious the new exodus would be when the people were commanded to forget the former things (first exodus) and to have eyes and ears only for this new act of God (Isa. 43:18 f). Indeed, the desert which had occasioned so many problems during the first exodus would now be completely transformed. It would be levelled out and traversed with a great road. Every valley would be filled and every hill brought down (40:3 f; 42:16). Under these conditions, how easy a journey through the desert would be! Water problems would also be dealt with. There would be rivers on the bare mountains, and the desert would become like a watered garden with beautiful trees (41:17–20; 48:21). And, in contrast to the time when they fled before the Egyptians as refugees, on this occasion 'you shall not go out in haste, and you shall not go in flight, for the LORD will go before you, and the God of Israel will be your rearguard' (Isa. 52:12; cf. also 55:12–13).

How much more glorious the new exodus would be than the first! And it is thus that the LORD works. It means that the people would completely misunderstand the first exodus, and with it the LORD himself, were they always to commemorate that and be grateful for it alone. On the contrary, the first exodus should direct their eyes towards the future to expect yet greater and more glorious things of the LORD. The LORD is like this. He is not trapped in the deeds he has already done. He is directed towards the future, towards the complete fulfilment of all his promises in a way that would be so glorious that he would reveal his glory in all its fullness then. The way in which God repeatedly fulfils his promises, each time in a more glorious and surprising way than can be deduced from the promises themselves,[21] is a testimony to God's future orientation. Consequently it is not surprising that the deliverance from sin has been interpreted in the Christian church as yet another liberation from the Egyptian house of bondage (on the basis of John 8:32–36).[22]

In Deutero-Isaiah especially there is a link between the new exodus and the new creation. The new exodus is even described in creation terms. A striking example is to be found in Isaiah 51:9–13, where the two motifs of a new creation and a new exodus are interwoven. In Isaiah 41:20 as well the word for creation, *bara'* (to create), is used to say something about the new exodus. We read about a new creation repeatedly in the Old Testament; e.g. Hosea 2:17; Isaiah 65:17–25 (which also explains Isa. 11:6–9); Ezekiel 47:12. In Isaiah 65:17 we read: 'For behold, I create new heavens and a new earth; and the former things (the first creation)[23] shall not be remembered or come to mind', because all attention will be focused on the new thing that will be so much more splendid. A further special characteristic of the new creation is that the LORD will then reign over all nations (Isa. 2:2–4; 19:16–25; 60:1 f). And because he is the only true God, his people (and he himself) wait with bated breath for that day. For this reason it is not only the bride (the Christian community) that calls for his coming, but the Spirit also (Rev. 22:17). In the pericope in which Paul deals with the yearning of creation and the sighing of the community for the coming of Christ, we read that the Spirit intercedes for us with inexpressible sighs (Rom. 8:26). Indeed the picture of Christ as the bridegroom and the community as the bride, which is a continuation of the Old Testament picture of God as the man and Israel as the woman, and the fact that everything reaches its climax in the marriage of the Lamb (Rev. 19:7 f), suggests that it is virtually self-evident that even Christ and the Father long for the new earth. Truly, in his revelation in words and deeds, and in *the* Word which is also the deed of God, namely Jesus Christ, we learn to know the God who directs us towards the future, because God himself also moves in that direction and he too is on his way to the complete fulfilment of his purpose with creation.

Preuss has rightly come to the following conclusion from these scriptural data and many others. Future orientation and future expectation, which are eschatology as Preuss understands it, are not strange or peripheral to the Old Testament, nor are they a late appearance on the scene. On the contrary, the LORD himself is the basis and the origin of the future orientation of the entire biblical message. The faith of Israel had as one of its most characteristic features this alignment to the future, and the reason for this must be sought in their faith in the LORD, which means in the LORD himself. The LORD is that God who reveals himself in the history that he creates with the world and with his people. Since he creates this history with a clear purpose in mind, all his activities in word and deed are directed towards the future. Preuss concludes that we ought not, therefore, to speak of faith in the LORD *and* future expectation, but faith in the LORD *as* future expectation, because faith in the LORD *is* future expectation.[24]

In the previous section reference has already been made to Rendtorff's proposition that at the time when the canon of the Old Testament was closed there was no suggestion that the history of the LORD with Israel and with the world had come to an end, but rather that the later Old Testament writings looked forward to the final revelation of the LORD in the future.

Elsewhere I shall consider the strikingly comprehensive meaning of Jesus Christ as the fulfilment of the promises of God.[25] Jesus' first 'sermon' witnesses to this: 'The time is fulfilled, and the kingdom of God is at hand: repent and believe the gospel' (Mark 1:15). When Jesus says 'The time is fulfilled', he means that the entire expectation of the Old Testament, expressed in a whole complex of promises, is only now being fulfilled in himself. For this reason he follows these words with the statement: 'and the kingdom of God is at hand'. The kingdom of God means the lordship of God which was awaited in the Old Testament with increasing intensity. That God's rule was now near at hand, is a comprehensive statement. It must not be seen as the fulfilment of a single promise, but as the fulfilment of the entire expectation of the prophets. Indeed, should God reign on earth, all their expectations and promises would be totally fulfilled. Paul could therefore also say 'when the time had fully come' (Gal. 4:4), and while he uses a different Greek word, he also means quite comprehensively that, in contrast to the provisional nature of the Old Testament, Christ's coming was the decisive event. This comprehensive and final meaning of Christ's coming is stressed in other New Testament traditions as well. According to Matthew 5:17 Christ had not come to 'abolish the law and the prophets', but to fulfil them. The law and the prophets is a reference to the whole of the Old Testament (Matt. 7:12). The same emphasis is found in the early apostolic preaching. According to Luke, Paul, preaching in the synagogue in Antioch, said: '... they did not recognise him nor understand the utterances of the prophets which are read every sabbath' (Acts 13:27). A few verses later: 'And we bring you the good news that what God promised to the fathers, this he has fulfilled to us their children by raising Jesus' (v. 32–33). Here we hear that through the death and resurrection of Jesus Christ 'the words of the prophets' and 'the promises made to the fathers' were fulfilled. It is striking that Paul does not refer to specific promises in the Old Testament, which the apostles, Paul included, usually do elsewhere, but apparently saw the entire complex of promises given in the Old Testament fulfilled in Jesus Christ. C. H. Dodd has said in this connection that the apostles 'ransacked' the Old Testament to pile up proofs that everything that had been said by the prophets concerning the final stages of God's purposes had been fulfilled in Jesus Christ. And H. Ridderbos (with reference to Mark 1:15) declared that one thing is clear, namely, that these words include everything that the prophets prophesied and that Israel had expected from the earliest times.[26] I will argue in Part 2 of this series that the fact that the diversity of prophecies in the Old Testament can be focussed in a single point of fulfilment rests in the strikingly unified structure of these promises.

In summary, one can say that Jesus Christ is the full and final revelation of God (John 14:9; Col. 2:9–10) because the kingdom of God (God's rule) came with him (Matt. 12:28). For this reason the church does not await further revelations; in this sense Jesus Christ is the measure and test of all that the church says and does.

But a further striking fact is that the end of the world did not come with the coming of Jesus Christ or with his death and resurrection. World history continues. And while the apostles certainly did not anticipate a period of 2000 years when they preached about the future, they did nevertheless, like Jesus, expect a definite period of time to elapse. The reason for this must be found in the fact that the fulfilment of the promises was not seen in the first or second coming of Jesus, but in Jesus Christ himself. He is called the 'last One' (*Eschatos*). Because he is not confined to a particular point in time, but creates a specific history (through his first coming, the coming of the Holy Spirit, his return), this entire history is seen as eschatology, as the fulfilment of God's promises and the realisation of his creation goal. But once more this means that from its birth the church immediately turned its eyes to the future. It was not of course exactly like Israel in this respect, for while its eyes were on the future, its feet were on the rock – first coming of Jesus Christ, and especially his resurrection. And while Israel also journeyed into the future on the sure basis of the exodus, this was only an event that directed them to the future, whereas the Christian community lived from the hand of a Person, Jesus Christ, who is himself the fulfilment of God's purposes for the church as the new humanity, and who will lead them into the future. The difference between the future expectation of Israel and that of the church is that the church had the fulfilment of God's goal for creation both behind it and before it, while Israel only had it before them. Indeed, the covenant never really took form in the history of Israel because they were never truly God's covenant people, that is, his faithful partners. In fact their repeated and persistent disobedience led to their ultimate fall, which did not mean that they were finally excluded from God's salvation, but that their unique position in relation to other nations had come to an end. In contrast, the church lives as the body, or people, of him in whom the covenant is fulfilled. At present he works in us through the Holy Spirit in order to fulfil in us also the covenant that he fulfilled *for* us in his death and resurrection. Meanwhile he takes us by the hand into the future towards his second coming when he will not only achieve God's purpose *in* us and the world, but *with* us and the world.[27]

So here we have an interesting state of affairs. In the light of the apostolic message that the promises had been fulfilled in Jesus Christ, we might have been able to explain the future orientation of the Old Testament from the fact that Christ had not yet come. But in the New Testament we now encounter the situation where Christ has indeed come, and the 'law and the prophets' have been fulfilled, but the community is still, in a certain sense at least, just as much directed towards the future as were Israel in the Old Testament. This must be seen as yet another indication of the future orientation of God himself. God has a definite objective (the covenant, the kingdom, the new earth, or whatever we choose to call it) that he wishes to reach. On the one hand Christ, in his own person, is this goal. He is God-with-us, and thus our God; and he is *the* man, and thus the representative of the new humanity – but representative in a real sense, as the one who makes the new humanity present. On the other hand Christ has also been elected to realise this goal in us and in the rest of creation. Indeed, in the beginning God made an earth and placed people on it in order to live with them in joy. So Christ may certainly come to take over our failure and make it good, but not in such a way that he displaces us, causing us to fade out of the picture while he alone fulfils the covenant with God. No. Christ is the covenant, and fulfils the covenant in such a way that we can be involved in it once again, and so that the covenant is fulfilled *for* us and *in* us and *with* us in the world. This purpose of God to live with people and not only with Jesus Christ is the driving force behind the church's continuing expectation. And the reason why the expectation of the church is now more urgent and tense than ever, rests in the fact that the coming of Christ, and thus the fulfilment of God's purpose with creation in its final form, is *near*.

This means that the covenant has already been fulfilled *for* us in Christ, in that he has made peace for us, in our name, with God by reconciling our sins and ending our enmity; moreover the covenant is now being fulfilled *in* us, in that Jesus Christ is working in us through the Holy Spirit to make effective the ending of our enmity towards God, to reconcile our sins, and to enable us to experience the renewal of our lives. This means that in contrast to Israel, who time and again missed the fulfillment of God's goal so that it never took on a concrete form, the covenant is already fulfilled for the church, and is now being fulfilled, and therefore does not lie only in the future. What has already been achieved stimulates the anticipation that that which must yet be achieved will be easily accomplished and might therefore happen soon, at any time (therefore the *nearness* of Christ's return). It is this that acts as a strong stimulus to our expectations. Moltmann has rightly said that we might have managed somehow to reconcile ourselves to the suffering and misery which we experience, had we not known what was awaiting us. But the fact that we know what God has stored up for us in the future makes it impossible for us to be really happy and to be at peace in the present. We will not truly be at peace and rest until we come before his throne on the new earth. This explains the urgent expectations of the early Christians. And the deepest reason behind it all is God himself who refused to abandon the work of his hands. For this reason the New Testament speaks of the 'eager longing' of creation for the return of Christ, and of Christians who 'groan inwardly', and of the Spirit who intercedes with 'sighs too deep for words' (Rom. 8:18 f). It is striking that Paul includes the impersonal creation in this longing. It is an interpretation of faith that pictures plants and animals languishing under natural phenomena such as storms and drought. And this presupposes the new earth where there will be neither devastating storm nor drought. Equally striking is the urgency of this expectation. 'Eager longing' is an emotionally loaded expression. We hear too of the way in which creation groans in travail, an expression which points strongly towards the future, to the birth which it anticipates. The community also sighs to be adopted publicly as God's children, so that it might no longer be his children only by faith. At present, they are exposed to the ridicule of the unbelievers and they long for an end to the suffering they experience even though they are God's children. (Here we are trying to express the intolerable and unnatural situation in which we live at present: *God's* children who suffer!) That the community sighs for the 'redemption of the body' has, of course, nothing to do with the Greek idea that the soul must be released from the body. Paul uses 'body' here in the sense of life (as in Rom. 12:1 and 1 Cor. 15), that is, life in a most comprehensive way. Thus what the community is looking forward to so eagerly (v. 23) is that their whole life will be totally redeemed. They are indeed only saved 'in hope' at this stage, which is to say they are saved to look forward to their full inheritance. The call in Revelation 22:17 is directly related to these thoughts: 'And the Spirit and the bride say, "Come!".' There, as in Romans 8, the longing of the Spirit and the longing of the church for the coming of Christ are mentioned in one breath. The fact that in that last chapter of the Bible, Christ himself says three times, 'I come quickly', linked with other expressions (see, behold, yes), indicates the urgency with which he too looks forward to his coming (v. 7, 12, 20).

The expectations of the New Testament are more pressing because the goal has already been reached, and is now being reached, so that there is a firm basis under foot for stretching forward towards the complete fulfillment which cannot be so far away. And this pressing expectation is again grounded in God himself.

Indeed it is he that has already begun to raise the dead in the resurrection of Jesus Christ. In this he has shown himself historically (i.e. in a definite event) the master of our last, and thus our greatest, enemy. For this reason theological literature often refers to the resurrection of Christ as an anticipation of the consummation, the fulfillment of a promise which not only directs us towards the future, but allows us to experience the future now. To understand this better it will be helpful to consider Pannenberg's fifth proposition on the doctrine of revelation.[28] He shows that Jesus identified himself particularly with the prophetic-apocalyptic background which was fairly generally accepted in his times. He distinguished himself from the apocalyptic writers by means of his message about a near end, and he distinguished himself from John the Baptist in that he did not speak of the near end only in terms of judgment and a call to repentance. He in fact brought about the decisive eschatological moment and promised the eschatological salvation. The clearest and most decisive point of agreement between Jesus and the apocalyptists was, however, the resurrection from the dead. The mere fact that the disciples of Jesus interpreted his appearances to them after his crucifixion with the words, 'He is risen', shows their direct association with the prophetic-apocalyptic convictions. It was the highest expectation of the apocalyptists that the general resurrection of the dead would accompany the end of the world. So when Jesus appeared to the disciples, they were convinced that he had risen and that in him the end had already appeared. By way of illustration, Pannenberg refers to the conversion of Paul. The sheer fact that Jesus had appeared to him convinced Paul that he had risen from the dead and that if he had risen then his claim to divine authority was automatically proved, since in him, at least in a limited and preliminary way, the end had already been reached. The close interdependence in Paul's thinking between the resurrection of Christ and the general resurrection is evident from 1 Corinthians 15–16, where we read: 'For if the dead are not raised then Christ has not been raised.' In this sense, the resurrection of Christ fitted in directly with the apocalyptic expectation that there would be a general resurrection. This explains why Paul's argument in this verse usually seems to us to be back-to-front. To our mind, Christ's resurrection ensures the general resurrection. And in itself this is, of course, correct. But originally there was no direct expectation of his resurrection, while there was of a general resurrection (Dan. 12:2). Today a secularised westerner would probably interpret Christ's appearances as those of a spirit or 'ghost'. However, someone who reckoned on this general resurrection would be able within this framework to interpret Christ's appearances as his resurrection and to see in Christ's resurrection the beginning of the general resurrection.

But because the general resurrection was understood as the sign of the end, this act of God did not merely direct the eyes of the believers towards the future – it riveted them there! This meant that in contrast to Israel in Old Testament times, they already stood within the end, they were experiencing it, and could expect that at any moment what had happened to Christ could happen to all. Even though they would not be raised, since they were still alive, they would be gloriously changed (1 Cor. 15:51 f). So once again God was not engaged in fulfilling isolated promises, but was bringing in the end. And, by the way, it seems to me unnecessary to place so much emphasis on the resurrection of Christ as an *anticipation* of the end. If one sees Christ himself as *the* end, the Last One (Rev. 1:17; 2:8; 22:13), and therefore his whole history as eschatology, then he and his resurrection are already the end, even if the end in all its details has not yet happened. In which case we really are living *in* the end and not merely after a few anticipatory events, which might strengthen our faith but which would leave us living in an 'empty' time. Therefore this act of God, the raising of Jesus Christ, becomes the tremendous boost that already imparts to us a share in the end and stimulates our longing for its full consummation. And indeed, the Holy Spirit performs this function. It is those who have received the Holy Spirit ('who have the first-fruits of the Spirit') who await their full inheritance even more eagerly (Rom. 8:23). Thus it is God who draws us into the future through the promises which he has already fulfilled. Our direction towards the future is determined by God's direction towards the future. It is, therefore, not surprising that in the New Testament he is called 'the God of hope' (Rom. 15:13), the God who does what he promises (Rom. 4:21), because he is faithful (Heb. 10:23). And in the light of the preceding discussion, there is nothing in the New Testament that directs us more forcibly towards the future than the name 'the God who raises the dead'. In Romans 8:11 we read of him 'who raised Christ Jesus from the dead', and of him it is said: 'He who raised Christ Jesus from the dead will give life to your mortal bodies also...'. Elsewhere too God is spoken of as 'God the Father who raised him from the dead' (Gal. 1:1; Rom. 4:17).

Along with this one can think of Jesus' earthly ministry, in which he not only preached and forgave sins but intervened in a fallen creation and in the physical needs of people.[29] Here we have nothing less than a realisation of the end, a reaching towards the new earth in which there will be no more struggle, or tears, or death. While Jesus was performing these miracles in the power of God and in this way was giving substance to the rule of God on earth, he was at the same time kindling the fires of hope in the hearts of his disciples as they looked for his return, at which time the earth would be renewed and righteousness would dwell among men.

The preceding discussion has been an attempt to give a broad biblical-theological foundation to Moltmann's view that the essential difference between God and the gods lay not in the fact that God revealed himself, but that the gods were 'epiphany gods' ('show-gods') over against Israel's God who was the God of promises.[30] The heathen also believed that their gods appeared, but for them the deepest meaning of the appearance was in the appearance itself. By appearing to them the god put them at ease with the conviction that his eternal presence would protect them against threatening powers. Because the meaning of an appearance was found in the appearance itself, the heathen revered the place where it occurred, usually making it into a cultic centre.

Although the LORD also appeared to his people, it became progressively clearer that the meaning of these appearance did not lie in the appearances themselves, but in the promises which he gave to his people and which directed them towards the future. In contrast to the gods, the LORD did not merely console his people with his eternal presence, thus giving a special meaning to the present and sanctioning the status quo, but on the contrary, by means of his promises he created among his people a feeling of being still far from home in the present and set them on a course towards the future. For this reason the people never came to a final rest, even after they had entered Canaan. While the reason for this unrest must to a great extent be found in their sin and disobedience, an aspect to which Moltmann gives insufficient attention, it is clear from the New Testament especially that Canaan was not God's final goal for them. (Cf. the interpretation of Abraham's call and hope that is given in Heb. 11:8–16 and that was referred to earlier in this chapter.) This promise of a richer and better future was in itself responsible for a great deal of unrest in Israel's history. And the promise that through Jesus Christ we will be given a new earth in which there will be righteousness is equally responsible for the unrest of the church in the world. The church cannot come to rest in any particular status quo because God's peace and justice are nowhere fully realised. Indeed, nowhere is there a community of people who love God with all their heart and soul and who do to others only what they would like to have done to themselves. As opposed to a theology of resignation or rest (which, in the light of our discussion, exhibits strong heathen elements)[31] Moltmann posits the God of hope, whom we see most clearly in the resurrection of Jesus Christ from the dead. Christ is not only a comfort in suffering, although he is this as well,[32] but is also a protest against suffering, on the grounds of God's promise that death, the last, greatest enemy, shall be conquered and destroyed (1 Cor. 15:26). Through calling death and, implicitly, all suffering and injustice, our enemy, the risen Christ has declared himself the enemy of death and of all injustice and suffering. Believers are followers of Christ and consequently they too are the enemies of death and suffering and injustice. But this means that over and above the *rest* that the LORD brings into the lives of his people (peace with God and peace with man), an *unrest* is also implicit in faith because the God of hope creates in us a longing for the future in which there will be no more death nor injustice nor suffering (Rev. 21). And for this reason the Christian is, in this sense, restless; not patient, but impatient; not subdued, but in rebellion. Anyone who hopes in Christ cannot be at rest in this reality, but is opposed to it and suffers under it. Peace with God means precisely being at variance with the world in which we live. As has already been said, were we aware of nothing other than the reality in which we live, we would have been able to adapt ourselves in one way or another to it. But because God has given us such glorious promises, and because God, our God, is accompanying us into the future, we cannot live in harmony with this reality – whether it be in Asia, or Europe, or Africa. The new earth will look different and a Christian can never escape that fact. Christian hope makes the church a great 'creator of unrest', or at least it should make it such, in every society on earth because in no society are the promises of God fully realised or his law fully obeyed. In this light it becomes clear that it is not only rebellion against God that is sin, but also the paralysing contentment and acceptance of a situation in which God's promises have not yet been fulfilled. Harvey Cox has reminded us that sloth in the service of the Lord is sin.[33]

In this paragraph we have consciously concentrated on a few specific promises of God in order to show that Bultmann and his fellows are mistaken when they wish to limit the object of Christian hope to God himself in contrast to particular expectations that God would fulfil. Bultmann's well-known idea is that a Christian knows *that* he hopes and that *God* is his hope, but that he does not know for *what* he hopes[34] and that the Christian is unable to make a single definite statement about his personal future. It is interesting to compare with this the view of H. W. Wolff.[35] He stresses that it is fundamental to the Old Testament as well that the LORD is the hope of mankind. Even the statistics relating to the words used for hope indicate that in by far the greater number of cases it is the LORD himself who is the object of hope. It is on these grounds that he speaks of the personal involvement of hope, that is, that hope is fixed in a person, the LORD. But then Wolff draws completely different conclusions from those of Bultmann. The LORD is the object of Israel's hope precisely because it is he who gives and fulfils specific, concrete promises. In the same context in which Wolff speaks of the LORD as Israel's hope, he refers to the concrete promises made to them and fulfilled: their becoming a people, the possession of the land, the monarchy, the exile and return, their special calling among the nations, the new Jerusalem, the new covenant, the new earth. Wolff then continues: Anyone who abandons the God of hope (*Deus spei*) and devotes himself to the idol hope (*Deus spes*) which he fills with the content of the merely human does one of two things: he either, in an inhuman way, demands too much of man, or, lamentably, he relativizes the Christian expectations of the new earth. The hope which the prophets and apostles looked forward to contains a new creation which radically transcends all human potential. In this way the Scriptures encourage man to make what contributions he can towards the fulfillment of that hope and at the same time to leave aside those things that work against this hope. Wolff then uses the image of someone reaching out for the 'new world' across the sea (America, a couple of centuries ago). With his own feet he would walk to the harbour on this side and begin to row in the little boat available to him, but with the awareness that many other powers (the wind at least) would have to come to his aid before he would be able to land in the new world. God's promises deliver us from two possible disillusionments, Wolff concludes. On the one hand they free us from the 'comfort' of a 'beyond' (*jenseits*) which disappoints us because it regards the present as unalterable (or simply loses sight of it altogether AK). On the other hand they free us from a 'comfort' that sets out in its own strength to bring about a 'heaven on earth', but which also disappoints us because it expects too much of man and as a result achieves nothing. This means that the LORD, as our actual hope, and the concrete promises which he gives and fulfils are inseparably united and that it is our hope in the LORD, the God who is directed towards the future, that will motivate us to begin taking small steps in the direction of the fulfilment to which he calls us for which he has enabled us.

PROCESS THEOLOGY

Eventually we have to come to the point where we investigate the possibility of an eschatological doctrine of God. Without going into it in too great detail at this point, the concept concerns God's involvement with his creation as he moves towards the fulfilment of his purpose with it – a perspective which dominates this entire study. In order to evaluate the possibility of such an approach it may be helpful first to clarify some modern trends.

First of all we will give attention to a modern trend in theology which yields a number of original insights about God and is seemingly strongly directed towards the future. This is the so-called *process theology*.[36] This theology has its origin and inspiration principally in the process philosophy of A. N. Whitehead and C. Hartshorne. It is characterised by a strong reaction against the old idea of a static reality and a static God. It sees the whole of reality, and man in particular, as events in a single great process. Against the old Aristotelian conviction that the universe consists of substances fixed entitites such as molecules, trees, animals, it proceeds from the modern concept of physics that the universe consists essentially of events. Reality, both in the totality of things and in every part, is a succession of events. It is striking that from this point onwards process theology follows precisely the same route as Aristotelian theology in order to arrive at God – the method of analogy. The latter theology argued that if reality is basically static and is comprised of fixed entities, God, the cause and guarantor of reality, must be the ultimately fixed, unchangeable and eternal being. In principle this view of God is thus formed from a particular view of reality. We have already observed the impact this had on the doctrine of God and especially the way in which the fathers handled some basic teachings of the Scriptures. Process theologians follow the same method. In a genuinely philosophical way they proceed from what they now regard as the basic structure of reality, its event character. If everything is event and the whole of reality is a great process in which relationships dominate, then God must be supremely process-orientated and must be involved in some decisive way with this great process. God is thus seen as the God who is involved, who shares in, and guarantees the process.

It would not be difficult to find particular points of agreement between such a view and the position adopted in this book. That God is really involved in history, that God has an inner sympathy with his creatures and in Christ has suffered for them because he is love, that God derives pleasure from his creatures, these are all convictions that have been presented in this study and are supported by an abundance of scriptural evidence. And yet when two people say the same things, they do not necessarily mean the same. There are in fact unbridgeable differences in principle. Gunton has even questioned whether the gospel could ever be expressed in terms of process theology. For the purposes of this study we shall confine ourselves more especially to its view of God.

Its view of God is entirely too passive to be able to do justice to the biblical testimony. In the unbroken forward-striving process in which reality is involved, God is assigned the task of experiencing and remembering the process in its entirety. Since every new event is influenced by preceding events, God influences the process in this way. This influence is regarded on the one hand as very important, since a development unrelated to the past would show a deficiency in order. But on the other hand, the free process as such, as well as the forms in which the process is realised, are *given*. God is not their origin, but makes use of them. As a result God is only the final and limited organiser of the elements that are given to him. It is impossible to express in these terms the biblical message that God is the Creator who constantly takes the initiative in the history of salvation (covenant, reconciliation, conversion, consummation). And this does not even begin to approach the biblical view of the future. The entire idea of a definite goal towards which the entire process is moving is lacking, as well as the glorious sound of the gospel which declares that God is so great that he cannot even fulfil his promises completely within our broken reality, but will leave us amazed when, with the return of Christ, he brings in a new earth.

Process theology does have a certain value, but this value is mainly negative, in that it is yet another protest against the Greek metaphysics of being which made the living God of Israel a dead, static, immoveable 'supreme being'. As such, this new direction in theology is a call to the church and theology to take seriously God's involvement with history and to throw off the dead weight of its Aristotelian past. On the other hand, B. Engelbrecht is right in asking his rhetorical question: 'What attractions are to be found in Whitehead's vision of God that are of particular significance to the experience of the world as a dynamic process, which cannot be accommodated within the framework of the traditional theistic concept of God?' (Engelbrecht should not be misunderstood to imply the Aristotelian view when he speaks of 'the traditional theistic concept of God'.) He goes on to say that the irreparable loss in the view of God in process theology is that it abandons the clear biblical distinction between God and the world, between Creator and creation.[37] That this loss is irreparable is evident, among others, in Gilkey in his contention that there is no place for a mercy that transcends the norms of life or that accepts reality (us) on quite new terms. At exactly the points where a more dynamic approach to the doctrine of God ought to be the strongest, this method seems to be most feebly developed: e.g. the love of

God, which is described in a most uninspiring way as God feeling our feelings.[38] We have here a good example of the danger of attempting to replace a static concept of God with just any dynamic view and not with the dynamism of the God of Israel. We cannot adopt just any dynamic view of God, any more than (as we indicated earlier) we can deduce a principle from the 'exodus' according to which everyone must always be on the move and everything must always change.

PANNENBERG

A second direction in theology that warrants attention is Pannenberg's thinking about God and the future.[39] In a remarkable way he approaches the doctrine of God from the perspective of the future. According to Pannenberg, God is 'the power of the future'. He reacts against what he calls traditional theistic thinking about God. This regarded God as one being among other beings, a being-in-itself, an almighty, complete (*fertiges*) being. From various quarters this view of God and especially the idea of God as the supreme being is being repudiated. It is precisely this idea of an almighty being that has been rejected for the sake of the freedom of man (Sartre). Nor can Pannenberg accept Tillich's idea of God as the ground of being, since if one is to speak of the biblical God it has to be in personal terms and Tillich's impersonal concept of God does not allow for this. Pannenberg therefore reaches back to the Marxist philosopher, Ernst Bloch (who lived in Tübingen for some years and has had a great influence on various young theologians, among them J. Moltmann). Bloch drew attention to the future and hope as indispensable features of our lives. He starts out from the future as the fundamental dimension of life which means that the future and hope determine the present, especially the way in which people live out the present. But as a Marxist, Bloch rejected the God of Israel and tried to construct his principle of hope (*Prinzip Hoffnung*) without reference to God. Pannenberg shows, however, that the need for God remains undiminished in Bloch's thought, since without God there is no guarantee that the future will determine the present. Without God as the power of the future the various aspirations and frustrations of man might eliminate the priority of the future over the present.

In reality, Pannenberg argues, the existence of the God of Israel is characterised precisely by his orientation to the future ('*Futurum als Seinsbeschaffenheit*'). It was he who through his promises repeatedly opened up Israel's present into the future without ever being exhausted in those 'little' realisations, for he is the power of the ultimate, eschatological future. Pannenberg regards the kingdom of God as the reign of God and places a lot of emphasis on the fact that Jesus proclaimed this kingdom as coming in the future.

Pannenberg acknowledges that Jesus also spoke of the presence of the kingdom of God (cf. e.g. Matt. 12:28; Luke 17:21, which should be translated 'the kingdom of God is in your midst'), but then it was the presence of the *coming* kingdom of God. Futurity, in fact the imminent future, is fundamental in Jesus' preaching. Pannenberg thinks that Jesus was mistaken as regards the nearness of the future, but the abiding significance of this preaching is the idea that the future determines the present, in contrast to the traditional idea that the past and the present determine the future. It is precisely because the future, the kingdom of God is *near*, that it has an imperative claim upon the present. Read, for example, James 5:8: 'Establish your hearts (present) for the coming of the Lord is *at hand*' (future).

By virtue of Jesus' preaching about the coming kingdom of God as the future reign of God, Pannenberg is convinced that we cannot think of the being and existence of God apart from this rule. This does not imply that God could not be God apart from the existence of finite beings, for God certainly can do without anyone or anything else. But it does mean that while there is a creation of finite beings, it is inherent in God's being to have power over them. The deity of God is his rule.

Jesus' preaching about God's sovereignty was of course not new. This theme forms an essential element in Old Testament preaching. But what was new was his understanding that God's claim on the world, and therefore his deity as well, is to be viewed exclusively in terms of his coming rule. As a result it is necessary to say that in a restricted but important sense God does not yet exist. Since his rule and his being are inseparable, God's being is still in the process of coming to be.[40] In this light, it is a mistake to conceive of God as an objectified being who already exists in his fulness. Consequently, the current critique directed against the traditional theistic idea of God as a being who exists somewhere in the way other beings do, is correct. Indeed, if the mode of God's existence is correlated with his coming rule, we must not be surprised that God cannot be 'found' in our present reality. Since God is himself the content of his promises and thus of the salvation that he has promised, we await God in and from the future.

It may well be asked then whether God exists in the present. His kingdom (reign, and so according to Pannenberg, himself) may well be near, but it is still coming and he is the power of the *future*. To the question as to whether or not God already exists, Pannenberg answers: 'In any case God exists only in the way in which the future is powerful over the present, because the future decides what will emerge out of what exists in the present. As the power of the future, God is no thing, no object presently at hand, which man could dissociate himself from and transcend. God appears neither as one being among others, nor as the quiescent background of all beings, the timeless being underlying all objects. Yet is being itself perhaps to be understood as in truth the power of the future? As the power of the future, the God of the Bible is always in advance of all speech about him, and has already outdistanced every concept of God. Above all, the power of the future does not rob man of his freedom to transcend every present state of affairs. A being presently at hand, and equipped with omnipotence, would destroy such freedom by view of his overpowering might. But the power of the future is distinguished by the fact that it frees man from his ties to what presently exists in order to liberate him for his future, to give him his freedom.

'The power of the future, and it alone, can be the object of hope and trust, since the future dominates the "here and now". The future is the power which is in rebellion against the present and which releases the forces which overcome the present. It is for this reason that the power of the future is able to save and preserve.'[41]

In order to make this clearer Pannenberg considers the meaning of God's eternity. God is not only the future of our present, but he was the future of every other present, including those long past. And he was the future of these past times not in the sense of a distant future which regularly moved further away, but in such a way that he realised the immediate historical future of every period or event. (Or, stated in more biblical terms, he at least provisionally fulfilled his promise, AK) God was therefore the future of even the remotest past. This means that in this sense he did indeed exist before the present time and before every present time, although he will only finally prove his deity in the future coming of his kingdom. He was always the future which determined every present. In this way the future of God also introduces his eternity. Thus far Pannenberg.

A few comments need to be made. First of all it should not be suggested that for Pannenberg God does not exist. One can say that Pannenberg equates God's existence and his rule and then conclude that because God's kingdom has not yet come, God in this sense does not yet exist. Elsewhere too, Pannenberg equates God's existence with his final demonstration of himself, and in this sense too God does not yet exist because he must still demonstrate himself. And to give a further example, he also equates God's existence with his promised salvation, so that in the sense that God's promises are not yet fulfilled, he does not yet exist.

The actual problem here is the equating of God's existence with his rule, God's existence and his final proof of himself, God's existence and his promise of salvation. It is striking that these 'equations' are stated as points of departure, rather than as reasoned propositions. Pannenberg does not take the trouble to show that one is really the same as the other and I do not believe he can succeed in doing so. Take for example the first equation between God's being and his rule.[42] Pannenberg begins by simply stating that God's existence apart from his reign is unthinkable. He follows this up by saying that in terms of the philosophy of religion this means that the being of the gods is their power. To believe in one god means to believe that one power dominates all. He quotes Luther to the effect that only the god who can create heaven and earth is the true God. Therefore the deity of God is his rule.

In terms of the history of religion this may be a valid argument, but from the perspective of biblical and systematic theology there is much more that needs to be considered. Earlier in this study we dealt with the absence of God. This, however, did not call his deity into question. The perplexed psalmist wrestled *with* God over his absence until God once more appeared.[43] Then too, specific cases were cited in which God deliberately withdrew from his people on account of their sins. Mention was made of the exile, which as it progressed was experienced by the exiles as a contradiction of the deity of God, as a 'proof' that the gods of Babylon were stronger than their God. But a prophet came to them during the exile, and thus before God had proved his deity by taking his people back home, with the comforting message: 'The LORD is the everlasting God, the Creator of the ends of the earth . . . they who wait for the LORD shall renew their strength' (Isa. 40:28 f).

It was promised, indeed, that God would prove himself anew in the future, by means of a new exodus, as the absolute superior of the Babylonian gods and all other gods; but the fact that God was not reigning at that particular moment, or that the people were not then experiencing his rule, had no bearing on his existence or his deity. What is true is that if God does not also control the future, then the comforting words which the prophet brought to the people would have been empty and futile. But this does not mean that because his rule and his proofs of himself were not yet visible he in a certain sense did not exist. In fact, he had deliberately concealed himself from his people on account of their sins and had used Nebuchadnezzar to take them away into captivity. Pannenberg is not correct when he equates the existence of God with his reign, his proofs of himself, and his salvation. And if he is willing to abandon these 'equations' he will not need to suggest that in a certain sense God does not yet exist.

But a second comment is necessary. Pannenberg sees the consummation too exclusively in terms of the future. The expressions which declare that the kingdom of God has already come are too easily dismissed with the observation that it is the *coming* kingdom that has arrived and that it is an *anticipation* of the end. The reason for this attitude on Pannenberg's part is that he clings to the old idea that eschatology is concerned with the last things which according to him include the resurrection of the dead, a view which he shares with the Jewish apocalyptic writers. When Jesus Christ was raised from the dead this is seen as a breaking in of the end of history, as an anticipation of the end. Were Pannenberg convinced that Jesus Christ himself is the Eschatos, the last, the end, he would have seen the whole of Jesus' life and history as eschatology. Only then would he be able to do full justice to the statements which stress that the kingdom of God has already come during the earthly ministry of Jesus, and that Jesus is now, already, confessed as Lord, meaning that the last days did in fact dawn with the birth of Jesus Christ and we are even now living in the end. God already rules in the Lordship of Jesus Christ.

A third and final comment is that Pannenberg does not write clearly enough and seemingly not personalistically enough about God. God as the power of the future, or often simply God as the future, is an unusual expression and suggests an impersonal God. This in itself is unnecessary because Pannenberg emphasises, against Tillich for example, that we cannot speak impersonally about God and that man is only called a person on the grounds of the biblical message that he is made in the image of God, because God is actually and fundamentally personal. Anyone proceeding from this point of view does not really need to speak of God in such 'unusual' ways. That the future has power over the present is clearly correct. The future and what will happen in it determines the present and gives to man the courage and the scope to be human and to fulfil his calling. Where there is no future, and this means those cases where the future has no power over the present, there is no meaning in life and man is dehumanised. Without a future man cannot live meaningfully and cannot be human.

But the gospel informs us that God has power over the future by declaring in advance what will happen, but more so by determining what will happen (Cyrus in Deutero-Isaiah). This fact made Israel's present bearable and meaningful again. They could endure the further humiliation and misery of the exile because God, who has the power over the future, had promised to open up the future for them and to lead them back to their own land. Of course, later on God did much greater and more glorious things (Christ, the Holy Spirit). He has promised also to give us the new earth. But all this can be quite adequately expressed by saying in thoroughly biblical terms that God has power over the future, that God keeps his promises. Anyone speaking of God in this way does not need to resort to impersonal expressions such as God as the power of the future, or simply, God as the future.

The conclusion to which we are driven is that Pannenberg's doctrine of God cannot be regarded as an acceptable 'eschatological doctrine of God'. Other facets of his theology were touched on in chapter 3, regarding the signs of God. While here and there positive and significant insights emerge from his theology, one feels that taken as a whole it is unacceptable.

A further brief reference must be made to the idea that God has power over the future. The decisive question is whether one understands this power of God over the future correctly. In chapter 3 where attention was given to the counsel and providence of God, it was shown that the providence of God is a comfort to the believer in need (Matt. 10:28 f). This is the way in which this biblical insight should be used. It is not a sort of blanket explanation of the world in viture of which one views everything that happens as God's will.

Anyone who levels things out in vague generalisations by attempting to explain everything and all possible circumstances as the will of God always ends up in the impossible situation that there are more exceptions than rules, more things that are inexplicable and that clash with the picture of God that is given to us in his word, than there are comforting confirmations that he is directing everything. This approach contributed greatly to unbelievers rejecting the almighty God in favour of the freedom of man, and to believers transferring the sovereignty of God in one way or another to some time in the future in order to escape the conflicts presented by the pain, misery, injustice, murder, assault, rape and deceit in the world. Anyone who tries to use the omnipotence and providence of God to propose a meticulously prepared divine plan which is unfolding in world history (L. Boettner) will always be left with the problem that other believers might not be able to discern the God of *love* in the actual course of world events. Of course, part of the reason for this might be that God's love is hollowed out and robbed of its full biblical content, which includes punishment for sin. But the fact that one cannot explain everything in this way is confirmed by the fact that such a 'plan' does not reduce but increases the problems surrounding a theodicy. (Theodicy means the attempt to justify God midst all the misery and injustice in the world.)

Moltmann made two important comments in connection with the providence of God. In an essay on the relationship between hope and planning he says that we must learn to distinguish between the promises of God and the providence of God. The promises of God do not rest on his providence, but his providence is in the service of the fulfilment of his promises. 'The deterioration of Christian hope began in the history of theology and philosophy with the disintegration of the promise of the God who makes history into a general providence of God over history.'[44] Earlier on, too, he referred to this and maintained that in place of the faithfulness of God from whom we await the fulfilment of the promised future, a concept was introduced of a divine plan that was established from time immemorial and was only unveiled in history. In place of an historical theology there developed a theology of history, and in place of an historical eschatology there developed an eschatological view of history.

These dangers have already been considered in chapter 3. But now it must be emphatically stated that, with regard to God and the future, the Scriptures do not present the future as something which materialises according to a 'plan' but according to the covenant. The Scriptures are not concerned with a plan of God worked out in detail beforehand and worked out afterwards (in history) with minute precision 'because God would at least do what a good architect would do' (Boettner). Instead the Scriptures are concerned with a purpose which God accomplishes, or a goal that he reaches because he is able to (being almighty) and will (being faithful – Heidelberg Catechism, q. 26), but which he reaches by way of the covenant; that is, in a way in which man would have definite responsibilities (the 'two parts' of the covenant). There are distressingly many things that happen on earth that are not the will of God (Luke 7:30 and every other sin mentioned in the Bible), that are against his will, and that stem from the incomprehensible and senseless sin in which we are born, in which the greater part of mankind lives, and in which Israel persisted, and against which even the 'holiest men' (Heid. Cat. q. 114) struggled all their days (David, Peter). God has only one course of action for this and that is to provide for its atonement by having it all crucified and buried with Christ. To try to interpret all these things by means of the concept of a plan of God, creates intolerable difficulties and gives rise to more exceptions than regularities. But the most important objection is that the idea of a plan is against the message of the Bible since God himself becomes incredible if that against which he has fought with power, and for which he sacrificed his only Son, was nevertheless somehow part and parcel of his eternal counsel. So it is better to proceed from the idea that God had a certain goal in mind (the covenant, or the kingdom of God, or the new earth – which are all the same thing viewed from different angles) that he will achieve with us, without us, or even against us. To use a few examples: together with us he brings the world to faith in himself; without us he gives us the new earth; and against us he will make his church one in the truth.

THE BEING OF GOD

One could compile a list of divergent 'definitions' which, over the centuries right down to the latest theological developments, have been introduced to describe the being of God. The reason for this divergence is possibly that the word 'being' is a difficult and abstract term. This is further complicated by the fact that the Bible itself does not use it for God. On the other hand one cannot escape the need to enquire after the being of God, as is evident from the countless attempts to do so during the course of history. Virtually every theologian who has attempted to think about God has tried to express what the being of God is. And this is not surprising. The biblical witness to God is so rich and diverse, he is spoken of from so many different perspectives, spoken to under such a variety of circumstances, and, above all, he moves into action in such a rich array of situations, that the questions rise irresistibly: Who is he? What is he like? What is unique in him? What makes him *God* as distinct from all creatures?

Many have asserted that God is indefinable and some have even suggested that it is wrong to try to define his being (thus himself) in any summary way, either because of the great diversity in the witness to God or because he is too exalted for us to describe. Our language would be too inadequate and even sinful, for God is too holy. There is a measure of justification for this attitude. God is after all a person and to define a person is certainly something different from defining a stone or a dog. But against this reluctance is the evident fact that the prophets of Israel and the apostles of Jesus Christ were not struck dumb when they had to speak of God. The Bible is a very substantial book and its principal theme is God! And every word in it that is written about God is written by men in human language. The fact that God cannot, like some created being, be the object of our investigations should caution us against speaking of him in ways that we use of stones and trees. But this should not prevent us from speaking of him in human, albeit imperfect, language. And in fact everyone admits this, because even those who have felt most strongly about the indefinable nature of God also wrote and preached about God and prayed to God and in doing so certainly did not merely attempt to say unimportant things about him. It would be somewhat foolish at this stage to ask whether it is possible to speak about the being of God. Our whole book up to this point has assumed that it is possible to express in words what it is that makes God God. Naturally not everything that is said about God can be described as his being, for there is always the difference between his being and his attributes. Nevertheless, whatever words may be used for his attributes, they are always approached from the perspective of his being, or with a view to his being.

The history of man's reflection on the being of God is not a history that sparkles with lively biblical expressions. On the contrary, it was the Greek concept of God as an eternal being that played a more important part than the biblical way of speaking about the living God. Earlier on reference was made to Bavinck's description of the being of God. Elsewhere he writes: 'God is the real, the true essence, the fullness of essence, the sum-total of reality and perfection, the totality of essence, to which all other essence owes its origin, an ocean of essence, unbounded and immeasurable, the absolute Being.'[45] Of course this description of God is not necessarily an absolute contradiction of the biblical message. And Bavinck's emphasis on the aseity of God could have the virtue of expressing the independence of God. He is not dependent on us and we can depend on him because he is sufficient in himself. But the role that this type of expression played in theological thought must be questioned. When Bavinck follows the above-mentioned presentation of the existence (being) of God with the assertion that this description of God is to be preferred to expressions such as personalness, love, fatherhood, then it is clear that his priorities are not correct. Indeed there is the arresting statement of the Japanese theologian, Kitamori: 'Frankly, no concept is so remote from the biblical concept of God as "essence". Those who know God as revealed to Jeremiah and Paul notice immediately that God defined as "essence" is missing one vital point: his real essence, his true heart. The pain of God which Jeremiah saw, the love in the cross which Paul saw – this is the essence of God, this is the heart of God. Consequently, the "essence" of God presented in classical Trinitarian doctrine may be called an essence without essence.'[46] One does not need to identify oneself with all Kitamori's views to accept this assertion that the actual being of God, that which makes him God in the testimony of the biblical writers is precisely what is missing in the traditional discussion of the being of God.

Because God is a living Person it is both possible and desirable to attempt to speak about him from various aspects. Since we have dealt with four views of God in the four chapters of this book, one can define his essence in terms of any or all of the chapters.

In terms of chapter 1, it is possible to define his essence as his gracious intolerance of the gods. God does not allow any gods beside him. Indeed, the first of the ten commandments expresses God's being in these terms, which is not strange. 'You shall have no other gods before me.' This intolerance is a revelation of his grace and love. God is indeed the only true God. He is completely incomparable, so that a person who serves other gods beside him betrays him and in so doing loses any hope of salvation and happiness. Because God knows this, because he has proven himself to be the absolute superior of the gods, because it has become clear from the history of Israel that the gods cannot do what gods should be able to do – protect, rescue, care for, and give happiness – for these reasons God refuses to surrender his people and his world to the gods. This would be the end of their happiness and their hope of a better future. He is implacable on this point because he loves his people and his world. He alone is God and he alone may be served and glorified, because he alone can save, because he alone loved the world so much that he gave his only Son, so that all who accept his gift can have eternal life (John 3:16). 'This fanatical (if you want to call it that) cry, "no other God" is the unity of the Testaments.'[47]

In terms of chapter 2 one can say that the essence of God is love. It would have been in harmony with biblical modes of expression if this description had been predominant in the history of theology. The contrary is true. The conviction that God is in his essence love has played only a small part in history, and in Protestant scholasticism virtually no role at all. That God in his external relationships concentrates on people and treats them in love is something unique. Indeed it is just this that man does not deserve. While we might assume that we should be beside ourselves with surprise and excitement that God cares about us, the contrary often happens. When God gives his greatest gift, Jesus Christ, the Jews reject him. When Jesus enters his own realm his own people refuse him (John 1:11 f). And the greatest mystery of all is that God then led him by the way of the cross. If the crucifixion of Jesus had been a *divine necessity* which was gratefully recognised and applauded as such by Israel, even that would have been the most glorious miracle of all times. But the fact that he died rejected and unwanted, taunted with the words, 'Saviour, save yourself!', makes it something totally inconceivable! Anyone who comes to know this God can no longer define his essence, that which makes him God, in abstract terms. Even if these terms can be biblically interpreted as a background to his love, his essence remains his love, his self-sacrifice in Jesus Christ. That God is essentially love is evident from the history of Israel where he remains loving in the midst of his wrath. After raging against Israel in a more than justified anger and condemning them to a destructive exile, without any change on their part, he bursts out with the words: 'How can I give you up, O Ephraim!

How can I hand you over, O Israel! How can I make you like Admah!...
My heart recoils within me...I will not execute my fierce anger, I will not
again destroy Ephraim; for I am God and not man, the Holy One in your
midst' (Hos. 11:8 f). Here the uniqueness of God consists in the fact that
he is not man. A man would have acted differently. He would have
persisted in his anger and would have executed his decision without
hesitation. But God declares: 'I am no man. My anger is the anger of the
God of *love*, and I have no wish to take my anger to its limits; I shall
(unlike man) "change" by being true to my unchangeable essence: love
and compassion.' When a person breaks out in anger he is unrecognis-
able. He becomes brutal. But when God breaks out in anger, he remains
the God of love and we still know him by his words: 'How can I...' (In
passing, that God 'changes' means here that he is different from man. If
God had remained 'unchangeable' in this situation he would have been
like a man, human, anthropomorphic.) God's essence is his love.

In terms of chapter 3 it can be said that the essence of God is expressed
in the fact that he reveals himself in history and is really involved in it.
From the manner in which the Bible calls him love it is evident that his
love is more than a concept, an ideal, a feeling. His love is an act, a
completely remarkable act: 'God is love. In this the love of God was made
manifest among us, that God sent his only Son into the world, so that we
might live through him.' And, as if that were not clear enough, there is a
repetition: 'Herein is love...that he loved us and sent his Son to be the
expiation for our sins' (1 John 4:8–10). And to make everything even
clearer, this act of God is not his only loving deed – as though we were
fortunate that he awoke in a good mood one morning and did something
exceptionally favourable to us. No; it was the climax of his whole history
with the world, a history comprising loving actions throughout. Creation
itself was an act of love. On account of his perfect goodness, he did not
wish to keep his joy to himself, but in his free love made a being alongside
of himself who would be able to share his joy with him. He intervened in
Israel's history, leading them out of their misery and oppression to a land
'flowing with milk and honey'. In contrast to the gods surrounding
Israel, the uniqueness of God was repeatedly shown in the fact that he did
things, that he kept his promises. He actually does the things appropriate
to a God. He even does those things that should have been characteristic
of the other gods (e.g. rain-making was supposed to be a speciality of
Baal), but which they actually were unable to do. Even his Name,
Yahweh, is related to a verb, a word meaning 'happen'. He is the One
who, supremely, makes things happen, the God of action. His actions are
actions of love, of salvation, of protection, actions that open up the future
for those who trust in him.

In terms of chapter 4 we can define the essence of God as the God who
has power over the future, who is faithful and keeps his promises, and
who, through his power over the future, opens up the present and gives
meaning to life. Zimmerli suggests that God accompanied Israel as their

leader into the future and that this determined the entire history of Israel. Indeed even the act of creation as such indicates that God was doing something with an eye to the future. And for this reason creation was not an end but a beginning. And so also the new creation in Jesus Christ was not an end but a new beginning (the new man, being *renewed* in the image of God). And even the new earth is not an end, but the real beginning, our first opportunity to do our actual work in a completely unhindered and unfettered way: to serve God and to glorify him. There are two things which make this future so enticing and which make 'the vale of tears' in which we live at present both bearable and even opportune: the wonderful promises of God and the fact that he is faithful and will certainly keep his promises; in his own unique way he will fulfil them more richly and gloriously than can ever be imagined from the promises themselves. God's richness and his faithfulness make him different from us, make him different from the gods, make him God. Israel lived with its attention focussed on the future; the church looks ahead because God himself is on his way towards the future and because God himself does not yet enjoy the pleasures of the new earth or of the achievement of his purposes or of the covenant in its full realisation. It is not only we who wait for his glorious future, for he himself is not yet all in all and he too is accordingly awaiting the full joy that he has promised and will give.

We have successively defined God's essence as his incomparability, and accordingly his gracious intolerance (as a result of his love); his love; his act and acts of love; and fourthly, his faithfulness in fulfiling his rich promises. If this is the kind of being God is, and if this is how his deity should be described, then one word is also enough: God is *love*. It is a love on which people may count, a love in which he has freely bound himself to achieve his goal, a love that means that he does not abandon the work of his hands, a love that enables us to trust him even in the midst of the present terrible spiritual and worldly need of mankind, and a love that allows us to hope confidently that he will remain faithful into all eternity – faithful to himself and therefore faithful to us, to whom he has bound himself, and faithful to our future. If this view of God can be called 'eschatological', then an eschatological doctrine of God does indeed flow from the biblical witness to God.

INSTEAD OF AN INTRODUCTION

This book begins deliberately without an introduction. In such an introduction it would have been necessary to deal with material which would on the one hand have been more formal in character, and on the other, more 'theological'. Since the book has been written for the 'ordinary man', and not only for those trained in theology, the subject itself was tackled immediately without any preliminary remarks. Therefore, anyone who does not wish to read further may relax, because he will miss nothing of the content of the book. What follows consists of explanations regarding method of work, point of view, and a few more formal observations.

Yet the following comments are important for a theological appraisal of what has been offered here.

In a certain sense these chapters have not been offered as a 'doctrine of God'. The approach is different from the way in which comprehensive accounts about God are usually presented. Traditional subdivisions dealing with the being of God and then his attributes have not been followed. This does not mean that such a procedure is rejected. It only means that in this book a different approach is deliberately offered, with the intention to cover the entire biblical message. It may be called a *Biblical, historical* theology.

There is a further sense in which this is not a 'doctrine of God' in the traditional meaning. As is clear from the table of contents, the book is not about 'God-in-himself', but about 'God and...', about God in certain *relationships*. This was a decision in principle. While God does exist over and above his relationships and his actions, and is thus more and greater than his deeds and relationships, it is only through his deeds and relationships that we know God. And it is the *true* God, or rather God in his fullness, that we know in these deeds and relationships. So we do not need to look for the actual God behind his revelation. We do not need to look behind God's revealed will for his actual (secret) will. God is not solitary, but a being-in-community. He lives in relationships towards his creatures. To search behind this revealed God for the true, hidden and actual God is unbiblical. This would be an abstraction, just as it is an abstraction to try to find his image (man) behind and outside of the relationships in which man lives.

The four relationships under which we have considered God (to the gods, to man, to history and to the future) are of course not the only possibilities. There is in fact an element of arbitrariness in the selection of these four. Such arbitrariness does not contain serious dangers, however, provided that throughout the investigation one manages to remain faithful to the biblical witness. Because God is the *living* God, i.e. a Person, one can quite easily begin at any point of the biblical witness. If one listens faithfully to that witness, allowing oneself to be led forward by it, one will conclude at the same point where one began: with God himself, the God of love. It is this fact that makes it possible to gain a true view of God without necessarily dealing with 'everything' about him. There is a certain centrality in the doctrine of God, and in fact in all theology, and *here* all roads do indeed lead to Rome. More data would not create a different picture of God.

Why then have *these* four relationships been chosen? Anyone familiar with the contemporary discussion about the doctrine of God will realise that the choice is, after all, not so arbitrary. In my judgment it is these aspects of the doctrine of God that are, on the one hand, the burning issues of our times, and on the other, are those that have been most neglected in the traditional approach to the doctrine. (By traditional I mean first and foremost the Reformed doctrine of God, but it is also true that few of the great doctrines of our faith have been as uniformly treated in the church as a whole over the centuries.) The relationship between God and the gods is at the heart of the contemporary discussion about salvation outside the church, salvation through other religions, the word of God in and through other religions. The relationship between God and man is, on the one hand, at the heart of the discussion about the universality and worldiness of salvation, about the way in which the kingdom of God is to come. On the other hand, the 'humanity' of God never completely came into its own in either Reformed or Roman Catholic theology before the middle of this century. God and history stand at the heart of the discussion about the meaning of history, the revelation of God, the relationship between faith and reality, and the question as to whether it makes sense to believe in God. The new interest in the relationship between God and the future, which is reflected particularly in the theology of hope, was not only a passing phenomenon of the sixties (when the year 2000 was looked forward to with such eagerness), but has also persisted through the more sober seventies in the realisation that we might not have so long on this planet as we used to think, and in any case, not in the form that we enjoy it now. This has made the question of the future, and of the God who has the future in his hand, an even more urgent issue.

These four relationships in which God is depicted have, therefore, been consciously chosen to try to bring out the reality of God in the most pertinent way possible. In the biblical witness God is always the One who makes the difference, the One who is decisive. Our modern experience of God as the One who stands at the periphery of life, as an unimportant factor who at the most has some relevance for our inner lives, is alien to the faith of Israel and is a sign that somewhere there is a colossal deficiency in the church's proclamation of God. By concentrating on these four relationships I have endeavoured to acknowledge the centrality of God in life and at the heart of history. So I have deliberately spoken of God in completely concrete terms by repeatedly bringing into the discussion his will for society. That somewhat less attention is given to the meaning of God for our inner lives, flows from the situation and the pietistic convictions of most of the Afrikaner people in South Africa. To let the emphasis fall on this aspect would be like carrying coals to Newcastle. This does not mean that it is not equally important. In Western Europe, for example, the emphasis might be completely reversed.

It must be emphasised again that a lack of systematisation is occasioned by the subject under discussion. To deal with God is to be obliged to return repeatedly to the same matter from different angles. For this reason, issues such as the proofs of God, his plan or purpose, his providence and his orientation towards the future, come up for discussion more than once. An attempt is made here and there to indicate this by means of cross-references.

It is inevitable that some readers will find a disproportionate prepon-
derance of Old Testament material. Various reasons can be given for this
feature. First of all, my own previous works have been strongly coloured
by the New Testament. The prominence of New Testament material in
my thesis especially is responsible for this. This earlier concentration
means that one is driven now to concentrate on a somewhat neglected
field in one's own thinking – the Old Testament. Along with this is the
fact that far better works have appeared in recent years on God in the Old
Testament than on God in the New Testament in both biblical and
systematic theology. It appears that the treatment of God the Father in
the New Testament has been almost completely neglected in New Testament theology and in the more comprehensive works only a few pages at
the most are devoted to him. This is a deficiency in New Testament
theology which will have a progressively damaging effect on systematic
thinking about God. The systematic theologian remains irrevocably
dependent on Old and New Testament theologians.

I am still uncertain as to whether this can be called an 'eschatological'
doctrine of God. My original plan was to approach the doctrine of God
from an eschatological perspective. However, it became progressively
clearer that one cannot without further explanation simply speak of an
'eschatological doctrine of God'. The term eschatology has too many
meanings for this to be possible and there are too many possibilities that
still remain unused. On the other hand one particular concept can so
easily dominate the scene when one concentrates on a special theology,
such as the theology of hope, the theology of revolution, the theology of
the world, or political theology. The danger inherent in this is that the
breadth and depth of theology as *Word* theology, as a listening to the
Scriptures in all their breadth and depth may be allowed to slip by. For
this reason I deliberately did not begin with a particular eschatological
aspect, but with the comparison between God and the gods, a theme
which in my judgment has been seriously neglected in the history of the
doctrine of God, and as a result of which the incomparability of God has
not come into its own. This was followed by God and man, and God and
history. But it also became increasingly clear to me that every chapter
was in a sense an 'eschatological' approach and this because each chapter
manifests an historical approach, since God reveals himself in history.
Because God is known with increasing clarity through his progressive
revelation[48] it means that, while one is following his history with Israel,
one realises more and more clearly who he is and what he is like. But
because God does not make history for the sake of making history, but
has a goal in mind, that is to say, because history is what he does by way of
the covenant along with his people in the fulfilment of his promises and
prophecies, neither he himself nor the history that he makes can be
approached from any other direction than from the perspective of the
goal that he has in mind and towards which he is moving. Therefore, if
eschatology is concerned with a goal and in this sense with the future (cf.

the forthcoming *Jesus the End*), then it is unavoidable that a genuinely historical approach to the revelation of God will result in an eschatological doctrine of God.

If in this special sense it is an eschatological doctrine of God that is offered here, then the question arises as to why, relatively speaking, Jesus Christ receives so little attention in the study. The theological reasons for this were given in chapter 2. But the question remains whether this is not a departure from the way that was taken in my thesis *Jesus Christus die Eschatos*, which is to be published in an abridged form as Part 2 of this series: *Jesus the End*. There Jesus Christ is absolutely central. *He* is the Eschatos, the *goal* of God for the world. And I stand by this wholeheartedly. But here the emphasis is placed on a different word in this sentence. The endeavour now is to discuss the goal of *God* for the world. That God has a goal in mind for the world, that *he* reaches this goal in Jesus Christ is also to be found in my thesis, although more in the background. And sooner or later this had to be worked out.

A further question that has often been asked in recent years in connection with the doctrine of God and Christology, is whether they should be approached from above (*von oben*) or from below (*von unten*). The classical approach, according to which God revealed himself in the history of Israel and Jesus, the second person of the Trinity become man, should be regarded as an approach 'from above'. In contrast to this it is then argued that one should ask 'from below' whether it makes sense to speak of God and whether there are any reasonable arguments as to why his existence and his revelation in the history of Israel and in Jesus Christ should be accepted as credible. So in Christology one would also have to begin from below, which is to say, not with the second person of the Trinity who became man, but with the man Jesus who lived in Palestine, and whose disciples gradually found out some extraordinary things about him and after a number of (so-called) appearances began preaching that he had risen from the dead. Pannenberg, more than any other contemporary theologian, has shown the value of such an approach from below. There is today a fairly widespread conviction that it is unreasonable to believe in God, that it is a leap in the dark which a person can only take against his better judgment. Pannenberg has done a great deal to show that this is not true and that it is thoroughly reasonable to believe in God, that it is in any case more reasonable to believe that God does exist than to believe that he does not. And yet Moltmann and Berkouwer have shown that it is a false antithesis to place the approach 'from below' against the approach 'from above' in this way and to demand a choice between the two.[49] In fact, while Moltmann does not state it in so many words, I have the impression that he would suggest that one should approach Christ from behind (Israel) and from before (the resurrection). In the same way I am convinced that 'from above' *or* 'from below' is a false antithesis as far as the doctrine of God is concerned. One cannot work completely from below, because then the gospel would have nothing more to say to man than he already knows. The gospel itself would be misunderstood in such an approach. And to work only from above is equally impossible – even the prophets could not do this. The proofs of God in Deutero-Isaiah (chapter 3) are sufficient evidence of this. In the time of Deutero-Isaiah, when Cyrus was called and used by God, there was abundant evidence for regarding faith in God as entirely reasonable. Those who did not believe in God were not behaving reasonably: they were committing sin in fact and were accordingly guilty before God. This is but one of many examples of the possibilities that indeed exist for working from below as well. But it is, of course, only possible when God first works from above. Rather than working from above or from below (or better: *while* working from below *and* from above), the essential matter is to attempt to understand the witness that has been handed down (and in this way to work 'from behind') and to understand the present in the light of the future that is opened up by this witness (and in this way to work 'from before').

As has already been stated, this study is not dogmatics in the ordinary sense of the word. One could define it rather as biblical historical theology with a dogmatic approach. Its aim is to reach ordinary people who do not have a scientific interest in the Bible, but who wish to understand something of the Christian faith. Experience has shown me that ministers in large congregations often have relatively little time to read in preparation for their sermons. As a result, their need for preaching material is one of the reasons why considerable attention has been given here to the exegesis of scriptural passages. And of course, God himself has a pastoral heart and perhaps he would not wish one to attempt to write about him with too much scholarship – as though with our little extra learning we might be able to write better of him than the simple direct witness of the Bible. This is not to deny the value of genuine, deep thought about God, but anyone who thinks really deeply will be able to express it in relatively simple words because God is love, as is concretely illustrated in the cross of Golgotha.

So far as the title *Here Am I* is concerned a brief word is necessary. I was grateful that I was able to find a title in the book of Isaiah because I have learned so much about God from this prophetic book (Isa. 52:6; 58:9; 65:1. Cf. also 40:9, for essentially the same expression, but in the prophet's mouth). The cry is one of joy, with which God presents himself to his disheartened people, languishing in a long exile. In their need God appeared to them after their long wait during which they had almost perished in doubt. Similarly, I wished to speak about God in an exclamation, a call. Anyone who learns to know God, learns to call out about him. He is wonderful; he is incomparable; he is love.

A final word about this book as the first of a series. Under the general title *A believer's reflection* I hope over the coming years to consider all the important aspects of our faith. The whole series will be written for the man in the street, and will be an attempt to throw light on our faith from various angles so that people may be able to understand what they believe (*fides quaerens intellectum*). This book has originally been published in Afrikaans in 1975.

Notes

1 God and the gods

1. J. Schmitz (ed): *Das Ende der Exportreligion – Perspektiven für eine künftige Mission.*
2. One ought not to repudiate the link between the gospel and Platonist philosophy so formally that it merely results in the rejection of (Greek) *terms* in theology. The real need is that such philosophical terms should be given a new, unique content from Holy Scripture, in a way far more radical than has usually been done.
3. H. D. Preuss: *Verspottung fremder Religionen im Alten Testament.*
4. Besides Preuss, W. Zimmerli: *The Old Testament and the World*, p. 23.
5. This interpretation assumes that Genesis 1 had achieved its final form by the time of the Babylonian captivity, but is not necessarily bound to such a late date.
6. H.-J. Kraus: The Living God, in: F. Herzog (ed): *Theology of the Liberating Word*, p. 99.
7. As to whether these gods really existed or not, this will be considered later. Ebeling has rightly observed that the second commandment does not read: 'There are no other gods beside me', but means rather: 'Beside the LORD there are for you no other valid gods.' This neither acknowledges nor denies the existence of other gods, because Israel did not distinguish between 'to-be-in-itself' and 'to-be-for-me' (between 'Sein an und für sich' and 'Sein für mich'). Israel therefore did not ponder over the abstract question of the existence of the gods. G. Ebeling: *Wort und Glaube*, Zweiter Band, p. 291–292.
8. C. J. Labuschagne: *The Incomparability of Yahweh in the Old Testament.* Preuss in turn makes considerable use of Labuschagne.
9. G. von Rad: *Old Testament Theology*, Vol. II, pp. 240–1, has indicated the interesting meaning that 'create' has in Deutero-Isaiah. It is used synonymously with elect, redeem, deliver, and all these concepts are used for the one great event in Israel's history: the liberation from Egypt. In this way for Deutero-Isaiah even creation is interpreted soteriologically.
10. Alongside the well-known theologies of the Old Testament, recent references have been made in *this* connection by, i.a. H. D. Preuss: *Jahweglaube und Zukunftserwartung*, p. 9–39 and 195, and Labuschagne: *Incomparability*, p. 89 f and especially 92 f.
11. That biblical promises and prophecies are in no way on the same plane as predictions that come true, has been clearly demonstrated by Old Testament scholars. I intend to elaborate on this in *Jesus the End*, part 2 of this series.
12. Preuss: *Verspottung*, p. 52–56, has shown in particular that the exodus was a contest between the LORD and the gods of Egypt, but a contest in which the LORD was so totally in control that the presentation in Exodus 1–12 is full of the mockery of these gods. As has already been shown in connection with Genesis 1:14 f, the *absence* of any references to the gods in Exodus 1–12 (as well as at the entry into Canaan) is the most acute form of mockery. Cf. also Labuschagne: *Incomparability*, p. 75 f.
13. Labuschagne: *Incomparability*, p. 91.
14. In chapter 3 the proofs of God are considered more fully.
15. Von Rad: *Old Testament Theology*, Vol. II, p. 249.
16. J. Blauw: *The Missionary Nature of the Church*, p. 66. On the other hand, Blauw means more than mere differences in form when he makes this distinction. But both are *mission*. D. J. Bosch: *Witness to the World* has recently refined this distinction into an

even more accurate description of the difference between the Old Testament and the New (pp. 79 f).

17. Von Rad: idem., pp. 249–250.
18. I gained this impression from a personal discussion with Pannenberg. 'That the history of religion can be understood as the course taken by God to reveal himself' we read in *The Idea of God and Human Freedom*, p. 115. Especially O. Eissfeldt, El and Yahweh, in: *Journal of Semitic Studies* 1, 1956, p. 25–37, has made a great deal of the positive relationship between Yahweh and El. We will return to this later.
19. W. Zimmerli: *Grundriss der alttestamentlichen Theologie*, p. 33.
20. J. Ridderbos: *De Psalmen II*, p. 326.
21. They are called 'the sons of God' (Job 1:6 f), or 'heavenly beings' (Ps. 29:1), 'the most of heaven' (1 Kgs. 22:19), 'the council of the holy ones' (Ps. 89:7). There might also be links with the seraphs of Isaiah 6:2. Cf. H.-J. Kraus, *Psalmen* 2 Teilband, p. 571.
22. This meaning does not come adequately to the fore in most commentaries, both old and modern – e.g. in the I.C.C., and F. Delitzsch (as representing the older ones) and in A. Weiser (D.A.T.D. Die Psalmen), J. Ridderbos and H.-J. Kraus, (as more modern commentaries).
23. Eissfeldt interprets 'the LORD' in v. 22 as secondary (*El and Yahweh*, in *Journal of Semitic Studies 1*, 1956, p. 29). But this fact is actually of the greatest importance, because it indicates how the writer of Genesis 14 interpreted this encounter. Since both the church and the theologian have to deal with the text as it is before us, 'the LORD' must be understood as the *meaning and intention* of the writer. Thus El is *eliminated* here as well, by the LORD, so that no one might imagine that beside the LORD there is another, named El.
24. Cf. ch. 4 of *Jesus the End*, Part 2 of this series.
25. Cf. ch. 2 of *Jesus the End*.
26. H. Berkhof: *Christelijk Geloof* – Een inleiding tot de geloofsleer, p. 281–335; P. Schoonenberg: Berkhof en het Credo, in *Weerwoord*, p. 127–135.
27. Cf. i.a. T. Ling: *The Significance of Satan*, p. 3.
28. J. Ridderbos: *De Psalmen II*, p. 512 weakens the meaning with the explanation that demons are here (in Ps. 106 and Deut. 32) used contemptuously as synonymous with the idols, but then in a footnote mentions Leviticus 17:7 as an example of possible worship of demons.
29. W. Foerster in *T.D.N.T. II*, p. 18.
30. J. Feiner und M. Löhrer (eds): *Mysterium Salutis* Band II, p. 273; E. Stauffer in *T.D.N.T. III*, pp. 101–2.
31. For most of the details cf. H.-J. Kraus: *Psalmen* I Teilband, p. 197 f and H. D. Preuss: *Verspottung*, p. 97 f, 105 f, 112 f.
32. W. H. Schmidt: *Das erste Gebot*, p. 24, note 38, points out that Israel did not by any means apply all statements relating to El or Baal to the LORD, and (on p. 16, note 20) that El and the LORD were never fully identified.
33. Labuschagne, *Incomparability*, p. 109.
34. W. H. Schmidt: *Das erste Gebot*, p. 19.
35. W. H. Schmidt: *Das erste Gebot*, p. 25.
36. Preuss: *Verspottung*, p. 99–100.
37. Cf. H. Berkhof: *Christelijk Geloof*, p. 156–164.
38. P. 109 f.
39. Preuss: *Verspottung*, p. 237. Cf. also p. 9 f in this chapter.
40. H. Bavinck: *The Doctrine of God*, p. 147.
41. Idem p. 149.
42. J. Ratzinger: *Introduction to Christianity*, p. 79.
43. On the sea as threat, cf. *Jesus the End*, ch. 4.
44. For a great deal of this material I am indebted to G. C. Berkouwer: *General Revelation*, ch. 7, and E. Haenchen: *Die Apostelgeschichte*.
45. H. Berkhof: *Christelijk Geloof*, p. 114.
46. E. P. Meijering: Relatie en Begrensdheid, in *Weerwoord*, p. 115, note 1.

47. W. Pannenberg: The Appropriation of the Philosophical Concept of God as a Dogmatic Problem of Early Christian Theology, in: *Basic Questions in Theology*, Vol. II, pp. 119–183. The following numbers between brackets in the text refer to pages in this article.

48. In *Mysterium Salutis, Band II*, p. 2 4. The whole of the second paragraph on this page is illuminating.

49. Labuschagne: *Incomparability*, p. 144–148.

50. Preuss: *Verspottung*, p. 284–285.

51. Idem p. 90.

52. Cf. i.a. L. A. Snijders: *Jesaja* Deel I.

53. For this and the following thoughts cf. i.a. G. von Rad: *Old Testament Theology* Volume II, pp. 80–98.

54. Preuss: *Verspottung*, p. 77.

55. Pannenberg: *Basic Questions in Theology*, Vol. II, p. 181.

56. Cf. H. M. Kuitert: *De Mensvormigheid Gods*, pp. 191 f.

57. H. D. Preuss: *Jahweglaube und Zukunftserwartung*, p. 24.

58. Preuss: *Verspottung*, p. 130 f.

59. Idem. p. 214.

60. *Church Dogmatics* II, 1.

61. H. H. Rowley: *The Faith of Israel*, p. 62.

62. There is an inclination these days among Old Testament scholars not to regard the exodus as a single event, but rather as the infiltration of various tribes at different times, which later were united as a single nation in Canaan. Cf. i.a. A. R. Hulst: *De Geschiedenis van Israel in de Theocratie*, in: *Woord en Werkelijkheid – Over de Theocratie*, p. 29 f. In such a case it would be an even greater marvel and sign of his gracious love that God should choose precisely this people.

63. J. Pfammatter in: *Mysterium Salutis*, Band II, p. 285.

64. E. Brunner: *Dogmatics* Vol. I, pp. 183 f, 187.

65. Idem pp. 200–4.

66. Cf. K. Barth: *Church Dogmatics* II/1 p. 276: 'If we say with 1 John 4 that God is love, the converse that love is God is forbidden until it is mediated and clarified from God's being and therefore from God's act what the love is which can and must legitimately be identified with God.'

67. J. Pfammatter in: *Mysterium Salutis Band II*, p. 278.

68. I have set out my objections to Berkhof's minimalist Christology in the form of questions in: Jesus nie God nie? 'n Aspeck uit Berkhof se Christologie, *Theologia Evangelica*, VII 2, July 1974, p. 130–140, an article unfortunately only available in Afrikaans.

69. J. Jeremias: *The Parables of Jesus*, pp. 145 f. A number of the thoughts on the parables that follow are drawn from this book.

70. Ibid. p. 128.

71. F. J. Schierse in: *Mysterium Salutis*, Band II, p. 91 f. This does not mean a division between the God of Israel and 'the God of the New Testament'. The Pharisees had a radically wrong understanding of the God of Israel.

72. Luke 18:14 according to TEV.

73. F. J. Schierse in: *Mysterium Salutis, Band II*, p. 92.

74. J. Moltmann: *The Crucified God*, p. 244.

75. I have some difficulty with Meijering's criticism of Berkhof, in which he suggests that Berkhof oversimplifies the problem of creation. Meijering presents as alternatives: *either* we know God's will from his being (which would imply that God was potentially the Creator from all eternity), *or* we must interpret God's being from his (incidental) will – which in Meijering's view cannot be sustained because God's being would then change with his will, and because the question would again arise: on what grounds would God will something new? (*Weerwoord*, p. 112–113). First of all, it is somewhat strange to pose God's will and his being against each other in this way, since we only know God through his words and deeds in which his being and his will are simul-

taneously disclosed. Then further, there is the question whether M. does not think of God too philosophically, as though he were a sum of potentialities which he might then convert into actualities. Thirdly one could ask whether it is correct to repudiate the alternative that 'God's being must be interpreted from his (incidental) will' with the question: On what grounds might God will anything new?, and answer: If it is on grounds of himself, his will is any case interpreted from his being. The mistake appears to me to be in M.'s failure to consider that people do indeed interpret God's being from his (revealed) will, while it is also true that his will proceeds from his being. I would then propose that M. opts for the second alternative, but rephrase it as follows: God's being is *known* from his will, but God's will proceeds from his being. To suggest that God could not will any *new* things would be to make of him a thing, a ground of being, instead of the living God of Israel. *New* things (creation, incarnation) do not *change* his will, but are acts of his will that give form to his being in new situations.

76. Labuschagne proposes this dating, *Incomparability*, p. 84, and it is accepted by Preuss – *Verspottung*, p. 115. Other dates would not alter the structure, nor, therefore, this interpretation.

77. Labuschagne: *Incomparability*, p. 84. On the righteousness of God in the general and all-embracing sense I have written in *Ek is wat ek is*, p. 63 f, and will not go into the matter again here.

78. A. J. Heschel: *The Prophets*, Volume II, p. 67.

79. Cf. J. L. Mays: *Amos – A Commentary*, p. 75.

80. G. von Rad: *Old Testament Theology* Vol. I, p. 322. The following few thoughts are also borrowed from von Rad.

81. A. A. van Ruler: *Theologisch Werk*, Deel IV, p. 120–121.

82. A. A. van Ruler: Gerechtigheid en Rechtvaardigheid, in: *Kernwoorden van het Christelijk Geloof*, p. 52.

83. A. A. van Ruler: *Theologisch Werk*, Deel IV, p. 124.

84. *Kernwoorden*, p. 54. This is an exceptionally penetrating and orthodox article.

85. D. H. Meadows et. al.: *The Limits to Growth*.

86. The end time, the signs of the times, the return of Christ, and all that relates to these things, will be dealt with in Part 2 of this series: *Jesus the End*.

87. E. Stauffer in: *T.D.N.T.* III, pp. 101–2. Cf. also J. Pfammatter in: *Mysterium Salutis*, Band II, p. 273.

88. Cf. F. Zündel: *Johann Christoph Blumhardt – Zeuge der Siegesmacht Jesu über Krankheit und Dämonie*. Cf. also Barth's appreciation of Blumhardt.

89. K. Koch: *Between Christ and Satan*.

90. H. Berkhof: *Christ and the Powers*, p. 19. Many of the following ideas are borrowed from, or inspired by this book.

91. O. Weber: *Grundlagen der Dogmatik*, Erste Band, p. 234.

92. K. Barth: *Church Dogmatics* IV 2, pp. 543–4.

93. In: *Mysterium Salutis*, Band II, p. 235.

94. G. C. Berkouwer: *Sin*, chap. 1.

2   God and man

1. U. Mauser: *Gottesbild und Menschwerdung*, p. 23 f.

2. The Septuagint is the Greek translation of the Old Testament, made before Christ, mainly for the sake of the Jews living scattered around the Mediterranean Sea, and who frequently could no longer read Hebrew.

3. W. Maas: *Unveränderlichkeit Gottes*, pp. 91 f, 121 f; H. M. Kuitert; *De Mensvormigheid Gods*, p. 78 f; Mauser: *Gottesbild*, p. 23.

4. H. M. Kuitert: *De Mensvormigheid Gods*, p. 69.

5. Most of these facts are taken from Kuitert: *De Mensvormigheid Gods*, pp. 5–6; and Mauser: *Gottesbild*, pp. 18–19.

6. Quoted by Mauser: *Gottesbild*, p. 18.
7. Idem p. 20 f.
8. A. J. Heschel: *The Prophets Volume II*, chaps. 2 and 3, is the source of many of these thoughts, besides Kuitert and Mauser.
9. H. M. Kuitert: *De Mensvormigheid Gods*, p. 58 f.
10. Cf. for this presentation, among others, Mauser: *Gottesbild*, p. 23; H. Braun: *Wie man über Gott nicht denken soll*, p. 58 f.
11. Mauser gives a very good survey of the attitude of modern Biblical theologians to the anthropomorphisms in: *Gottesbild*, pp. 28–45.
12. Cf. H. M. Kuitert: *De Mensvormigheid Gods*, p. 236 f.
13. W. Maas: *Unveränderlichkeit Gottes*, p. 122 shows the boundless arbitrariness with which the Septuagint translated these forty texts – or sometimes simply omitted the word for repent! Words such as reflect, be gracious, have compassion, stop, admonish are often used as translations for repent!
14. Cf. H. M. Kuitert: *De Mensvormigheid Gods*, p. 191 f for various views and literature.
15. J. Ratzinger: *Introduction to Christianity*, p. 79. Ratzinger offers a well-worth reading survey of the history of the interpretation of this text, but comes back eventually dangerously close to the old static Greek concept.
16. T. Boman: *Das hebräische Denken im Vergleich mit dem griechischen*, pp. 34–37.
17. W. Maas: *Unveränderlichkeit Gottes*, p. 24.
18. Idem p. 26.
19. H.-J. Kraus: *Psalmen 2*. Teilband, passim.
20. P. A. Verhoef: *Maleachi, Commentaar op het Oude Testament*, p. 21 f.
21. W. Maas: *Unveränderlichkeit Gottes*, p. 28 f.
22. Among others, H. Bavinck: *The Doctrine of God*, pp. 142 f.
23. Idem p. 86.
24. Idem p. 146. It is quite remarkable that a second 'als het ware' (as it were) in the Dutch original (*Dogmatick* Vol. II, p. 128) is left out in the translation (*The Doctrine of God*, p. 151).
25. Much of the material following is taken from or inspired by Mauser: *Gottesbild*, chap. 3.
26. C. van Gelderen and W. H. Gispen: *Het Boek Hosea, Commentaar op het Oude Testament*, passim.
27. Cf. H. W. Wolff: *Dodekapropheton I*, on 7:13, *Biblischer Kommentar Altes Testaments*.
28. A. J. Heschel: *The Prophets*, Vol. II, pp. 51–52.
29. A. van Selms: *Jeremiah*, Deel I, *De Prediking van het Oude Testament*, passim.
30. This thought must not be rejected as unworthy even for theological reasons. If God could explain sin and point to a cause for it, he could not have punished it. What makes sin *sin*, and therefore entirely punishable, is precisely that it is unnecessary, and that there is no reason for the person who commits it to do so, and he is therefore wholly guilty. G. C. Berkouwer has written very clearly on this in *Sin*, chap. 1, although H. Berkhof, in *Christelijk Geloof*, p. 213, has rightly pointed out a definite defect in Berkouwer's doctrine of sin – a defect, however, that does not alter the issue.
31. Translations and commentaries differ over whether it is not perhaps a word of Jeremiah himself. If this is the case one must assume that this *change* in the LORD was to begin with a great problem to Jeremiah, and that he only gradually came to an understanding of the *time* of the truth, to which attention will now be given. Cf. Mauser: *Gottesbild*, p. 94 f and especially p. 96 f.
32. See A. S. vd. Waude on true and false prophecy in G. C. Berkouwer and A. S. vd. Woude: *Wat is Waarheid?* p. 13 f.
33. This last sentence is from Mauser: *Gottesbild*, p. 97.
34. Mauser: *Gottesbild*, p. 23; Maas: *Unveränderlichkeit Gottes*, pp. 91 f; 12 f; Kuitert: *De Mensvormigheid Gods*, p. 78 f.
35. Jonah 3:10–4:3.
36. K. H. Miskotte: *When the Gods are Silent*, p. 132.
37. Cf. H. Braun: *Wie man über Gott nicht denken soll*, chap. 4, for Philo's view on this – a view that has had a tremendous influence on theological thought up to the present.

Even H. Ott: *Der Persönliche Gott*, pp. 143 f and 206 f is still determined by the idea that the invisibility of God is a matter of course – as is F. Flückiger: *Theologie der Geschichte*, pp. 11, 58 f.

38. Th. C. Vriezen: *An outline of Old Testament Theology*, pp. 249–250.
39. We frequently use the idea that God is Spirit (John 4:24) in an out and out Greek philosophical way, as though for both John and Paul Spirit (spirit) was opposed to matter, whereas in fact it is opposed to flesh. H. M. Kuitert: *De Mensvormigheid Gods*, p. 200 f, has gone into it more fully, and has shown that God as a spiritual being is not in the least contrasted with the visibility or form of God. The term *'bodiliness'* which Kuitert uses of God, can evoke misunderstanding (especially in relation to the Greek dualism of body-soul and matter-spirit) but he has himself warned against this and has explained 'bodily' with 'concrete' (p. 215).
40. I intend coming back on this problem in *Jesus the End*, ch. 5.
41. K. Barth: C.D. II, 1, p. 229 f. This does not mean that one can go along with everything that Barth has written about anthropomorphisms; e.g. when he writes on p. 222 'As a characteristic of human language about God "anthropomorphic" necessarily has the comprehensive meaning of that which corresponds to the form of man, and does not, therefore, correspond to God.' The question is what the imago dei then means. Barth retains too much of the Greek philosophical assumption that God is essentially invisible and therefore unknowable, that every revelation comes down to a certain loss (or diminution) of his deity, that in Jesus Christ God is therefore necessarily still concealed, because in him he enters what is alien. (e.g. p. 53 f.)
42. K. Barth, C.D. II, 1 p. 266 below.
43. There is no difference here between the glory of the LORD and the LORD himself (v. 18 and 20).
44. A number of the thoughts in these pages come from G. C. Berkouwer: *The Return of Christ*, ch. 12, esp. p. 362 f.
45. H. M. Kuitert: *De Mensvormigheid Gods*, p. 251 f.
46. Berkouwer: *The Return of Christ*, p. 38.
47. Kuitert: *De Mensvormigheid Gods*, pp. 162–163.
48. Idem p. 263.
49. W. Pannenberg: *Basic Questions in Theology*, Vol. II, p. 162.
50. E. P. Meijering: *Orthodoxy and Platonism in Athanasius – Synthesis or Antithesis?* e.g. p. 186.
51. And it is clear that Meijering says this in the Netherlands political situation from a positively *right* position, and *against* a 'theology' of revolution working with (as Meijering formulates it) a few Biblical-theological concepts (sometimes quoted in Hebrew and sometimes not) and assuming that all problems can be solved with a wave of the hand. There is something biting in Meijering's formulations against the group on the far left. Die Onveranderlikheid van God, *Kerk en Theolgie*, April 1974, p. 134.
52. Idem p. 134.
53. M. Löhrer in: *Mysterium Salutis*, Band 2, p. 311. In German the last few words read: '... wirklich im andern *wird*'.
54. Pannenberg: op. cit. p. 162.
55. W. Mas: *Unveränderlichkeit Gottes*, p. 132 f, shows the struggle in Origen, who never comes further than a quasi-incarnation, because in his fierce contest with Celsus, he in fact holds to the same unbiblical point of departure: that God is essentially unchangeable, and therefore could not *really* become man.
56. H. Küng: *Menschwerdung Gottes*, p. 640; W. Pannenberg: *Basic Questions*, Vol. II, p. 163, who shows that there is a definite link between the unchangeableness of God and Pelagianism!
57. How impossible it was for Origen to really hear what is said in Philemon 2, on account of his philosophical appriori can be seen, e.g. in Mass: op. cit. p.134 f.
58. P. 109 f.
59. I intend dealing with the doctrine of the Trinity in Christology because both historically and theologically that is the proper place.

60. P. 41 f and 46 f.
61. Cf. G. C. Berkouwer: *The Work of Christ*, p. 284 f.
62. Berkhof develops the idea of Jesus as the new man, God's new creation, but his doctrine of God apparently reflects no influence of this minimalised Christology.
63. Cf. H. Küng: *Menschwerdung Gottes*, pp. 622 f, 637 f.
64. H. Ott: *Der Persöhnliche Gott*, p. 32 f, uses the faithfulness of God in a remarkable way in support of the truth (validity) of theology. Among other things he argues that the continuity that flows from the unfaithfulness of God as a personal 'Verhaltensweise' makes possible the rationality of theology.
65. A. J. Heschel: *The Prophets*, Volume II, which contains the second part of his original work, *Die Prophetie* (1936). Cf. especially chaps. 1–3. Much of the material in the following pages comes from or is inspired by Heschel and J. Moltmann: *The Crucified God*, p. 267 f.
66. H. Küng: *Menschwerdung Gottes*, p. 631. He discusses the matter on pp. 622–631.
67. Heschel: *The Prophets*, Vol. II, p. 11.
68. Moltmann: *The Crucified God*, p. 272.
69. Th. C. Vriezen: *An Outline of Old Testament Theology*, p. 157 f.
70. W. Zimmerli: *The Old Testament and the World*, p. 65 f.
71. Heschel: *The Prophets*, Vol. II, p. 25 f.
72. G. C. Berkouwer: *Verdienste of Genade?* p. 20 has also pointed out this radical difference.
73. Th. C. Vriezen: *An Outline*, p. 154.
74. W. H. Schmidt: *Das erste Gebot*, p. 19.
75. H. D. Preuss: *Jahweglaube und Zukunftserwartung*, p. 41.
76. H. Küng: *Menschwerdung Gottes*, p. 624 f.
77. G. C. Berkouwer: *The Triumph of Grace in the Theology of Karl Barth*, pp. 297–312.
78. G. C. Berkouwer: *A Half Century of Theology*, p. 246 f.
79. H. Bavinck: *Gereformeerde Dogmatiek III*, p. 348.
80. W. Maas: *Unveränderlichkeit Gottes*, p. 136 f.
81. Berkouwer: *A Half Century of Theology*, p. 247 f.
82. Moltmann: *The Crucified God*, p. 191.
83. C. van Genderen and W. H. Gispen: *Het Boek Hosea*, passim.
84. In this I agree with Miskotte's criticism: *Het lijden is in God – over Jürgen Moltmann's trinitarische kruistheologie, Rondom het Woord* 15, 4, 1973, p. 36 f.
85. Moltmann: *The Crucified God*, pp. 150 f, 190 f, 216: 'God suffered in the suffering of Jesus, God died on the cross of Christ' is oversimplified and does not take sufficient account of the fact that the Word became *man*.
86. P. 63 f.
87. P. 2 f.
88. H.-J. Kraus: *Biblisch-theologische Aufsätze*, p. 154 f.
89. G. C. Berkouwer: *Man: The Image of God*, p. 85 f, discusses this whole matter in the Reformed tradition. Much of the material in the remainder of this discussion is inspired by the chapter in Berkouwer entitled, 'The meaning of the Image'.
90. H. W. Wolff: *Anthropology of the Old Testament*, p. 93.
91. In *Jesus the Last*, ch. 5, I intend coming back on this.
92. J. A. Heyns: *Die Nuwe Mens Onderweg*, p. 86 f apparently takes exactly the opposite point of view when he speaks of the law as the boundary between God and man, in the sense that the law prohibits to man those acts that God lays claim to for himself, and for himself alone. On page 87 he says that 'the ten commandments indicate what man may not do, because God alone may do it'. Rather than adopting an absolute contradiction between these two positions, I would call to mind the fact that God is both *like* man and *different* from him. God is the uncreated Creator, man the creature. God has his meaning in himself; man receives his through his relationship to God. On the other hand man is created in God's image, and there is (and must be) a definite agreement between God and man. I would therefore not expect to find agreement in every respect, any more than Heyns would look for total exclusiveness. We will rather

have to pay attention to the actual message of the Scriptures in order to discover in what respects God and man are also incomparable, and in what respects his life must take form in our lives.

93. P. 11 f and 48 f.
94. F. Flückiger: *Theologie der Geschichte*, p. 59, has summarised it perfectly.
95. G. C. Berkouwer: *Man: The Image of God*, p. 114 f. Much of what follows is inspired by the subsequent pages in Berkouwer.
96. F. P. Pop: *Apostolaat in Druk en Vertroosting – De Tweede Brief aan de Corinthiërs. De Prediking van het Nieuwe Testament*, p. 112–113.
97. H. M. Kuitert: *De Mensvormigheid Gods*, p. 221 f.
98. G. von Rad: *Old Testament Theology*, Vol. I, p. 145 f.
99. P. 84 f.
100. In a sermon on Psalm 23, Jüngel says that God Almighty, the Creator of heaven and earth, is called: 'my shepherd'. It is obvious that a sheep is not afraid of his shepherd. The sheep takes his presence for granted, to the extent that it grazes with contentment in his presence. E. Jüngel: *Geistesgegenwart*, p. 12. In this sermon the nearness of God is brought out beautifully.

3 God and history

1. I hope to deal with election in a subsequent volume.
2. Important names are: W. J. Hamilton: *The New Essence of Christianity*; T. J. J. Altizer: *The Gospel of Christian Atheism*; and written by both of them: *Radical Theology and the Death of God*. G. Vahanian: *The Death of God*, 1961 can be regarded as the beginning of this direction in theology; D. Sölle: *Stellvertretung* (English: *Christ the Representative*) and several later publications. In a certain sense, H. Braun and P. van Buren as well.
3. D. Sölle: *Christ the Representative*, p. 131 f.
4. This is the heart of what Berkouwer aims to say about man in *Man the Image of God*. See especially chapters III, VI, and X.
5. M. de Jonge: *De Brieven van Johannes*, De Prediking van het Nieuwe Testament, pp. 207–208.
6. I have dealt with this in the Church and Politics, *Theologia Evangelica*, XII, 1, April 1979.
7. F. Flückiger has pointed out the illegitimate and dangerous one-sidedness of the latter in *Theologie der Geschichte*, pp. 178–179.
8. The discussion following is inspired especially by G. Von Rad: *Old Testament Theology* Vol. I, p. 398 f, Vol. II, p. 374 f; and B. J. Oosterhoff: *De afwezigheid Gods in het Oude Testament*.
9. J. H. Kroeze: *Het Boek Job*, p. 28.
10. H. Ott says that it is part of the faith (and is a specific experience of faith) that at times, if not mostly, we miss a direct and tangible experience of God. *Der Persönliche Gott*, p. 153.
11. H.-J. Kraus in: F. Herzog: *Theology of the Liberating Word*, p. 97. It is, of course, possible that, like the 'Most High' God, this was derived from Israel's environment (W. H. Schmidt: *Das erste Gebot*, p. 31), but then it would be interpreted in a unique and original way, to suit the special character of the LORD.
12. Th. C. Vriezen: *An Outline of Old Testament Theology*, p. 169.
13. H. D. Preuss: *Jahweglaube und Zukunftserwartung*, pp. 16, 17. His expression about God: 'sein Wesen ist Wirken' (his being is acts). I can only accept with Barth's reservations: i.e. that God does not exist only in his works, but is *more* than his works, and also exists without and outside of his works. The ontological element in God may never be minimalised, but neither may it be conceived as a static 'being' and dominate the doctrine of God as in Greek thought. Cf. K. Barth, C.D. II, 1, p. 257 f. I have no doubt that Preuss himself would agree with this.

14. Preuss: op. cit. p. 24.
15. G. Von Rad has dealt with this repeatedly: see, for example: *Gottes Wirken in Israel*, p. 213–229; *Old Testament Theology*, Vol. II, pp. 99–118.
16. H. D. Preuss: *Verspottung*, p. 26.
17. O. Cullmann: *Christ and Time*, p. 51 f.
18. Hartmut Gese has shown that there were in fact at least two views of history in Mesopotamia. The older one saw history as an indeterminate sequence of eras, arbitrarily repeated according to the will of the gods, and were classified as times of salvation and times of disaster. *Von Sinai zum Zion*, p. 87, below. The later view emerged as a result of the insight that there is a connection between an act and its consequences, so that history was no longer an arbitrary *Abfolge* (sequence) of events, according to the pleasure of the gods, but a *Folge* (result) of human deeds, in which the act and its consequences were so closely linked that they formed a unity (p. 89). In spite of this more balanced view, Gese acknowledges that there can be no thought of a concept of a *goal-orientated* history (p. 86). In this respect Israel's view of history is unique (p. 95). Gese has also pointed out the tremendous *uncertainty* in which the Mesopotamians lived, as a result of their view of history, precisely because it was dominated by the opaque and changeable will of the gods (p. 86). Earlier mention was made of the *positive* meaning that the unfortunate concept of the 'unchangeableness' of God acquired when it was seen against the arbitrariness of the heathen gods. Here we have a further good example of this.
19. *Gottes Wirken in Israel*, p. 219.
20. Cf. J. L. Mays: *Amos – A Commentary*.
21. W. Zimmerli: *The Old Testament and the World*, p. 12.
22. Th. C. Vriezen: *An Outline*, p. 136: 'And throughout the course of history God intervenes at critical moments.
23. The forthcoming: *Jesus the End*, ch. 2.
24. Among others: *Mysterium Salutis* Band II, pp. 232, 239, 247 f.
25. Th. C. Vriezen: *An Outline*, p. 140–141; H. Berkhof: *Om het Verbond*, p. 4.
26. God has indeed a need for fellowship, and in *this* sense an inward drive towards community. But it is his own, freely self-imposed need, that was not thrust on him from without, and it is a need which belongs to his being, and is satisfied by his being, in his trinitarian fellowship, and for the satisfaction of which he was not obliged to turn to anything outside of himself.
27. Cf. G. C. Berkouwer: *Faith and Sanctification*, pp. 180–185.
28. I intend to deal in Part 2, *Jesus the End*, ch. 2, with Jesus as the content of the covenant, and reconciliation as the restoration of the covenant.
29. H. D. Preuss: *Jahweglaube und Zukunftserwartung*, p. 78.
30. *Basic Questions in Theology*, Vol. I, p. 20; cf. also G. von Rad: *Old Testament Theology*, Vol. II, p. 118.
31. Cf. for example, G. C. Berkouwer: *The Providence of God*, chap. V, and *Sin*, chap. 1.
32. This is the basic structure of eschatology I intend to put forward in *Jesus the End*.
33. Specific aspects of the providence of God are dealt with later.
34. K. Dijk: *Van Eeuwigheid Verkoren*, p. 49 f, inclines in this direction.
35. *C.D.* II, 1, p. 608 f.
36. Among others, O. Cullmann: *Christ and Time*, p. 62 f.
37. G. C. Berkouwer: *Divine Election*, p. 116, with a reference to H. Bavinck.
38. H. Venema: *Uitverkiezen en Uitverkiezing in het Nieuwe Testament*, p. 160.
39. e.g. in H. Ott: *God*, p. 29 f.
40. H. Ott: *Die Antwort des Glaubens*, p. 95.
41. G. Ebling: *Wort und Glaube* zweiter band, p. 272.
42. E. Jüngel, *Unterwegs zur Sache*, p. 100.
43. H. Ott: *Die Antwort des Glaubens*, p. 98.
44. I would not say *impossible*. I think that H. G. Hubbeling has succeeded in showing that it is not (yet) proved that after Kant all proofs of God should be regarded as

disproved. Cf. p. 164–178 in *Wat is Waarheid?*, edited by G. C. Berkouwer and A. S. van der Woude.

45. H. H. Rowley: *The Faith of Israel*, p. 40 f.
46. More references to texts can be found in H. D. Preuss: *Jahweglaube*, p. 32 and a discussion of the meaning of the exodus in the message of the Old Testament, in R. Bÿlsma: *Schriftgezag en Schriftgebruik*, p. 20 f.
47. C. J. Labuschagne: *The Incomparability of Yahweh in the Old Testament*, p. 92.
48. This has been referred to briefly in chap. 1, p. 20 f.
49. C. Westermann: *Isaiah 40–66*, p. 15 f; and G. von Rad: *Gottes Wirken*, p. 154 and 218 f.
50. C. J. Labuschagne: *The Incomparability*, pp. 116–117.
51. G. von Rad: *Old Testament Theology*, Vol. II, p. 248; H.-J. Kraus: *Biblisch-theologische Aufsätze*, p. 160–168.
52. Cf. Part 2 of this series: *Jesus the End*, ch. 5.
53. 195 f.
54. German: Die Wege Gottes in der Weltgeschichte nach dem Zeugnis der Propheten, included in the volume: *Gottes Wirken in Israel*, p. 213–229.
55. Thus in another article from 1958 which reflects a remarkable similarity with the previous article on this point. Cf. op. cit. p. 154–155.
56. H.-J. Kraus: *Biblisch-theologische Aufsätze*, p. 164–178 and 134–150.
57. G. Ebling: *Wort und Glaube*, p. 257 f, and J. Moltmann: *The Crucified God*, p. 211 f, have referred to this in recent times.
58. G. C. Berkouwer: *The Work of Christ*, p. 192.
59. C. H. Dodd: *The Apostolic Preaching and its Developments*, p. 25. It is clear from a comparison between the preaching of Peter and Paul that Paul saw many more aspects of salvation in various historical events in Jesus' life than Peter. For example, in Peter's preaching (in the Acts) Jesus dies; but according to Paul, he dies for our sins, and *we die with him*; according to Peter, Christ was raised by God, but according to Paul, he was raised for *our justification*, and we are raised together with him; according to Peter Christ is exalted to the right hand of the Father, but according to Paul, *we are exalted together with him, and he intercedes for us there* – to mention only a few examples which reflect something of the development of apostolic preaching.
60. I will show in Part 2: *Jesus the End*, ch. 5, that Paul was convinced that the gospel had reached all people in his time, and indeed that Pentecost represented the preaching of the gospel to all people (i.e. to the representatives of all the known peoples of the time). This can perhaps be best understood by remembering that the biblical promises are usually repeatedly fulfilled.
61. Something of this in H. Bavinck: *The Doctrine of God*, p. 393.
62. H. Ridderbos: *Heilsgeschiedenis en Heilige Schrift*, p. 34 f.
63. *Jesus the End*, ch. 5.
64. For the extraordinary importance that the prophet has for the church *today*, read H. Küng: *The Church*, pp. 396, 433 f; and G. Hasenhüttl: *Charisma – Ordningsprinzip der Kirche*, pp. 185–198.
65. What follows on Pannenberg is a rewritten version of part of an article of mine in Ned. Geref. Teologiese Tydskrif XV, 2, March 1974, under the title: *Pannenberg en Jüngel – Huidige tendense in die Godsleer*.
66. In contradistinction to this, see Pannenberg's later work on the doctrine of God: *The Idea of God and Human Freedom*. J. W. V. van Huyssteen has given a good introduction to Pannenberg's thought in his thesis: *Teologie van die Rede – Die funksie van die rasionele in die denke van Wolfhart Pannenberg*, and in German: I. Berten: *Geschichte – Offenbarung – Glaube, Eine Einführung in die Theologie Wolfhart Pannenbergs*.
67. Barth would, of course, not have spoken of 'Christendom' in this connection, but rather of the gospel or the God of Israel. But provisionally, I use Pannenberg's terms in this presentation of his views.
68. *The Idea of God and Human Freedom*, p. 100 f. The thought in these analogies plays an important part with Pannenberg. Cf. e.g. p. 88, as well as *The Apostles' Creed*, p. 20, and for greater detail: *Basic Questions in Theology*, Vol. II, pp. 126 f, 137, 247.

Also: *Gottesfrage Heute*, ed. F. Lorenz, p. 51.
69. *The Idea of God and Human Freedom*, p. 101 f.
70. Ibid. p. 104. The translation 'God' does not do justice to 'Gottesdanke' in *Gottesdanke und menschliche Freiheit*, p. 34.
71. Cf. e.g. A. M. K. Müller and W. Pannenberg: *Erwägungen zu einer Theologie der Natur*, p. 35–36 and 42.
72. *The Idea of God*, pp. 83, 105.
73. He shows that since the time of Plato, in one way or another, the stars (or nature in general) or the soul (or man, especially as a moral being) have been decisive in the proofs of God. Ibid. p. 80 f. If the first realm (nature) is now eliminated (temporarily at least), the latter realm (man) is all that is left.
74. Ibid. p. 105 f.
75. Ibid. pp. 88–89. Cf. also p. 86.
76. Ibid. p. 86 f.
77. Ibid. p. 92. On p. 113 f he shows that freedom must indeed be *received* from a supra-human reality. Cf. also *Gottesfrage heute*, ed. F. Lorenz, p. 56–57.
78. Ibid. p. 23.
79. While I had already made these remarks on 14.9.1973 (cf. Ned. Geref. Teol. Tydskrif XV, 2, March 1974, p. 105, comment before note 1), it is interesting to observe that I used almost exactly the same words as Berkouwer used in his criticism on the matter: *A Half Century of Theology*, p. 169 below – 170 above, which came out at the end of 1974.
80. Ibid. p. 23. Clearer still in: *Gottesfrage heute*, ed. F. Lorenz, p. 58, lines 10–12 p. 63.
81. Here Pannenberg agrees with Max Scheler, A. Portmann, A. Gehlen, M. Landmann, H. Plessner and E. Bloch. Cf. his *Basic Questions in Theology*, Vol. II, p. 216.
82. *The Apostles' Creed*, p. 24 f.
83. Cf. also the conclusion of B. Welte in: *Die Frage nach Gott*, ed. J. Ratzinger, p. 29.
84. J. W. V. van Huyssteen: op. cit. p. 64.
85. *Basic Questions in Theology*, Vol. II, p. 225.
86. *The Apostles' Creed*, p. 24.
87. In addition to the following presentation in the text itself, see also: *Einführung in den Glauben*, p. 23 where Kasper says that the dialectal theology smothered the legitimate objectives of the liberal theology rather than resolving them; p. 27: man is to himself an open question; p. 32 f: the 'Weltoffenheit' of man, the necessity of the question concerning meaning founded in *anthropology*; p. 41: God as the power of the future. Further, Kasper: *Glaube und Geschichte*, p. 92 f: the unity in principle between salvation-history and secular history; p. 114: the freedom of God – revealed on the cross – which makes man free; God, therefore, does not threaten the freedom of man.
88. *Einführung in den Glauben*, p. 30.
89. *The Idea of God*, p. 105.
90. *Einführung*, p. 34 f.
91. Ibid. p. 38 f.
92. Thus W. Kasper: *Glaube und Geschichte*, p. 112.
93. *Gottesfrage heute*, ed. F. Lorenz, p. 52. I find this a particularly illuminating article with regard to what Pannenberg's intentions are with his signs of God. Ott's brief discussion of the Gottesaufweise, emphasises also that they are not compelling proofs, but aids (*Antwort des Glaubens*, p. 98–99). He shows that the fact of God's absence proceeds from the being of God – as does Jüngel. In *Der Persönliche Gott*, p. 124–125 Ott offers a very interesting 'proof of God': *e communicatione gentium*.
94. G. C. Berkouwer: *Een halve eeuw theologie*, p. 245. Unfortunately this section is not included in the English translation: *A Half Century of Theology*.
95. E. Jüngel, *Unterwegs zur Sache*, p. 88.
96. H. M. Kuitert: *The Necessity of Faith*, ch. 2.
97. In a personal conversation with Pannenberg in June 1974 he stressed that his 'opposition' to Barth has been over-emphasized. He, himself, is convinced that in certain respects he expands on Barth.

98. P. 8 f and 151 f.
99. *God in Nature and History, New Directions in Faith and Order* (Bristol 1967) p. 26: The statement of the problem in this document is followed here.
100. I have made considerable use of this in *Jesus the End*, ch. 3.
101. A. S. van der Woude: *Ware en valse profete in Israel*, in *Wat is Waarheid?* ed. G. C. Berkouwer and A. S. van der Woude, p. 18.
102. German text can be found in G. C. Berkouwer: *The Providence of God*, pp. 162–3.
103. Idem p. 164.
104. Quoted in part by C. F. J. Muller: *Die oorsprong van die Groot Trek*, p. 46. Prof. Muller will, I trust, permit two remarks in this connection. The first is his personal promise that he will publish more of this little known archival document in a future publication; and the second, that I have great difficulty with the sentence that follows directly after the reference to the above-mentioned letter: 'In December of the same year, by taking a solemn oath and achieving a great military victory, the Voortrekkers showed to the Afrikaners of the time and to later Afrikaners, that like Israel in the Old Testament they were moving under divine guidance and protection in their great undertaking.' My problems are that the *Afrikaners* are said to provide the proof here, whereas in the Bible it is *God* that does so; and furthermore that the Afrikaner people are so easily compared with Israel.
105. Cf. the article by C. F. A. Borchardt in *Teologie en Vernuwing* (ed. Borchardt, Eybers, König).
106. Though at the congress on the Interpretation of History held at the University of South Africa Pretoria, in March 1979, it once more became clear how difficult it is to reach any form of agreement on this issue. The papers read at this congress are published by the University as: *The Meaning of History*, ed. A. König and H. Keane.
107. *New Directions in Faith and Order* (Bristol 1967), p. 29.
108. Gaudium et Spes. German text in Rahner and Vorgrimler: *Kleines Konzilskompendium*. English text in W. M. Abbott: *The Documents of Vatican II*.
109. This, of course, does not mean that everything accompanying these movements was also to be ascribed to God. This has already been touched on in connection with Babylon, which was later punished by the Lord for the way in which they had treated the people in captivity.
110. G. C. Berkouwer: *Sin*, ch. 1.
111. Cf. among others, the Heidleberg Catechism, question and answer numbers 26–28; and the Belgic Confession, article 13.
112. In *Gottesfrage heute*, F. Lorenz (ed.), p. 55.

4 God and the future

1. A number of references may be found in H. D. Preuss: *Jahweglaube und Zukunftser-wartung*, p. 208 note 10, and p. 210 f.
2. H. H. Rowley: *The Faith of Israel*, p. 165 f.
3. This is a deficiency in the otherwise excellent work of Preuss: *Jahweglaube*.
4. Cf. the forthcoming Part 2: *Jesus the End*, ch. 1.
5. Cf. among others, H. D. Preuss: *Jahweglaube*, the last chapter under the title Jahweglaube *als* Zukunftserwartung (Faith in Yahweh *as* expectation of the future).
6. Idem p. 103 f, 211.
7. O. Cullmann: *Christ and Time*, Part 1. See also O. Cullmann: *Salvation in History* for considerable shades of emphasis and elaborations of his viewpoint.
8. H. D. Preuss: *Jahweglaube*, p. 94, with reference to Cullmann's footnote 110.
9. S. L. Parmar: The Limits-to-Growth Debate in Asian Perspective, *The Ecumenical Review* XXVI, 1 Jan. 1974, p. 33 f.
10. Quoted by N. Lohfink: *Die Priesterschrift und die Grenzen des Wachstums, Stimmen der Zeit*, 7 July 1974, p. 435 f.
11. Cf. H. Boer: *Pentecost and Missions*, p. 118–130.

12. Macht euch die Erde untertan, *Orientierung*, H. 12/13, 38, 1974, p. 137 f.
13. W. D. Marsch: *Zukunft*.
14. H. Ott: *Der persönliche Gott*, p. 133.
15. W. Zimmerli: *Grundriss der alttestamentlichen Theologie*, p. 17 f.
16. All these aspects are dealt with by H. D. Preuss: *Jahweglaube*.
17. R. Rendtorff: The Concept of Revelation in Ancient Israel, *Revelation as History*, ed. by W. Pannenberg, p. 23 f. Many of the following facts are taken from these pages by Rendtorff.
18. Cf. chap. 3 on the proofs of God.
19. H. D. Preuss: *Jahweglaube*, p. 14 f. Many of the facts in the following pages are derived from this work by Preuss.
20. A. Deissler in: J. Feiner und M. Löhrer (eds.): *Mysterium Salutis 2*, p. 246 f.
21. On the way in which God fulfils his promises I intend writing in greater detail in *Jesus the End*, ch. 5.
22. Equally striking is the title of one of Luther's writings: The Babylonian captivity of the church, in which the papacy is described as the kingdom of Babylon! *Luthers Werken, Werken van Dr. Martin Luther I*, p. 13.
23. It is possible that the 'former things' here as distinct from Isaiah 43:18 means the former anxieties. Cf. v. 16. But in this case as well the LORD directs the eyes of his people towards the new Jerusalem and the new earth, to the glory that awaits them there.
24. Preuss: *Jahweglaube*, p. 208 f, 213.
25. *Jesus the End*, ch. 1.
26. C. H. Dodd: *The Kingdom of God and History*, p. 24–25. H. Ridderbos: *The Coming of the Kingdom*, p. 13.
27. Cf. the structure of eschatology in *Jesus the End*, ch. 3.
28. W. Pannenberg (ed.): *Revelation as History*, p. 145 f.
29. Cf. *Jesus the End*, ch. 3.
30. J. Moltmann: *Theology of Hope*, p. 95 f.
31. Reformed theology traditionally fostered an attitude of resignation in the face of disappointments and disasters, and thereby restricted the contribution of Christians to a better world. Resignation is not a biblical concept.
32. J. Moltmann: *Theology of Hope*, pp. 21, 223 f. That Jesus Christ is also comfort in suffering does not, of course, emerge strongly in *Theology of Hope*, but this would appear to be one of the things that Moltmann wanted to say in *The Crucified God*. Yet his contrasts are sometimes unnecessarily strong. e.g. hope 'does not calm the unquiet heart, but is itself this unquiet heart in man' (p. 21).
33. H. Cox: *God's Revolution and Man's Responsibility*, p. 37 f.
34. W. Schmithals: *An Introduction to the Theology of Rudolf Bultmann*, pp. 320–4.
35. H. W. Wolff: *Anthropology of the Old Testament*, pp. 151–5.
36. Cf. for the following presentation and critique especially. L. Gilkey: Process Theology, *Vox Theologica* 43, 1, 1973, p. 5–29; P. Schoonenberg: *Process or History in God? Louvain Studies IV*, 4, Fall 1973, p. 303–319; B. Engelbrecht: The Dipolar God of Process-Thinking, *Journal of Theology for Southern Africa*, 5, Dec. 1973, p. 29–46; C. Gunton: Process Theology's Concept of God – An Outline and Assessment, *The Expository Times* LXXXIV, 10 July 1973, pp. 292–296.
37. B. Engelbrecht, op. cit. 43–44.
38. L. Gilkey: op. cit. p. 28.
39. In chapter 3, in the discussion on the signs of God, attention has been given to another aspect of Pannenberg's doctrine of God. For the following presentation consult especially W. Pannenberg: *Theology and the Kingdom of God*, p. 51 f, and *Basic Questions in Theology*, Vol II, p. 234 f.
40. W. Pannenberg: *Theology and the Kingdom of God*, p. 56.
41. W. Pannenberg: *Basic questions in Theology*. Vol. 2, p. 242 f.
42. *Theology and the Kingdom of God*, p. 55.
43. Cf. the discussion of the God-is-dead theology in chap. 3.

44. J. Moltmann: *Hope and Planning*, p. 184.
45. H. Bavinck: *The Doctrine of God*, p. 126.
46. K. Kitamori: *Theology of the Pain of God*, p. 46.
47. K. H. Miskotte: *When the Gods are Silent*, p. 131.
48. G. C. Berkouwer: *The Person of Christ*, p. 131 f.
49. J. Moltmann: *The Crucified God*, pp. 87–107; G. C. Berkouwer: *A Half Century of Theology*, pp. 64 f, 71 f, 234 f.

Bibliography

(Commentaries consulted are not included)

Abbott, W. M.: *The Documents of Vatican II*, London 1972.

Barth, K.: *Church Dogmatics*, II 1 and IV 2, Edinburgh.
Bavinck, H.: *Gereformeerde Dogmatiek*, Kampen 1928.
Bavinck, H.: *The Doctrine of God*, Grand Rapids 1977. (This is a translation of the first half of Vol. II of *Gereformeerde Dogmatiek*.)
Berkhof, H.: *Christ and the Powers*, Scottdale 1962.
Berkhof, H.: *Christelijk Geloof – een inleiding tot de geloofsleer*, Nijkerk 1973.
Berkhof, H.: *Om het Verbond, Miniaturen no. 3*, 'S-Gravenhage,1966.
Berkouwer, G. C. en v. d. Woude, A. S. (red.): *Wat is Waarheid? Waarheid en Verifikasie in Kerk en Theologie*, Kampen 1973.
Berkouwer, G. C.: *Divine Election*, Grand Rapids 1968.
Berkouwer, G. C.: *Faith and Sanctification*, Grand Rapids 1952.
Berkouwer, G. C.: *General Revelation*, Grand Rapids 1973.
Berkouwer, G. C.: *Man The Image of God*, Grand Rapids 1972.
Berkouwer, G. C.: *The Person of Christ*, Grand Rapids 1954.
Berkouwer, G. C.: *The Providence of God*, Grand Rapids 1961.
Berkouwer, G. C.: *The Return of Christ*, Grand Rapids 1972.
Berkouwer, G. C.: *Sin*, Grand Rapids 1971.
Berkouwer, G. C.: *The Work of Christ*, Grand Rapids 1976.
Berkouwer, G. C.: *A Half Century of Theology – Movements and Motives*, Grand Rapids 1977.
Berkouwer, G. C.: *The Triumph of Grace in the Theology of Karl Barth*, Grand Rapids 1956.
Berkouwer, G. C.: *Verdienste of Genade?*, Kampen 1958.
Berten, I.: *Geschichte – Offenbarung – Glaube, Eine Einführung in die Theologie Wolfhart Pannenbergs*, München 1970.
Blauw, J.: *The Missionary Nature of the Church*, London 1964.
Boer, H.: *Pentecost and Mission*, London 1961.
Boman, T.: *Das hebräische Denken im Vergleich mit dem griechischen*, Göttingen 1968.
Braun, H.: *Wie man über Gott nicht denken soll – dargelegt an Gedankengängen Philos von Alexandria*, Tübingen 1971.
Brunner, E.: *Dogmatics*, Vol. I, London 1970.
Bijlsma, R.: *Schriftgezag en Schriftgebruik – Een hermeneutiek van de Bybel*, Nijkerk 1964.

Cox, H.: *God's Revolution and Man's Responsibility*, London 1969.
Cullmann, O.: *Christ and Time, The Primitive Christian Conception of Time and History*, London 1967.
Cullmann, O.: *Salvation in History*, London 1967.

Dodd, C. H.: *The Apostolic Preaching and its Developments*, London 1960.
Dodd, C. H. e.a.: *The Kingdom of God and History*, London 1938.
Dijk, K.: *Van Eeuwigheid Verkoren – De belijdenis der praedestinatie*, Delft 1952.

Ebeling, G.: *Wort und Glaube, zweiter Band – Beiträge zur Fundamentaltheologie und zur Lehre von Gott*, Tübingen 1969.

Feiner, J. und Löhrer, M. (ed.): *Mysterium Salutis – Grundriss heilsgeschichtlicher Dogmatik*, Band II, Einsiedeln 1967.
Flückiger, F.: *Theologie der Geschichte – Die biblische Lehre von Gott und die neuere Geschichtstheologie*, Wuppertal 1970.

Gese, H.: *Vom Sinai zum Zion – Alttestamentliche Beiträge zur biblischen Theologie*, München 1974.

Hasenhüttl, G.: *Charisma – Ordnungsprinzip der Kirche*, Freiburg 1969.
Herzog, F. (ed.): *Theology of the Liberating Word*, New York 1971.
Heschel, A. J.: *The Prophets*, Vol. II, London 1971.
Heyns, J. A.: *Die Nuwe Mens Onderweg – oor die tien gebooie*, Cape Town 1970.

Jeremias, J.: *The Parables of Jesus*, London 1963.
Jüngel, E.: *Geistesgegenwart, Predigten*, München 1974.
Jüngel, E.: *Unterwegs zur Sache – Theologische Bemerkungen*, München 1972.

Kasper, W.: *Einführung in den Glauben*, Mainz 1972.
Kasper, W.: *Glaube und Geschichte*, Mainz 1970.
– *Kernwoorden van het Christelijk Geloof*, Kampen 1970.
Kittel, G.: *Theological Dictionary of the New Testament*, Grand Rapids 1964 and later (abb. T.D.N.T.).
Koch, K.: *Between Christ and Satan*, Berghausen 1972.
König, A.: *Jesus Christus die Eschatos – die fundering en struktuur van die eskatologie as teleologiese Christologie*, Pretoria 1970.
König, A. and Keane, H. (ed.): *The Meaning of History*, Unisa, Pretoria 1980.
Kraus, H.-J.: *Biblisch-theologische Aufsätze*, Neukirchen 1972.
Kraus, H.-J.: *Psalmen 2. Teilband, Biblischer Kommentar Altes Testament*, Neukirchen 1961.
Kuitert, H. M.: *De Mensvormigheid Gods – Een dogmatisch-hermeneutische studie over de anthropomorfismen van de Heilige Schrift*, Kampen 1967.
Kuitert, H. M.: *The Necessity of Faith*, Grand Rapids 1976.
Küng, H.: *Menschwerdung Gottes – Eine Einführung in Hegels theologisches Denken als Prolegomena zu einer künftigen Christologie*, Freiburg 1970.

Labuschagne, C. J.: *The Incomparability of Yahweh*, Leiden 1966.
Ling, T.: *The Significance of Satan*, London 1961.
Lorenz, F. (ed.): *Gottesfrage heute*, Stuttgart 1969.
Luther, M.: *Luthers Werken, Werken van Dr. Martin Luther* I, Kampen 1959.

Maas, W.: *Unveränderlichkeit Gottes – Zum Verhältnis von grieschisch-philosophischer und christlicher Gotteslehre*, München 1974.
Marsch, W. D.: *Zukunft, Themen der Theologie* Band 2, Stuttgart 1969.
Mauser, U.: *Gottesbild und Menschwerdung – Eine Untersuchung zur Einheit des Alten und Neuen Testaments*, Tübingen 1971.
Mays, J. L.: *Amos – A Commentary, The Old Testament Library*, London 1969.
Meadows, D. M. e.a.: *The Limits of Growth*, New York 1972.
Meijering, E. P.: *Orthodoxy and Platonism in Athanasius – Synthesis or Antithesis?*, Leiden 1968.
Miskotte, K. H.: *When the Gods are Silent*, London 1967.
Moltmann, J.: *The Crucified God*, London 1974.
Moltmann, J.: *Hope and Planning*, London 1971.
Moltmann, J.: *Theology of Hope*, London 1974.
Müller, A. K. M. und Pannenberg, W.: *Erwägungen zu einer Theologie der Natur*, Gerd Mohn 1970.
Muller, C. F. J.: *Die Oorsprong van die Groot Trek*, Tafelberg 1974.

Muller, C. F. J.: *Die Oorsprong van die Groot Trek*, Tafelberg 1974.
– *New Directions in Faith and Order*, Bristol 1967, Faith and Order Paper no. 50, Geneva 1968.

Oesterhoff, B. J.: *De afwezigheid Gods in het Oude Testament*, Apeldoornse Studies no. 1, Kampen 1971.
Ott, H.: *Der persönliche Gott, Wirklichkeit und Glaube* Zweiter Band, Göttingen 1969.
Ott, H.: *Die Antwort des Glaubens – Systematische Theologie in 50 Artikeln*, Stuttgart 1972.
Ott, H.: *God*, Edinburgh 1974.

Pannenberg, W.: *The Idea of God and Human Freedom*, Philadelphia 1973.
Pannenberg, W.: *The Apostles' Creed in the Light of Today's Questions*, London 1975.
Pannenberg, W.: *Basic Questions in Theology*, Vol. I and Vol. II, London 1970, 1971.
Pannenberg, W.: *Theology and the Kingdom of God*, Philadelphia 1969.
Preuss, H. D.: *Jahweglaube und Zukunftserwartung*, Stuttgart 1968.
Preuss, H. D.: *Verspottung fremder Religionen im Alten Testament*, Stuttgart 1971.

Rahner, K. und Vorgrimler, H.: *Kleines Konzilskompendium*, Freiburg 1967.
Ratzinger, J.(ed.): *Die Frage nach Gott*, Freiburg 1973.
Ratzinger, J.: *Introduction to Christianity*, London 1969.
Ridderbos, H.: *Heilsgeschiedenis en Heilige Schrift – Het Gezag van het Nieuwe Testament*, Kampen 1955.
Ridderbos, H.: *The Coming of the Kingdom*, Philadelphia 1962.
Ridderbos, J.: *De Psalmen II, Commentaar op het Oude Testament*, Kampen 1958.
Rowley, H. H.: *The Faith of Israel – Aspects of Old Testament Thought*, London 1956.

Schlier, H.: *Der Brief an die Galater, Kritisch-Exegetischer Kommentar über das Neue Testament*, Göttingen 1962.
Schmidt, W. H.: *Das erste Gebot – seine Bedeutung für das Alte Testament*, München 1969.
Schmithals, W.: *An Introduction to the Theology of Rudolph Bultmann*, London 1968.
Schmitz, J. (ed.): *Das Ende der Exportreligion – Perspektiven für eine künftige Mission*, Düsseldorf 1971.
Snijders, L. A.: *Jesaja deel I, De Prediking van het Oude Testament*, Nijkerk 1969.
Sölle, D.: *Christ the Representative – An Essay in Theology after the 'Death of God'*, London 1967.

Van Huyssteen, J. W. V.: *Teologie van die Rede – die funksie van die rasionele in die denke van Wolfhart Pannenberg*, Kampen 1970.
Von Ruler, A. A.: *Theologisch Werk* Deel IV, Nijkerk 1972.
Venema, H.: *Uitverkiezen en Uitverkiezing in het Nieuwe Testament*, Kampen 1965.
Von Rad, G.: *Gottes Wirken in Israel – Vorträge zum Alten Testament* (ed. O. H. Steck) Neukirchen 1974.
Von Rad, G.: *Old Testament Theology*, Vol. I, London 1977; Vol. II, Edinburgh 1970.
Vriezen, Th. C.: *An Outline of Old Testament Theology*, Oxford 1958.

Weber, O.: *Grundlagen der Dogmatik* Erster Band, 1955 Moers.
– *Weerwoord, reacties op Dr. H. Berkhof's 'Christelijk Geloof'*, Nijkerk 1974.
Wolff, H. W.: *Anthropology of the Old Testament*, London 1974.
– *Woord en Werkelijkheid – Over de Theocratie*, Nijkerk 1973.

Zimmerli, W.: *The Old Testament and the World*, London 1976.
Zimmerli, W.: *Grundriss der alttestamentlichen Theologie*, Stuttgart 1972.
Zündel, F.: *Johann Christoph Blumhardt – Zeuge der Siegesmacht Jesu über Krankheit und Dämonie*, Basel 1962.

Articles

Eissfeldt, O.: *El and Yahweh, Journal of Semitic Studies*, I, 1956.
Engelbrecht, B.: *The Dipolar God of Process-Thinking, Journal of Theology for Southern Africa*, 5 December 1973.

Gilkey, L.: *Process Theology, Vox Theologica*, 43, 1, 1973.
Gunton, C.: *Process Theology's Concept of God – An Outline and Assessment, The Expository Times* LXXXIV, 10 July 1973.

König, A.: *The Church and Politics, Theologia Evangelica*, XII, 1 April 1979.
König, A.: *Pannenberg en Jüngel – Huidige tendense in die Godsleer, Ned. Geref. Teologiese Tydskrif*, XV, 2 March 1974.

Lohfink, N.: *Die Priesterschrift und die Grenzen des Wachstums, Stimmen der Zeit*, 7 July 1974.
Lohfink, N.: *'Macht euch die Erde untertan?' Orientierung* H.12/13, 38, 1974.

Meijering, E. P.: *De Onveranderlikheid van God, Kerk en Theologie*, 25, 2 April 1974.
Miskotte, H. H.: *Het lijden is in God, Rondom het Woord*, 15, 4, 1973.

Parmer, S. L.: *The Limits-to-Growth Debate in Asian Perspective, The Ecumenical Review*, XXVI, 1 January 1974.

Schoonenberg, P.: *Process or History in God? Louvain Studies*, IV, 4, Fall 1973.

Scripture Index

Subject Index

Authors Index